Becoming Rwandan

CENTER FOR THE STUDY OF
GENOCIDE
& HUMAN RIGHTS

GENOCIDE, POLITICAL VIOLENCE,
HUMAN RIGHTS SERIES

Edited by Alexander Laban Hinton,
Stephen Eric Bronner, and Nela Navarro

Nanci Adler, ed., *Understanding the Age of Transitional Justice: Crimes, Courts, Commissions, and Chronicling*

Alan W. Clarke, *Rendition to Torture*

Alison Crosby and M. Brinton Lykes, *Beyond Repair?: Mayan Women's Protagonism in the Aftermath of Genocidal Harm*

Lawrence Davidson, *Cultural Genocide*

Daniel Feierstein, *Genocide as Social Practice: Reorganizing Society under the Nazis and Argentina's Military Juntas*

Alexander Laban Hinton, ed., *Transitional Justice: Global Mechanisms and Local Realities after Genocide and Mass Violence*

Alexander Laban Hinton, Thomas La Pointe, and Douglas Irvin-Erickson, eds., *Hidden Genocides: Power, Knowledge, Memory*

Douglas A. Kammen, *Three Centuries of Conflict in East Timor*

Eyal Mayroz, *Reluctant Interveners: America's Failed Responses to Genocide from Bosnia to Darfur*

Walter Richmond, *The Circassian Genocide*

S. Garnett Russell, *Becoming Rwandan: Education, Reconciliation, and the Making of a Post-Genocide Citizen*

Victoria Sanford, Katerina Stefatos, and Cecilia M. Salvi, eds., *Gender Violence in Peace and War: States of Complicity*

Irina Silber, *Everyday Revolutionaries: Gender, Violence, and Disillusionment in Postwar El Salvador*

Samuel Totten and Rafiki Ubaldo, eds., *We Cannot Forget: Interviews with Survivors of the 1994 Genocide in Rwanda*

Anton Weiss-Wendt, *A Rhetorical Crime: Genocide in the Geopolitical Discourse of the Cold War*

Ronnie Yimsut, *Facing the Khmer Rouge: A Cambodian Journey*

Becoming Rwandan

EDUCATION, RECONCILIATION, AND THE MAKING OF A POST-GENOCIDE CITIZEN

S. GARNETT RUSSELL

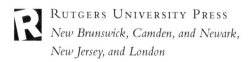

RUTGERS UNIVERSITY PRESS
New Brunswick, Camden, and Newark,
New Jersey, and London

Library of Congress Cataloging-in-Publication Data

Names: Russell, S. Garnett, 1980– author.
Title: Becoming Rwandan : education, reconciliation, and the making of a post-genocide citizen / S. Garnett Russell.
Description: New Brunswick : Rutgers University Press, [2019] | Series: Genocide, political violence, human rights series | Includes bibliographical references and index.
Identifiers: LCCN 2018058777 | ISBN 9781978802865 (pbk. : alk. paper) | ISBN 9781978802872 (hardcover : alk. paper) | ISBN 9781978802889 (epub) | ISBN 9781978802896 (web pdf) | ISBN 9781978802902
Subjects: LCSH: Education and state—Rwanda. | Education—Social aspects—Rwanda. | Citizenship—Rwanda. | Transitional justice—Rwanda. | Peace-building—Rwanda. | Reconciliation—Rwanda. | Genocide—Rwanda—History—20th century. | Rwanda—History—Civil War, 1994—Atrocities.
Classification: LCC LC95.R87 R87 2019 | DDC 379.67571—dc23
LC record available at https://catalog.loc.gov/vwebv/search?search Code=LCCN&searchArg=2018058777&searchType=1&permalink=y

A British Cataloging-in-Publication record for this book is available from the British Library.

♾ The paper used in this publication meets the requirements of the American National Standard for Information Sciences—Permanence of Paper for Printed Library Materials, ANSI Z39.48-1992.

www.rutgersuniversitypress.org

Manufactured in the United States of America

For my son, Rafa

Contents

ABBREVIATIONS

AERG	Association des Etudiants et Elèves Rescapés du Génocide (Association for Student Survivors of the Genocide)
A-level	advanced level
CEH	Comisión para el Esclarecimiento Histórico (Guatemalan Commission for Historical Clarification)
CNLG	Commission National pour la Lutte contre le Génocide (National Commission for the Fight against Genocide)
DRC	Democratic Republic of Congo
EAC	East African Community
FARG	Fond d'Assistance aux Rescapés du Génocide (Fund for Survivors of the Genocide)
GP	general paper
HRE	human rights education
ICC	International Criminal Court
ICTR	International Criminal Tribunal for Rwanda
ICTY	International Criminal Tribunal for the Former Yugoslavia
MINECOFIN	Ministry of Finance and Economic Planning (Rwanda)
MINEDUC	Ministry of Education (Rwanda)
NCDC	National Curriculum Development Center

NGO	nongovernmental organization
NURC	National Unity and Reconciliation Commission
O-level	ordinary level
RPF	Rwandan Patriotic Front
SDGs	Sustainable Development Goals
SLTRC	Sierra Leone Truth and Reconciliation Commission
TRC	Truth and Reconciliation Commission (South Africa, Peru)
UN	United Nations
UNESCO	United Nations Educational, Scientific, and Cultural Organization
UNICEF	United Nations Children's Fund

Becoming Rwandan

CHAPTER 1

Introduction

PERCHED ON A hilltop among city buildings, with verdant peaks visible in the distance, Green Fields is an elite and high-achieving government secondary school in Kigali, the capital of Rwanda. Built on a large tract of land, the school has newly refurbished buildings, a library, and a computer lab, and its grounds boast a soccer field and basketball courts. When the bell rings, students dressed in spotless matching khaki school uniforms hurry to their next class, chattering to friends along the way.

During a visit to the school one morning in October 2011, I sat with Emmanuel, who teaches political education and religion, in a sparsely decorated classroom. Emmanuel, a Tutsi survivor of the 1994 genocide, recounted in French his experience during the horrific violence of that period, including how he hid for three months with a Hutu family.[1] When I asked whether he encountered any difficult or sensitive topics in class when teaching about the genocide, Emmanuel cautiously explained the challenges he faced:

When we talk about the history of Rwanda, we must pay attention to avoid hurting the souls of others, because the hearts of certain people were hurt. So we must try to generalize without any particularities, because [otherwise] we run the risk of bringing up things that can cause division.

During the genocide, the country was divided in two, but
today, the country is in the process of putting itself back
together. ... For example, among the kids, we have those
who are survivors of the genocide, and the others are survivors of the war. There are orphans from both sides, so that if
we address them, we must take them as one group. So it's
very difficult to put them in one group without knowing
who is in which group and who isn't, all the while being
aware that they are the kids in front of you. So to talk about
the genocide, we can't concentrate on one side, saying that
the Tutsi are dead, the Hutu killed [them]. If you still bring
up the words "Hutu" or "Tutsi," that can bring back division. *We must be neutral, even if it's difficult. If a student poses a
question that deviates [from this usage], we must bring them to
reason, bring them back to the center. We must avoid a student
going outside of a subject and its parameters, because there are those
who still confuse genocide and war crimes.* (Teacher interview,
School 6, October 2011; emphasis added)

Emmanuel's observations illustrate some of the chief predic-
aments facing Rwanda's teachers: How do you teach about the
past in a way that brings people together rather than separates
them? The state views education as a vehicle for peacebuilding
and shaping a unified nation in the aftermath of the genocide.
While teachers are mandated to address the genocide and past
human rights violations, they must also avoid sowing what the
government views as "division" across groups. Indeed, when they
teach about the 1994 genocide committed against the Tutsi,
teachers can talk about violations of human rights only within
the context of the genocide. During the Rwandan genocide,
more than 800,000 Tutsi and moderate Hutu were massacred in
just one hundred days between April and July (Prunier 1995).
        Teachers are forbidden from discussing human rights issues
relating either to the civil war that led to the genocide or to the

killings by the Tutsi-dominated Rwandan Patriotic Front (RPF) following the genocide. They must avoid answering questions from students about moderate Hutu who were killed during the genocide or those who were killed subsequently by the RPF. And as they try to teach about the genocide committed against the Tutsi without mentioning the violent events before and after, teachers must also make no mention of ethnic identity. Moreover, they must do this in a room full of students who are either children of survivors of the genocide or children of the *génocidaires* (the French term for the perpetrators of the genocide).

The tensions and contradictions inherent in providing (and receiving) such an education lie at the heart of this book. Drawing on extensive field research, this book investigates the way in which the Rwandan state uses the country's education system to promote peacebuilding and reconciliation in the aftermath of the 1994 genocide. However, this approach is not a politically neutral affair and is used for political ends and as a way for the government to retain power. Although the RPF-led government ostensibly seeks to reconcile Hutu and Tutsi, perpetrators and victims, it also seeks to nurture new generations of Rwandans who embrace a particular form of national identity and view the past and the present through a lens that excuses or obscures the regime's own shortcomings.

As the chapters in this book reveal, in seeking to foster a generation focused on a unified and patriotic future rather than on the ethnically divisive past, the government has incorporated global models of peacebuilding and human rights. In this book, I explore not only the goals and policies of the government but also the complexities of executing a peacebuilding project through education. I present the perspectives of teachers and students who have grappled with the problems encountered when teaching and learning about citizenship, human rights, and reconciliation in a postconflict and authoritarian context. My findings demonstrate that although the Rwandan government utilizes global discourses in national policy documents, the way in which teachers and students engage with these global models distorts the intention of the government and the global agencies that promote these models, resulting in unintended consequences and fueling new tensions across social groups. As I explain in the following chapters, the results of this effort have been mixed. Although, on one hand, widespread violence has not returned to the country since the genocide, on the other hand, by forging a particular narrative and repressing open discussions of the past, the government of Rwanda may in fact be threatening sustainable peace in the long term.

The issues addressed in this book—such as how global models are used and interpreted at national and school levels and whether a censored view of a divided past can lay the foundation for a unified future—are relevant not only to Rwanda but to all conflict-affected countries that want to achieve peacebuilding, state-building, and transitional justice goals through education. Schools play a crucial role in socializing national citizens and in creating legitimate knowledge in most societies (Meyer 1977). In the aftermath of violent conflict, education systems are integral for rebuilding a nation and creating a unified identity (Bar-Tal and Rosen 2009; Davies 2004). In Rwanda, schools have been tasked with helping to unify students across diverse groups and disseminating the official narrative of the past. Indeed, my findings attest both to the power and the limitations of education as a peacebuilding and state-building tool.

PEACEBUILDING AND EDUCATION

The social science literature on peacebuilding focuses primarily on political, security, and economic developments in the aftermath of conflict.[2] Although scholars recognize the role that youth may play both in fueling conflict and in aiding reconstruction (Lederach 2006; McEvoy-Levy 2006, 2011), only recently have scholars begun to conduct in-depth empirical studies on the role of education in building social cohesion and facilitating peace and transitional justice in conflict-affected societies (see Bellino, Paulson, and Worden 2017; Novelli, Lopes Cardozo, and Smith 2017).

The notion of peacebuilding emerged from John Galtung's (1969) concepts of "negative peace" and "positive peace": negative peace refers to the absence of direct or personal violence, and positive peace refers more broadly to the absence of indirect or structural violence, which is embedded in institutionalized social structures. According to Galtung, the lack of violence does not necessarily translate into a longer-term state of peace in which the fundamental conditions that led to violence are addressed. Inspired by these insights, the peacebuilding field has sought to address the underlying social, economic, and political conditions that give rise to violence. In the UN report *An Agenda for Peace*, which helped promote the field to a global audience, UN Secretary-General Boutros Boutros-Ghali defined peacebuilding as "action to identify and support structures which will tend to strengthen and solidify peace in order to avoid a relapse into conflict" (Boutros-Ghali 1992, 4).

Boutros-Ghali's report, like many subsequent UN reports, did not place great importance on education as a peacebuilding tool, but that neglect has begun to be corrected. Discussions involving UN organizations, governments, donors, and nongovernmental organizations (NGOs) around the 2030 Agenda for Sustainable Development, the follow-up to the Millennium Development Goals, have focused on mainstreaming peacebuilding across social sectors. Sustainable Development Goal (SDG) 4.7 mentions human rights, global citizenship, and a focus on a culture of peace and nonviolence as important for achieving quality education; SDG 16 focuses on peace, justice, and strong institutions. UN Security Council Resolution 2282 and UN General Assembly Resolution 70/262 in 2016 on peacebuilding both mention the important role of youth in the prevention and resolution of conflict and refer to the importance of "sustaining peace" as linked to broader development processes. UN Resolution 2250 on Youth, Peace, and Security (2015) is devoted to the role of youth in maintaining peace. In addition, UNICEF's (United Nations Children's Fund) Peacebuilding, Education, and Advocacy Program, which ran from 2012 to 2016, focused on integrating peacebuilding activities into UNICEF's work with education and youth (UNICEF 2015).

As is now increasingly recognized, education systems serve as central institutions in the nation-building projects of post-conflict governments through the construction of a national identity and the dissemination of ideas about citizenship and the past conflict. States rely on education to socialize citizens into the dominant norms of society and to legitimize national civic identities (Dreeben 1968; Meyer 1977). A socially constructed national civic identity, or an "imagined political community" (Anderson 2006), is forged directly through the process of schooling and by teaching a common national history and language (Bendix 1964; Tyack 1966; Weber 1976). Education systems also play a key role in the process of political socialization and creating a civic identity for citizens (Almond 1963; Torney-Purta 2002). Civic education and history education are particularly important in the process of creating a common identity and promoting reconciliation (Bellino 2015; Davies 2004).

Influential works by education scholars, such as Kenneth Bush and Dana Saltarelli's *The Two Faces of Education in Ethnic Conflict* (2000), recognize the dual nature of education as both a driver and a solution to conflict (see also Burde 2014; King 2014). Indeed, some studies illustrate the positive effects of education in promoting intergroup tolerance, reconciliation, and understanding (Salomon 2006; Torney-Purta, Wilkenfeld, and Barber 2008). However, others highlight the fact that education can be used to perpetuate social inequalities and to incite intergroup conflict, whether through curriculum or unequal access to education (Buckland 2005; King 2014; Lange 2012). In some instances, governments use education as a political tool to promote ideologies, cultural values, and negative stereotypes about different groups (Buckland 2005; Johnson and Stewart 2007; Lange 2012; Alan Smith 2005; Alan Smith and Vaux 2003).

Some scholars have pointed to the link between education and reconciliation (Paulson 2011) and have argued that education systems can extend the reach of transitional justice mechanisms in a conflict-affected society (Cole 2007a). Lynn Davies (2017) argues for "justice-sensitive education" that helps students address past violations of human rights, understand the "truth" about a past conflict, and engage with the past to create a better future (3). Similarly, an edited volume by Clara Ramírez-Barat and Roger Duthie (2016) examines how transitional justice initiatives influence the education system across several country cases. However, few empirical studies have assessed the extent to which global models of peacebuilding and reconciliation for addressing past violence are implemented in national education policies and schools, as well as the contradictions and tensions that emerge in the implementation process. The crucial role that education systems play in broader peacebuilding and reconciliation processes thus remains underexamined.

As this book shows, in post-genocide Rwanda, the education system is considered an important tool for promoting the state-mandated version of reconciliation and unity and for disseminating notions of citizenship and human rights. The Rwandan *Education Sector Strategic Plan, 2006–2010* specifies that the overarching goal of the education sector is to "contribute to the promotion of a culture of peace and emphasize Rwandan and universal values of justice, peace, tolerance, respect for human rights, gender equality, solidarity and democracy" (Ministry of Education 2006, 8). However, although education is seen as a tool for reconstructing the past and building a shared future, teachers and students are expected *not* to mention specific details of the genocide, ongoing ethnic divisions and tensions, or human rights violations, and are instead encouraged to refer abstractly to terms such as "human rights" and "reconciliation." This points to the broader challenges inherent in trying to promote peacebuilding while restricting discussion around certain topics in a politically intolerant context. The empirical evidence presented in the following chapters shows the difficulties teachers and students face in trying to comply with such directives. The next section provides an overview of the education system in Rwanda leading up to the genocide and in the aftermath.

A SHORT HISTORY OF EDUCATION IN RWANDA BEFORE AND SINCE THE GENOCIDE

One reason the Rwandan government has sought to use the education system to promote reconciliation and a unifying national identity in the aftermath of the genocide is that the same system played a part in fueling the intergroup tensions that led to the genocide. The formal education system now tasked with effacing ethnic identity was a favored institution for both the construction and the manipulation of ethnic identity for decades before the explosion of violence in 1994. Indeed, the education system contributed to the division of the population by favoring one group over another in the precolonial and colonial periods. As several scholars have described, biased curricula and classroom practices inflamed tensions between Hutu and Tutsi through the construction of opposed ethnic identities (Bentrovato 2015; Gasanabo 2006; King 2014; McLean Hilker 2011; Njoroge 2007; Rutayisire, Kabano, and Rubagiza 2004).

Education in the Precolonial, Colonial, and Independence Eras
Before the arrival of the European colonialists and missionaries at the end of the nineteenth century, education in Rwanda took place primarily in the home and focused on language and

culture, including stories, singing, and poetry (Erny 2001; King 2014). Introduced during the reign of King Ruganzu Ndori during the seventeenth century, the first formal educational institution, *itorero*, or formal training schools run by the monarchy, sought to provide military, artistic, and moral education for future civic and military leaders, who were primarily Tutsi (Sundberg 2016; Vansina 2004). In pre-genocide Rwanda, the Hutu, Tutsi, and Twa historically made up approximately 84–90 percent, 9–15 percent, and 1 percent of the population, respectively (Straus 2006, 19).

Catholic missionaries established the first Western schools in Rwanda around the beginning of the twentieth century. While others, including Protestants, Presbyterians, and Seventh-day Adventists, also started schools, the Catholic Church remained dominant and highly influential in the education sector during the colonial period (Hoben 1989). By 1918, twelve mission schools had been established. Initially, these schools catered to poor peasants, primarily Hutu, since attending the missionary schools was viewed with suspicion by the elites (Erny 2003; Hoben 1989; King 2014). With the transfer of colonial power from Germany to Belgium in 1916, Belgium established several nonreligious schools to train the Tutsi elite for public service.

By the mid-1920s, when the Tutsi monarchy began allowing their children to attend the schools, Tutsi were favored over Hutu as "natural leaders" (Hoben 1989). As the Belgian colonialists and the Catholic missionaries alike favored Tutsi and believed them to be superior to Hutu, schools were used to train an elite group of Tutsi (Longman 2010). The goal of the Catholic missionary schools was to create a new Christian social class of elite Tutsi to run the colonial administration (Newbury 1988). Under the Belgians, the missionaries had almost complete control over the education system, implementing a system favoring the Tutsi and explicitly discriminating against the Hutu.

Under Belgian colonial rule there were three types of schools: *écoles officielles*, public schools funded and administered by the colonial state; *écoles libres subsidiées*, schools run by the missionaries but subsidized by the government and following the national curriculum and standards; and *écoles libres non-subsidiées*, privately funded missionary schools (Catholic and Protestant). As the majority of schools were the second type, *écoles libres subsidiées*, the Catholic and Protestant churches exerted a great amount of control over the education system during the colonial period (Hoben 1989). During the colonial period, both government and missionary schools gave preference to Tutsi students in order to cultivate the future elite class; access to education was severely restricted for the Hutu (Erny 2003; Longman 2010; Prunier 1995).

In the 1930s, the Belgian colonial government established a dual-tier education system, which further reinforced ethnic stratification by providing unequal types of schooling for the different ethnic groups. While Tutsi attended high-quality French-medium schools, in the rare instances when Hutu attended school, they were only admitted to inferior schools that taught in the regional vernacular of Kiswahili (Mamdani 2001).

The system of ethnic stratification and cultural division of labor created a society in which Tutsi were systematically favored over Hutu in the realms of employment and education (King 2014; Newbury 1988). In 1957, Hutu leaders drafted the "Hutu Manifesto," which demanded democratic reforms and railed against the "political, socioeconomic, and cultural monopoly" enjoyed by the Tutsi (Newbury 1988, 191). Increasing tensions between the groups helped foment the 1959 Hutu Revolution, which led to the end of the Rwandan monarchy. The election of the first Rwandan president, Grégoire Kayibanda, in 1961, marked a shift in power from the Tutsi minority to the Hutu majority.

Following Rwanda's independence from Belgium in 1962, a new constitution was promulgated that sought to expand educational access by guaranteeing free primary education for all school-age children (Erny 2003). During what became known as the First Hutu Republic (1962–1973), the Hutu-controlled government implemented a range of measures in order to widen access by Hutu to key economic and social opportunities such as education and employment. A policy of regional and ethnic quotas was implemented by which Tutsi were allocated only 9 percent of spaces in secondary schools, the civil service, and any sector of employment; nonetheless, in practice, Tutsi still tended to hold more than their allocated share (Prunier 1995, 60). During the Second Hutu Republic (1973–1990), General Juvénal Habyarimana, a Hutu who came to power in a military coup in 1973 before being formally elected as president in 1978, continued the policy of regional and ethnic quotas for postprimary education, explicitly discriminating against Tutsi and children from the south while favoring Hutu from the north (King 2014; Rutayisire, Kabano, and Rubagiza 2004).

Reforms introduced in 1979 revised the curriculum, replaced French with Kinyarwanda as the medium of instruction in primary schools, and sought to expand access to education. Enrollment in primary schools did increase, but secondary schooling was available only to wealthy elites (Erny 2003; McLean Hilker 2011; Obura 2003). Meanwhile, discrimination based on ethnic and regional quotas created new inequities within the education system, which in turn wrested economic and social power further away from the Tutsi. Political power was also taken from the Tutsi, most of whom found it difficult to get an education that would qualify them for elite political jobs.

Throughout the First and Second Hutu Republics, the government manipulated the curriculum in schools to serve political interests; history and civics courses were especially susceptible to manipulation and the propagation of stereotypes about Hutu and Tutsi (Gasanabo 2006; King 2014; Rutayisire, Kabano, and

Rubagiza 2004). For example, an analysis of school history textbooks in Rwanda from 1962 to 1994 found that they employed
a racist perspective that emphasized the biological, historical,
and cultural differences among the Hutu, Tutsi, and Twa (Gasanabo 2004, 2006). Biased classroom practices and a curriculum
that emphasized Hutu subjugation under Tutsi rule also stoked
intergroup tensions.

The 1994 Genocide and Post-Genocide Developments
Those tensions erupted in April 1994, when extremist Hutu
leaders initiated mass killings, drawing on an ideology of "Hutu
power" that envisioned a "Hutu nation" and portrayed the Tutsi
as the enemy and an "alien race" rather than as an indigenous
ethnic group (Mamdani 2001, 190). In this context, the notion
of "ethnicity" became a state-sponsored script and justification
for violence, whereby Tutsi were framed as enemies of the state
(Fujii 2009). During the genocide, more than three in four Tutsi
were killed—one of the highest death rates for an ethnic group
in the history of modern genocides. While government-backed
militia groups known as *interahamwe* led the killings, many ordinary Rwandans also participated in the slaughter. Scott Straus
(2006) estimates that 14–17 percent of the active adult male
Hutu population at the time of the genocide may have participated (118).

The genocide was halted in July 1994 only by the victory of
the RPF, which had been fighting the Hutu regime for several
years. Based in Uganda, the RPF comprised exiled Tutsi living
in Uganda, Burundi, and the Democratic Republic of Congo
(DRC). After the victory of the RPF, more than 2 million
Rwandans, most of them Hutu civilians, fled their homes to
escape revenge killings by the RPF (Prunier 1995). One scholar
estimates that the RPF killed between 25,000 and 45,000 Hutu,
both innocent civilians and suspected *génocidaires*, during and
after the genocide (Des Forges 1999, 18).

Following the genocide, the Government of National Unity, comprising both Hutu and Tutsi leaders, assumed power.[3] Pasteur Bizimungu, a Hutu member of the RPF, became president, and Paul Kagame, a Tutsi, became vice president and minister of defense. The new government instituted a policy of unity and reconciliation, eradicating ethnicity as a form of official identity: ethnicity was removed from national identity cards, and the government banned the use of ethnicity as a criterion for admission to school and for employment (Burnet 2009; Eltringham 2004; Longman and Rutagengwa 2004; Pottier 2002).

With the end of the genocide and the victory of the RPF, an estimated 700,000 Tutsi returnees, or so-called old caseload refugees, who had fled to other countries in 1959 and 1973, returned to Rwanda (Prunier 1995). Subsequently, in 1996 and 1997, approximately 2 million "new caseload refugees," Hutu who had fled in 1994 to Tanzania and to the DRC, began to return (Bruce 2007). Refugees who had been living in Uganda and Tanzania were primarily Anglophones, while those who had been living in the DRC and Burundi were Francophones. The return of refugees from surrounding countries and the fact that they spoke different languages had implications for the medium of instruction and for integrating students into the education system.

In the aftermath of the genocide, the international community and the government took a variety of steps to prosecute those guilty of crimes against humanity and to promote societal reconciliation. In November 1994, the United Nations Security Council established the International Criminal Tribunal for Rwanda (ICTR) in Arusha, Tanzania, to try the organizers of the genocide. The Rwandan government tried genocide suspects before domestic military and ordinary courts beginning in 1996. The government established the National Unity and Reconciliation Commission (NURC) in 1999; NURC is tasked with promoting social cohesion in Rwanda through re-education camps known as *ingando*, civic education programs known as *itorero*, and other unity and reconciliation programs.[4] In 2000, to accelerate the trials of the more than 130,000 genocide suspects housed in prisons built to hold a tiny fraction of that number, the government created the *gacaca* courts. *Gacaca*, which means "justice on the grass" in Kinyarwanda, combined a traditional precolonial local dispute resolution mechanism with a modern judicial structure. The *gacaca* system began operation in June 2002 and ended in 2012.

Paul Kagame became president in 2003, winning the election in a landslide, and under his rule Rwanda has enjoyed relative political stability and economic growth and has seen a continuing focus on reconciliation. But Kagame has also exercised his power in an increasingly authoritarian fashion. The government has placed limits on political opposition, freedom of the press, and freedom of speech and has threatened opposition politicians, journalists, and human rights advocates (Amnesty International 2017; Longman 2011, 2017; Reyntjens 2004; Waldorf 2011). In the 2010 election, Kagame was re-elected virtually unopposed after opposition candidates had been threatened and intimidated (Human Rights Watch 2010). In 2015, the senate voted in favor of a constitutional amendment to allow Kagame to seek a third presidential term; he was re-elected with 99 percent of the vote in August 2017. However, the election results were critiqued by outside observers for irregularities and for the oppressive political environment in which they took place (U.S. Department of State 2017). In the period before and after the election, the Rwandan government suppressed civil society groups, the media, and political opponents; its actions included the harassment of the two opposition candidates and the arrest and detention of Diane Rwigara, an independent candidate and activist who was disqualified before the election (Human Rights Watch 2018).

In addition to restricting the political space, the government has passed several laws restricting public discussion around ethnicity and genocide. This trend began in 2001, when the government passed a vaguely worded law against "sectarianism," forbidding "the use of any speech, written statement, or action that divides people, that is likely to spark conflicts among people" (Republic of Rwanda 2001). The 2003 Constitution reinforced the trend, forbidding "divisionism" in Article 33, which states that the "propagation of ethnic, regional, or racial discrimination or any other form of division shall be punishable by Law" (Republic of Rwanda 2003). In 2008, the Genocide Ideology Law was passed, forbidding discussion of ethnicity or division along ethnic lines. "Genocide ideology" is defined in Article 2 as "an aggregate of thoughts characterized by conduct, speeches, documents and other acts aiming at exterminating or inciting others to exterminate people based on ethnic group, origin, nationality, region, color, physical appearance, sex, language, religion or political opinion, committed in normal periods or during war" (Republic of Rwanda 2008a). In response to international criticism, the government revised the Genocide Ideology Law in 2013 to more clearly define the crime of genocide ideology as "any deliberate act, committed in public whether orally, written, or video or by any other means which may show that a person is characterized by ethnic, religious, nationality or racial-based with the aim to advocate for the commission of genocide" (Article 3). The revised law addresses criticisms about ambiguous language and requires that criminal intent to incite genocide ideology in public must be proven in order for someone to be accused (Uwizeyimana 2014).

Education in the Post-Genocide Period

The 1994 genocide devastated Rwanda's education system. A majority of the country's school buildings were destroyed, and more than two-thirds of the teachers at the primary and secondary levels either fled the country or were killed (Buckland 2005; Obura 2003). In the aftermath of the genocide, the government has not only worked to rebuild schools but has also introduced significant changes to education policy and curriculum, including expanding access to basic education; reforming the social studies, civics, and history curriculum to reflect the state project for reconciliation and unity; and switching from French to English as the language of instruction in primary and secondary schools.

The post-genocide regime has focused on expanding access to basic education for all children, regardless of ethnic background or gender. In order to expand enrollment, the government of Rwanda introduced universal primary education in 2003, followed by a nine years basic education policy in 2009; in 2011, the government committed to the provision of twelve years of basic education. In addition to expanding access to education, the government has undertaken reforms in the structure and content of the curriculum. The concerted focus of the RPF-led government on development is linked to the need to hold onto power in the absence of democracy. The provision of social services, such as the expansion of basic education and health care, is the RPF's only claim to legitimacy and one they use in their political campaigning (Williams 2017). Similarly, the switch from French to English in the schools is also linked to the need to consolidate power around an Anglophone minority of returnees from Uganda.

THE INTERPLAY OF THE GLOBAL, NATIONAL, AND LOCAL WITHIN RWANDA'S EDUCATION SYSTEM

While the education system was used by the colonial and post-colonial governments to maintain differences between ethnic groups, Rwanda's post-genocide government has tried to use education to mitigate intergroup conflict and promote reconciliation and a single, shared civic and nonethnic identity. In designing and then implementing its education policies, however, the government has had to contend with the interplay of the global, national, and local forces within the context of schooling. Two crosscutting themes emerge in this book that help explain the goals and the impact of the Rwandan regime's education policies: the government's readiness not only to draw on but also to manipulate global models, and the way in which global and national discourses can be reinterpreted at the local level, in the process creating unintended consequences and undermining the impact of the peacebuilding project.

Global and National Discourses

The Rwandan government selectively draws on global discourses in setting and articulating its national education policies in order to avoid a contested past, to promote a strong and unified national identity, and to garner broader external legitimacy. Although the government invokes global models of citizenship, human rights, and reconciliation, the global discourse is manipulated in the process of implementation and does not accord with the reality of teachers and students on the ground.

From the perspective of international relations realist scholars, nation-states act within the international system in their own self-interest and view global treaties and ideas about human rights to be largely irrelevant to their actions. Neoinstitutional sociological scholars, however, argue that nation-states are embedded in a larger world culture and draw on global models or "scripts" that elevate the individual, human rights, progress, and justice (Meyer, Boli, et al. 1997). Similarly, constructivist scholars examine the ideational spread and influence of global norms transmitted via international organizations and transnational civil society networks and the influence on national actors

(Finnemore and Sikkink 1998; Keck and Sikkink 1998; Risse-Kappen, Ropp, and Sikkink 1999). Post-genocide education in Rwanda comes into sharper focus when one uses these neoinstitutional and constructivist lenses.

A number of empirical studies have documented the rise in global norms around human rights (Keck and Sikkink 1998; Tsutsui and Wotipka 2004) and transitional justice mechanisms (Jelin 2003; Sikkink and Walling 2007) in the post–World War II era. Several studies have documented the inclusion of global norms around global citizenship (Buckner and Russell 2013), human rights (Meyer, Bromley, and Ramirez 2010; Russell and Suárez 2017), and transitional justice mechanisms (Russell and Tiplic 2018) within education policy documents, curricula, and textbooks. The increasing visibility, acceptance, and institutionalization of norms around human rights and transitional justice on an international scale have been referred to as the "norm cascade" (Finnemore and Sikkink 1998; Lutz and Sikkink 2000).

In this book, I argue that in post-genocide Rwanda, the state is very careful to position itself in relation to this norm cascade, selecting and negotiating global discourses to garner broader legitimacy and avoid internal discussions of contentious topics. The government engages with these discourses as part of the larger peacebuilding project within the education sector, offering a narrative of the genocide and an understanding of human rights that support their goals while silencing alternative memories and conceptions.

Perspectives from the Local Level

Teachers, students, and other local actors are far from passive actors in transitional justice and reconciliation processes; they actively engage, translate, and reject or reframe global and national norms around peacebuilding and reconciliation. By presenting the perspectives of genocide survivors, children of perpetrators and survivors, and returnees from other countries, this book demonstrates the ways in which local actors respond to global and national discourses and shift the intent and meaning of these models. Thus, my research reveals that even though the official Rwandan discourse on human rights and reconciliation is pervasive in policy and curricular documents, there is a dearth of genuine reconciliation, trust, and open discussion in the schools themselves.

Most sociological research around global norms focuses on the nation-state as the unit of analysis and examines the phenomenon of "isomorphism"—that is, how nation-states increasingly embrace norms and discourses similar to those taken up by other nation-states—across discourses and models (Meyer, Boli, et al. 1997). In contrast, anthropological approaches consider how actors "localize" or respond to global norms. For instance, anthropological perspectives on human rights discourse emphasize the ways in which local actors practice "vernacularization"—translating and contextualizing global conceptions of human rights for the local context (Goodale 2009; Goodale and Merry 2007; Merry 2006). Other scholars acknowledge the limits of a global-local binary for an analysis framework (Anderson-Levitt 2012; Russell, Sirota, and Ahmed 2019). Goodale (2007) suggests an approach between the global and the local that locates how human rights discourse is applied in practice. This book seeks to bridge the global and local binary by incorporating an analysis of how global norms influence discourses in national documents and how these norms are adopted among students and teachers.

The Rwandan government refers strategically to citizenship, human rights, and reconciliation within a specific context, framing and selecting global discourses to fit the national discourses around unity and reconciliation. As local actors in schools vernacularize or translate global discourses, certain global norms such as gender and global citizenship are prioritized, while discussions around multiculturalism and diversity are excluded. In Rwanda, the intention of reconciliation and peacebuilding is not always realized on the ground. National policies aiming to promote reconciliation and national unity in some cases serve to create new tensions across groups by suppressing discussions of the past.

The evidence presented in the following chapters illuminates the phenomenon termed "decoupling" by sociological institutional scholars (Meyer and Rowan 1977). Decoupling occurs when the norm or model that policy makers intended to be implemented is not the same as the norm or model that is embraced in practice. Decoupling between policy and practice tends to occur when policies are adopted as symbolic but are not implemented due to a lack of capacity or a lack of will (Bromley and Powell 2012; W. Cole 2012). Patricia Bromley and Walter Powell (2012) refer to a form of decoupling called "mean and ends," whereby policies are implemented but the link between the policies and the intended outcomes is tenuous. In Rwanda, decoupling occurs in two forms: where intended policies are not always implemented in the schools, and where the policies when implemented produce unintended consequences that are not aligned with the broader objectives of the regime's peacebuilding project or its desire to maintain power.

Situated at the intersection of theoretical debates on the role of education in transitional justice and reconciliation and the influence of global norms, this book provides insight into how and why local actors strategically draw on global norms, how these norms are interpreted in the classroom, and the forms of decoupling that occur. This book contributes the perspective of local actors and how they engage with these global norms that are mandated via state institutions.

The Research for This Book

The research for this book involved collecting data from both national and local levels while accounting for global and transversal influences (Bartlett and Vavrus 2016). I spent a total of eleven months in Rwanda between 2010 and 2012, both in the capital city of Kigali and in two rural field sites in different parts of the country.

To better understand the broader policy environment around the realm of education, I began my research with key informant interviews with government officials, policy makers, and academics. In addition, I gathered relevant policy documents for the education, development, and social sectors, as well as the current curriculum and textbooks. The policy documents and curriculum that I selected were in use at the time of research and were available on government websites. To ensure that I would be looking at textbooks currently and widely in use, I obtained copies of textbooks from the Ministry of Education's National Curriculum Development Center, from teachers in the schools I visited, and from local bookstores.

Since the vast majority of people in Rwanda live in the countryside, I chose two rural field sites to complement the time I spent in the capital. Close to the Ugandan border, one field site, in the Eastern Province, consisted of newly constructed towns mainly populated by Tutsi who returned from Uganda and Tanzania after the genocide. Most of the population in this area spoke English and was supportive of government language and nation-building policies. The other field site was a sharp contrast: an area within the Western Province, close to the border with the DRC, where most of the people were Hutu, many of whom had temporarily fled to the DRC following the genocide. This population spoke French and tended to be more critical of the regime in Kigali, which they viewed as supporting the Anglophone Tutsi returnee agenda at the expense of the majority of the population. The third field site was based in Kigali and included schools in both urban and semiurban areas in the periphery of the city with both Hutu and Tutsi students with mixed views about the government (see figure 1).

From a list of the schools in Rwanda provided by the Ministry of Education, I purposively selected fifteen secondary schools across three districts in order to reflect the diversity of schools in those districts: some were government-run, some private, and some religious (but all had to follow the national curriculum); some were in urban areas and some in rural areas; and the quality of the education provided ranged from high-achieving to average to low-achieving schools. In general, in the urban, higher-quality schools, students came from higher socioeconomic backgrounds, and many parents worked for the government, whereas in the rural, lower-quality government schools, the majority of students came from agricultural families and lower socioeconomic backgrounds (to confirm this common assumption, I asked students questions about their parents' employment). I surveyed 536 randomly selected students across these fifteen schools (see appendix A for more details on research methods).[5]

Despite the fact that not all students in Rwanda attend secondary school, I chose to engage with older, more mature students to generate in-depth and richer discussions around sensitive topics. I also included both lower and upper secondary students in order to capture a broad range of perspectives. An added benefit of working with secondary students was that, at the time of my research, my sample could include genocide survivors and "returnees" (those who had fled abroad before returning to Rwanda after the genocide).

To better interpret the findings from my survey, I then selected seven case study schools from the larger sample and spent approximately three to four weeks in each school conducting classroom observations and interviews with students and teachers.[6] In total, I conducted group and individual

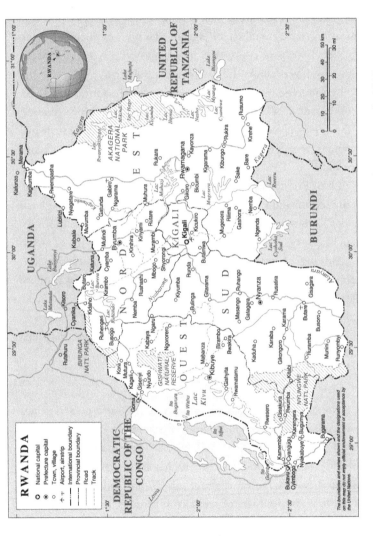

1. Map of Rwanda. *Source:* Map No. 3717 Rev. 11 United Nations, July 2015.

interviews with 109 students who had taken the survey. I selected a range of students to include boys and girls from different grades, as well as from different academic concentrations. In addition, I observed more than seventy hours of history, political education, and general paper (an interdisciplinary social sciences subject) classes and conducted interviews with twenty teachers of these subjects across the case study schools.[7]

I conducted interviews in English, French, Kinyarwanda, or a combination of those languages depending on the preference of the interviewee. However, in the rural areas, I relied on my Rwandan research assistants to translate the interviews in Kinyarwanda.[8] I carried out all of the interviews with teachers in English or French. For the students, the language used depended on the school and region: for example, in the urban and "higher-quality" schools, the students often spoke fluent English or French.

Although I never explicitly asked students or teachers for their ethnic identity—to do so is illegal in Rwanda—I was often able to infer their ethnic group from various identifying characteristics, such as if a student said that he or she was a returnee from Uganda or a genocide survivor. In some cases, teachers spoke openly about their ethnic identity.

THE ORGANIZATION OF THIS BOOK

In chapter 2, "The Role of Education in Transitional Justice, Peacebuilding, and Reconciliation," I provide an overview of the rise of transitional justice mechanisms in postconflict contexts globally. The education system—which is used to interpret the contested past, shape ideas about citizenship and human rights, disseminate the findings of truth commissions, and mold hopes for the future—is an important transitional justice mechanism that is often overlooked in favor of legal and political tools. I cite examples that range from the inclusion of discussion of apartheid and the truth and reconciliation commission in South African textbooks to the development of materials for children from the truth commission in Sierra Leone. I explain how in Rwanda, revisions to the history and civics curricula and the implementation of a new language policy have been used for broader peacebuilding and justice efforts. The chapter highlights how the Rwandan state strategically employs the education system and global rights discourse to address the legacy of the genocide, to build a new civic identity, and to avoid controversial issues of the past. In some instances, as the following chapters explore in depth, these efforts have achieved their goals, but in other cases, tensions and contradictions have emerged at the local level when national policies have been implemented, undercutting peacebuilding objectives.

Chapter 3, "Constructing Citizenship and a Post-Genocide Identity," discusses how the state uses the education system as part of its post-genocide peacebuilding project to create a new civic identity. Through an analysis of data from surveys conducted with students and interviews with students and teachers, I demonstrate that the school serves as a vehicle to build a new citizen in post-genocide Rwanda, one who has a nonethnic identity, speaks English, and has a regional and global orientation, but who is also patriotic and loyal to the Rwandan state. While the government attempts to fashion a new, unified Rwandan nonethnic identity, it also endorses the use of ethnic terms when referencing the 1994 genocide and to gain access to clubs and scholarships in schools. This contradiction has led to an emergence of new and unintended boundaries and new identities in schools. In fostering a nationalistic and obedient generation of citizens, the state has suppressed critical thinking and reckoning with the past and present, threatening to undermine the broader peacebuilding project by repressing instead of addressing underlying tensions.

In chapter 4, "Using and Abusing Human Rights Norms," I demonstrate the extent to which the state uses human rights discourses strategically and selectively as part of the broader peace-building project and to garner international legitimacy. By promoting a rights discourse and focusing on achievements in gender equality, the government draws both funding and support from the international community. Based on an analysis of national education documents and interviews with local actors, I argue that the government deliberately draws on human rights discourses in certain contexts, such as gender equality, but ignores violations of human rights in other contexts. For instance, violations of human rights during the genocide are highlighted in the curriculum but omitted when discussing the prelude to and aftermath of the genocide. More recent or current human rights violations are not mentioned in the curriculum, in textbooks, or in the classroom. Certain types of rights, such as women's rights and gender equality, are privileged, whereas discussion of group and minority rights is avoided. This inconsistency has led to a focus on gender equality at the expense of addressing other social inequities (related, for example, to ethnicity and language), negatively impacting the broader peacebuilding project.

In chapter 5, "Addressing the Genocide and Promoting Reconciliation," I demonstrate how the Rwandan government uses education as part of its strategy to address the past. While the RPF advances a tightly controlled official narrative around the genocide to promote reconciliation and unity, testimonies from students and teachers reveal narratives and lived experiences that diverge from the state-sanctioned version of the past. Although ethnicity is used to discuss the genocide, it is in other contexts a taboo subject, and critical discussion of ethnic identity is forbidden. This dichotomy results in contradictions and inconsistencies when teaching and learning about the genocide. Through an analysis of national documents, interviews, and school observations, I show how the state-sponsored narrative around unity and reconciliation is reframed and reinvented at the local level and how this suppresses open discussion among students and teachers, thereby limiting national unity. I argue that the Rwandan government's attempt to promote reconciliation and unity by mandating an official and narrow narrative around the genocide and muting ethnic identity in fact suppresses open discussion about the past and authentic reconciliation. Students and teachers know the official discourse around unity and reconciliation, but in private, they question the inconsistencies and contradictions. They are careful to censor themselves out of fear of legal consequences, not because they are infused with the spirit of genuine reconciliation.

In chapter 6, "The Potential and Limitations of Education for Peacebuilding," I restate the larger arguments of the book and discuss how the issues and tensions that have emerged in Rwanda are relevant to other postconflict contexts. The findings presented in this book raise questions about the efficacy of global discourses in promoting citizenship, human rights, and reconciliation when they are significantly diluted and reinterpreted at the local level. Rwanda highlights not only the use of global discourses but also the limitations of exporting global peacebuilding models to postconflict contexts. Countries often opt for techniques such as placing a moratorium on history education or promoting one-sided official narratives to avoid a controversial past. Alternatively, countries may rely on global models of human rights, citizenship, and peace education rather than delve into their national histories. This diversity in how states address the past highlights the difficult roles played by teachers—who must navigate their own positionality and experience to teach about the past—and the challenges faced by students, who may learn at home a different interpretation of the past than they are taught at school. The task for teachers is made even more difficult in authoritarian countries. In such contexts, a regime can compel or intimidate teachers and students to pretend to ignore contradictions in what is taught at school and to keep silent about discrepancies between what textbooks assert and what their families remember. But while criticism of those contradictions can be silenced, the realization among teachers and students that official accounts of the past and the present do not align is likely to impede efforts to promote reconciliation, unity, and a new civic identity.

CHAPTER 2

The Role of Education
in Transitional Justice,
Peacebuilding,
and Reconciliation

[We] are unable to forgive what [we] cannot
punish and [we] are unable to punish what
has turned out to be unforgivable.
—Hannah Arendt, *The Human Condition* (1985)

NUMEROUS SCHOLARS HAVE documented the
rise and institutionalization of transitional justice in postconflict
contexts, particularly since the end of the Cold War (see De Greiff 2012; Hayner 2011; McEvoy 2007; Minow 1998; Roht-Arriaza
and Mariezcurrena 2006). Transitional justice mechanisms
include both judicial and nonjudicial mechanisms—such as
criminal tribunals and truth commissions—that seek to address
the legacies of human rights violations. Transitional justice is
concerned not only with addressing the past but also with promoting a shared future. The United Nations began to recognize
the integral role of transitional justice processes and mechanisms
in peacebuilding endeavors with the release of the 2004 report
*The Rule of Law and Transitional Justice in Conflict and Post-conflict
Societies.* This document emphasized the necessity of "redress for

29

grievances" through "legitimate structures" for the "maintenance of peace in the long-term" (United Nations 2004, 3).

Scholars have also examined the link between transitional justice and broader peacebuilding and development initiatives (Kent 2016; Lambourne 2009; Mani 2008; Sriram 2007). Although that link has generally been seen as positive, scholars have noted that transitional justice processes may cause instability and perpetuate further conflict in some cases (Mani 2008; Sriram 2007). While previously viewed as a distinct field, transitional justice is now seen as a necessary part of the peacebuilding process (Sriram 2007). Wendy Lambourne (2009) argues that transitional justice processes must attend to the legal as well as the political, socioeconomic, and psychosocial aspects of justice in order to contribute to sustainable peacebuilding.

Despite the institutionalization of the field and the global spread of norms around transitional justice (McEvoy 2007; Sikkink and Walling 2007), the majority of empirical literature in the field of sociology, political science, and law has not examined the role that education systems perform in promoting justice and reconciliation in the aftermath of a violent conflict. Only recently have scholars begun to examine the crucial function that education systems can and should play in the aftermath of a violent conflict through in-depth empirical studies (see Bellino et al. 2017; Davies 2017; Ramírez-Barat and Duthie 2016).

This chapter begins by providing an overview of the global rise of transitional justice mechanisms. I then elaborate on the role that education plays in transitional justice and peacebuilding processes, highlighting global trends and key country cases, before reviewing the case of Rwanda. I examine the extent to which education systems have been integrated into broader transitional justice, peacebuilding, and reconciliation processes across different regional contexts. The chapter argues that education systems—which are used to interpret the contested past, shape ideas about citizenship and human rights, disseminate the findings of truth commissions, and mold hopes for the future—serve as an important transitional justice mechanism that is often overlooked in favor of legal and political tools.

THE GLOBAL RISE OF TRANSITIONAL JUSTICE

Ruti Teitel defines transitional justice as the "conception of justice associated with periods of political change, characterized by legal responses to confront the wrongdoings of repressive predecessor regimes" (2003, 69). However, other scholars, such as Naomi Roht-Arriaza (2006), view transitional justice as encompassing not only legal mechanisms but also the political, social, and cultural aspects of the manner in which a postconflict society deals with past human rights violations and mass atrocities. In other words, transitional justice incorporates the processes and the mechanisms through which a postconflict nation-state addresses a violent past. These mechanisms include the use of international tribunals, national courts, local or traditional forms of justice, truth commissions, amnesties, reparations, and various hybrid approaches.

The notion of *transitional justice* emerged in the wake of the Nuremberg and Tokyo war crimes tribunals at the close of World War II. At first, transitional justice was an exceptional event, but it became increasingly institutionalized in international law toward the end of the twentieth century (Teitel 2003). Since the end of the Cold War, there has been a notable rise in the use of various transitional justice mechanisms, including trials, truth commissions, reparations, lustration, memorials, and oral history projects (Jelin 2003; Sikkink and Walling 2007). International transitional justice norms and mechanisms have become progressively more common in postconflict and transitional societies. The rising influence and institutionalization of global norms around transitional justice and human rights constitutes what Martha Finnemore and Kathryn Sikkink (1998) refer to as a "norm cascade," or the broad acceptance of a norm. While transitional justice is often linked to international legal mechanisms or global models, recent scholarship has sought to understand how norms and practices around transitional justice are experienced by local and national actors (Hinton 2010; Shaw, Waldorf, and Hazan 2010).

Transitional justice is commonly used in attempts to foster peace and societal reconciliation in the aftermath of civil or ethnic conflict or collective violence. Transitional justice mechanisms also seek to promote recognition of past abuses, as well as civic trust (De Greiff 2012). The international community and scholars now view transitional justice as an integral part of the peacebuilding process (Lambourne 2009; Mendeloff 2004; Sriram 2007).

The progression of societal reconciliation or social reconstruction is often characterized in terms of the debate between justice and truth (Stover and Weinstein 2004). Is it possible to achieve justice and also restore peace? Scholars conceptualize justice as falling into two distinct categories: retributive and restorative justice. The purpose of *retributive justice* is that of "taming vengeance" by the transfer of the responsibility for punishment from the victims to the courts by holding individuals accountable for crimes; *restorative justice*, by contrast, aims to promote societal healing and is primarily victim-centered (Stover and Weinstein 2004). In general, it is assumed that retributive justice will address the justice requirement, while restorative justice will promote peace within society. However, some mechanisms include aspects of both retributive and restorative justice.

The eminent legal scholar Martha Minow (1998) theorizes an approach that goes beyond the justice/peace dichotomy by focusing instead on the notions of vengeance and forgiveness, thereby justifying a response to addressing mass atrocities that goes beyond criminal justice: "Between vengeance and forgiveness lies the path of recollection and affirmation and the path of facing who we are, and what we could become" (147). The focus on the emotions of vengeance and forgiveness calls for a better understanding of how individuals address their need for vengeance in order to achieve justice, while also forgiving, which is necessary for peace. This approach underscores the idea that the ideals of achieving justice and peace are not mutually exclusive and do not require specific mechanisms to achieve specific outcomes; a variety of processes across different settings can be employed.

COMMON TRANSITIONAL JUSTICE MECHANISMS

This section provides an overview of commonly used transitional justice mechanisms, ranging from judicial, such as trials, to nonjudicial mechanisms, such as truth commissions and education systems.

Judicial Mechanisms

Judicial mechanisms, such as national and international tribunals, aim to promote retributive justice and deter future crimes, as well as to rehabilitate or incapacitate indicted criminals (Roht-Arriaza 1995). While judicial mechanisms tend to focus on the retributive aspect of transitional justice, they may also have restorative goals, including the promotion of accountability, establishing the rule of law, creating symbolic norms, fostering societal reconciliation, and laying the foundations for enduring peace.

The Nuremberg and Tokyo trials in the 1940s were the first international tribunals established for the prosecution of international war crimes. In the early 1990s, the United Nations established ad hoc tribunals—the International Criminal Tribunal for the Former Yugoslavia (ICTY) and the International Criminal Tribunal for Rwanda (ICTR)—to address the genocide and ethnic cleansing perpetrated in those two parts of the world. Less than a decade later, the International Criminal Court (ICC) was established by the Rome Statute in 2002 as a permanent tribunal for the prosecution of crimes against humanity, war crimes, and genocide. The ICC has jurisdiction for massive human rights violations by state parties. By the end of 2017, 123 states had ratified the Rome Statute, indicating the global reach of the norm around transitional justice.

Additionally, hybrid courts, or "mixed tribunals," which include both international and national staff, have been established in Sierra Leone, East Timor, Kosovo, and Cambodia. Prosecutions for crimes against humanity have also been conducted in national courts—for instance, in Argentina, Rwanda, and Ethiopia.

Retributive justice views punishment in terms of a moral rationale that transfers individual feelings of vengeance and revenge into the court system, which assigns individual responsibility for collective guilt (Bass 2014; Roht-Arriaza 1995; Stover and Weinstein 2004). The punishment of the perpetrator is deemed necessary in order to achieve justice in society, which is linked to reconciliation. Furthermore, criminal trials or tribunals are now widely viewed as essential for instilling legal accountability and for promoting the rule of law in a new democracy. Criminal accountability provides the victim with a public forum to disclose the facts, an official record, and a sense of justice and catharsis (Kritz 1996; Minow 1998). Trials are also said to create or support global and symbolic norms that may prevent future conflict and lead to reconciliation and peace in the long term (Akhavan 2001).

Despite the apparent benefits of criminal justice mechanisms, trials are by no means a panacea. While trials are believed to deter future atrocities, this assumption has not been adequately tested with empirical evidence (Mendeloff 2004; Wippman 1999). Additionally, the assumed results of deterrence and retributive justice may be limited due to the problem of selectivity. In situations of mass collective violence, it is impossible to prosecute all offenders; thus, often only select leaders are prosecuted (Drumbl 2003).

Another limitation to criminal justice is that there is no criminology of mass violence, even though crimes of mass violence are being prosecuted (Drumbl 2003). The legal system focuses on the individual and does not address the implications of collective violence (Stover and Weinstein 2004). Further constraints on trials include the problem of retroactivity—in other words, the fact that the defendants may be on trial for breaching legal norms that were not formally established when the crimes were committed. Trials are also likely be to highly politicized and may not be immune to pressure from governments and other political actors (Minow 1998). The impact of trials and the reach of tribunals may be limited by a scarcity of both human and material resources and the lack of authority to apprehend indicted criminals. In general, international courts have indicted relatively few perpetrators and have tried and sentenced far fewer. While some empirical studies of international tribunals, such as the ICTY and the ICTR, have found that they contribute to peacebuilding (Akhavan 2001; Meernik and King 2001), other studies cast doubt on the effectiveness of trials and other transitional justice mechanisms to build sustainable peace (Mendeloff 2004; Vinjamuri and Snyder 2004).

Nonjudicial Mechanisms

An alternative approach to transitional justice focuses on nonjudicial mechanisms, such as truth commissions and reparations, that seek to promote restorative justice. Nonjudicial mechanisms serve as other sites through which to promote restorative justice and address aspects of collective forgiveness.

TRUTH COMMISSIONS. Truth commissions are officially authorized temporary and nonjudicial bodies charged with investigating widespread abuses. The aim of a truth commission is to establish a record of past events and, as Priscilla Hayner (2011) writes, to "lift the lid of silence and denial from a contentious and painful period of history" (20). More than forty official truth commissions have been established across a diverse range of countries— including Argentina, Guatemala, Germany, Sierra Leone, and South Africa (Hayner 2011). Truth commissions can be national or international, and they can have different and distinctive prosecution powers. In the case of the South African Truth and Reconciliation Commission (TRC), conditional amnesty was offered in return for a full disclosure of facts deemed to be politically relevant.

Truth commissions have an inherently different focus and mandate compared to trials. The aim of a truth commission is to focus on the victim, encourage truth-telling, foster individual healing and social repair, and engender restorative justice (Hayner 2011). By focusing on the victims of mass atrocities, truth commissions encourage the cathartic and therapeutic process of truth-telling in a public and official space. The act of testimony as well as the public acknowledgment of the wrong committed may allow for healing and reconciliation at both the individual and societal levels. Hence, compared to criminal trials, truth commissions foster restorative justice rather than retributive justice, and they focus on social reconstruction rather than retribution.

Truth commissions do not necessarily replace criminal trials; indeed, they can complement judicial processes or be utilized when judicial systems are weak (Hayner 2011; Kritz 1996). In some instances, truth commissions occur simultaneously with trials; in other cases, the evidence gathered by the commissions may be used for later prosecutions. For example, truth commissions and trials have proceeded concurrently in Sierra Leone and East Timor; in Argentina and Chad, in contrast, truth commissions were established before criminal trials (Roht-Arriaza and Mariezcurrena 2006).

REPARATIONS. Reparations can be used in conjunction with criminal proceedings and truth commissions. Reparations seek to redress past wrongs and represent a societal acknowledgment of past violations (De Greiff 2006; Hayner 2011; Roht-Arriaza 2004). Reparations may be material or moral in form. Material reparations include monetary compensation; restitution of property; and the provision of jobs, pensions, educational funds, and medical and psychological care. Moral or symbolic reparations include public apologies, memorials, justice, and truth-telling (Minow 1998; Roht-Arriaza 2004). Some scholars critique reparations for seeking to compensate for a wrong that cannot be undone (Roht-Arriaza 2004).

Reparations programs have been implemented to varying degrees in postconflict situations. Examples include monetary reparations for victims in Germany following the Holocaust; economic and symbolic reparations for families of the victims of the military dictatorships in Argentina, Brazil, and Chile; reparation grants for victims in South Africa; and a trust fund for victims in Sierra Leone (De Greiff 2006; Hayner 2011; Roht-Arriaza and Mariezcurrena 2006). In some instances, such as Guatemala, El Salvador, and Haiti, reparations were recommended by the truth commissions but were never implemented. In other cases, such as South Africa, the government delayed allocating the funds to victims; some apartheid victims had still not received monetary reparations in 2017 (Collins 2017).

Although reparations are usually focused on monetary compensation, in some countries reparations have specifically referred to the role of the education system in compensating for past wrongs. For instance, in Chile, the Truth and Reconciliation Commission recommended the provision of educational scholarships for the children of those who had been killed or disappeared during the military dictatorship (Lira 2006). In South Africa, the Truth and Reconciliation Act similarly promised educational benefits for apartheid victims (Colvin 2006).

Education for Transitional Justice

The education system is another nonjudicial mechanism that can be used to promote transitional justice. Minow (2002) argues that educational change must be included in any efforts to reconstruct society following intergroup conflict; "Education," she writes, "offers the chance to shape minds, hearts, and behaviors of succeeding generations" (2). When used in conjunction with other mechanisms, such as truth commissions or trials, education systems can teach the broader population about past atrocities. By themselves, changes to the education system or to educational policies may directly respond to past grievances or seek to rectify socioeconomic inequalities across formal, nonformal, and informal educational spaces.

Scholars increasingly view education systems as serving a central role in broader transitional justice, peacebuilding, and reconciliation processes (Bellino et al. 2017; E. Cole 2007a; Davies 2017; Ramírez-Barat and Duthie 2016). A country's education system can function not only as a venue to educate the public about past violations but also as an instrument that works in conjunction with other transitional justice mechanisms to address broader structural inequalities and discrimination linked to underlying causes of the country's conflict. Several empirical studies have documented the role that education plays in transitional justice through expanding access to education across diverse groups, teaching about the past conflict, and teaching about citizenship and human rights (see Bellino 2014; Paulson and Bellino 2017; Tibbitts and Weldon 2017). For instance, Julia Paulson and Michelle Bellino (2017) find that truth commissions are increasingly involving educational aspects in their work, particularly in terms of recommending the introduction of new curricular subjects and nonformal programs around human rights and civics.

Lynn Davies (2017) presents the notion of "justice-sensitive education," which seeks to address past human rights abuses, uncover the truth about a violent past, and promote a two-way gaze that looks to both the past and the future. She argues that in order to incorporate a transitional justice lens within the education sector, three types of changes must be made: *structural educational reforms*, which include changes to language policies, the integration of segregated schools, and the reallocation of teachers and resources; *changes in the curriculum*, including revision of the old curriculum and the adoption of human rights and citizenship education; and *reforms to the pedagogy and institutional culture*, which implies the promotion of critical thinking and the use of democratic and participatory teaching strategies.

STRUCTURAL REFORMS. While transitional justice often focuses on violations of civil and political rights, violations of economic, social, and cultural rights are often linked to historical inequities across groups and to the roots of the conflict (Laplante 2008). Addressing these structural inequalities and the underlying causes of conflict is a necessary condition to obtain what Johan Galtung (1969) terms "positive peace." Positive peace promotes social justice and includes redistribution, recognition, representation, and reconciliation—what Mario Novelli and his colleagues refer to as the "4Rs framework" (Fraser 1995; Novelli, Lopes Cardozo, and Smith 2017). In the context of education, this framework includes *redistribution* or access to equal educational opportunities and the distribution of resources; *recognition* of a range of diverse groups across ethnic, racial, gender, and linguistic differences, including in language policies and curriculum; the *representation* of these diverse groups in political governance for transformational change; and *reconciliation*, or dealing with the past and historical memory (Novelli, Lopes Cardozo, and Smith 2017).

CURRICULAR REFORMS. Aligned with both reconciliation and the recognition of diverse groups in the 4Rs framework is the reform of curricular content. Educational scholars have generally focused on the importance of reforms to history, social studies, and civics/citizenship curricula. Elizabeth Cole (2007a) argues that history education is related to the transitional justice process through officially addressing the past, preserving a collective memory, and promoting reconciliation and public deliberation. History education, and particularly history textbooks, provide an official record of past atrocities (E. Cole 2007a, 2007b; Paulson 2015). However, while history education has the potential to promote reconciliation, a certain level of reconciliation must exist in a society before contested narratives can be introduced in the classroom (E. Cole 2007a).

While history education often plays an important role in establishing a historical record, in other instances, postconflict countries rely on social studies or human rights education to construct a narrative of the past. In some countries, governments have eliminated history as a subject following the conflict (E. Cole 2007a). In Rwanda, the postg-enocide government placed a moratorium on history, while in South Africa history was not included as a separate subject in the first iteration of the post-apartheid curriculum. In other cases, such as in Guatemala or Peru, history has been incorporated into the social studies curriculum. Governments that view history education as contentious or politically sensitive often opt to include historical events under more general subjects such as social studies or civics, where there is no explicit reference to the role of the state in committing past abuses (E. Cole 2007b).

INSTITUTIONAL CULTURE. A third way of providing justice-sensitive education is to reform the institutional culture of the education system and the pedagogy teachers adopt. Scholars argue for the importance of student-centered pedagogy in developing engaged citizens (E. Cole 2007a) and, more particularly, in promoting human rights and civic engagement (Bajaj 2011a; Tibbitts 2002). Felisa Tibbitts (2008) emphasizes the importance of fostering knowledge and actions around human rights through interactive and student-centered methods, which are relevant to daily life and engage students in meaningful and participatory action. Similarly, Monisha Bajaj (2011a) characterizes human rights education as not only imparting knowledge about human rights but also developing skills for active civic engagement through participatory methods. Elizabeth Cole and Judy Barsalou (2006) claim that the pedagogy is more important than the content for promoting critical thinking, democratic participation, and long-term peacebuilding.

COUNTRY CASES

Given that in many conflict contexts, unequal and biased education fueled the conflict (Bush and Saltarelli 2000; Lange 2012), the incorporation of transitional justice into education systems has particular relevance. Most postconflict countries focus on the legal and political aspects of transitional justice and pay much less attention to educational aspects of transitional justice. Several countries, including South Africa, Sierra Leone, Peru, and Guatemala, have infused educational perspectives into the transitional justice process or transitional justice into the educational systems. This section briefly reviews four country cases to illustrate the range of engagement with the education sector and varying degrees of success. As these country cases illustrate, despite the intention of incorporating education into broader discussions around justice and reconciliation, a challenging political context or disagreement about how to address the past impeded progress.

South Africa

Following the end of apartheid, or institutionalized racial discrimination, and the transition to democracy in 1994, the newly elected government of Nelson Mandela formed the South African TRC in 1996 to address gross violations of human rights committed during the apartheid era. The mandate of the TRC was to focus on politically motivated human rights violations committed from 1961 through 1993.

However, structural inequalities linked to social, racial, and economic injustices committed during apartheid were not explicitly addressed by the TRC. In particular, the provision of substandard education to nonwhites was not included under the jurisdiction of the TRC or directly addressed in the testimonies. Felisa Tibbitts and Gail Weldon (2017) point to the contradiction that despite the fact that unequal access to education was critical to maintaining the system of apartheid, the formal transitional justice process did not focus on "the role of education in contributing to apartheid, nor on the ways in which the education system might respond to the requirements of a new, democratic South Africa" (447).

Despite these inherent limitations, the TRC served an educational role in disseminating findings about crimes committed during apartheid to the broader public. Although the TRC did not produce a final report for students or materials to teach about the commission in schools, the postapartheid curriculum and textbooks for history, social studies, and life orientation do mention the TRC and mass human rights violations as a topic of study (Russell, Sirota, and Ahmed 2019).

In addition, Tebojo Moja (2016) argues that educational reforms in South Africa function as a form of redress. Structural reforms to the education system, such as mandating the right to basic education in the 1996 Constitution to all groups, integrating formerly segregated school systems, and redistributing resources, sought to address past injustices and include a transitional justice lens within the education system (Christie 2016; Moja 2016). However, education systems in South Africa remain highly unequal and divided across racial lines and by socioeconomic background (Badat and Sayed 2014; Moja 2016). Although the education system has not fully addressed past grievances, the postapartheid South African government has attempted to integrate the transitional justice process into educational materials.

Sierra Leone

The decade-long civil war (1991–2002) in Sierra Leone between the Revolutionary United Front rebel group and the government resulted in the deaths of more than 50,000 people and the displacement of three-quarters of the population. The Lomé peace agreement, signed in 1999 between the government and rebel forces, called for a truth commission to address past human rights abuses. One such abuse was in the realm of education: unequal access to education was viewed as a driver of the conflict, and schools were greatly affected by the violence (Paulson 2006; Shepler 2014; Smith Ellison 2012).

Consequently, the Sierra Leone Truth and Reconciliation Commission (SLTRC), created by the Sierra Leone Truth and Reconciliation Act of 2000, considered reforms to the education system and recommended a number of changes. For instance, the SLTRC recommended making primary education free and compulsory, including human rights education in educational materials, and eliminating corporal punishment and discrimination in schools (Paulson 2006). The government introduced free primary education in 2001 and guaranteed the right to free basic education in the 2004 Education Act (Smith Ellison 2012).

The SLTRC was the first truth commission to focus specifically on the experiences of children during the conflict and to involve the participation of children in the hearings (Cook and Heykook 2010). In addition, with support from UNICEF and local nongovernmental organizations (NGOs), the SLTRC produced the first child-friendly version of its final report for both primary and secondary school students.

Despite the mandate for the inclusion of education reforms in the SLTRC process, scholars have found that often these reforms were disconnected from the SLTRC recommendations and did not have much concrete impact on Sierra Leone's schools and students (Paulson 2006). The child-friendly versions of the SLTRC's reports, for instance, were not widely disseminated or used in schools (Cook and Heykook 2010; Paulson 2006). This disappointing outcome reflected a lack of both initiative and resources from the government and partner organizations, and it meant that the government's ambitious plans to incorporate transitional justice into education materials and education into the transitional justice process were not fully realized.

Peru

The Peruvian Truth and Reconciliation Commission (TRC) was established in 2001 by the country's interim president, Valentín Paniagua, after the former president, Alberto Fujimori, fled to Japan following a corruption scandal. The TRC was tasked with investigating the mass human rights violations committed during the two decades of conflict from 1980 to 2000 between the government and the Maoist revolutionary movement Sendero Luminoso (Shining Path). The TRC was also mandated to investigate the conditions that led to the armed conflict and to discover the facts around mass displacement of the population and the deaths of an estimated 70,000 people (Theidon 2012).

In addition to investigating the structural conditions that led to the conflict, the TRC also included a forward-looking mandate to reform the school curriculum. Aspects of the TRC's final report, published in 2003, were incorporated into educational resources. For instance, following the release of the final report, the Ministry of Education produced a set of six workbooks (called *Recordándonos*) for primary and secondary students that examined the history of armed conflict and the work of the TRC. However, the workbooks were not distributed widely and were never officially approved by the ministry due to politically sensitive content around state violations of human rights and criticisms from the Ministry of Defense and Congress (Paulson 2017).

In addition to the *Recordándonos*, the Ministry of Education also revised the national curriculum in 2000 as part of a broader reform of the education sector. Under this reform, history as a subject was eliminated and replaced with an interdisciplinary social sciences subject. The new 2008 social sciences textbook did include some discussion of the armed conflict and the TRC (Paulson 2017). Despite the government's intention to integrate the findings from the TRC into educational materials, the politicized nature of the narrative of the past resulted in attempts to block the inclusion of the work of the TRC in educational materials. Ultimately, the government's efforts to incorporate the findings of the TRC into educational materials have had mixed results.

Guatemala

The 1996 peace accords brought an end to thirty-four years of violent armed conflict between the government and the indigenous communities of Guatemala. More than 200,000 people died as a result of what was known as the Conflicto Armado (Armed Conflict). The Guatemalan Commission for Historical Clarification (CEH or Comisión para el Esclarecimiento Histórico) was created as part of the peace process to investigate the mass violations of human rights. The CEH, which issued its final report in 1999, found that the vast majority of human rights violations were committed by the state's military and police forces against indigenous groups.

As part of the peace process, the government committed to increasing spending on education and reforming the curriculum to address issues of diversity and multiculturalism (Oglesby 2007). The CEH also brought attention to the role of Guatemala's education system in fueling the underlying inequalities and discrimination that led to the armed conflict (Bellino 2014). While the peace accords promised to improve the education system through increased investment, the government did not significantly increase spending on education or carry out comprehensive curricular reforms (Oglesby 2007).

Hence, education reforms for promoting transitional justice were recommended but never implemented. Schools and teachers teach about transitional justice in an ad hoc manner rather than by adhering to a systematic course of instruction endorsed by the state (Bellino 2015; Oglesby 2007). Although most textbooks produced since the peace accords address the past conflict (Oglesby 2007), there are no national curriculum standards requiring schools to teach about the past conflict and the CEH's findings.

MECHANISMS FOR PEACEBUILDING
AND TRANSITIONAL JUSTICE IN
POST-GENOCIDE RWANDA

Since the 1994 genocide, the Rwandan government, led by the RPF, has introduced both legal and nonlegal mechanisms intended to deliver transitional justice and foster reconciliation. The government has also expected the education system to play a complementary role to broader transitional justice processes, particularly through policy, curricular, and pedagogical reforms.

Legal Mechanisms

The first legal mechanism to deal with the mass atrocities of the genocide was established by the UN Security Council, which set up the International Criminal Tribunal for Rwanda (ICTR) in 1994. The purpose of the tribunal, which was located in Arusha, Tanzania, was to try the leaders of the genocide and those responsible for violating international humanitarian law at any point during 1994. Targeting government, military, business, media, and religious leaders, the ICTR ran for twenty years and cost US$1.5 billion. But its results were disappointing. By the time it closed in December 2015, the tribunal had indicted only ninety-two individuals and sentenced sixty-two.[1]

In 1996, the Rwandan government established a law for the prosecution of genocide-related crimes and began national trials. However, the judicial system was overwhelmed: by 1999, more than 130,000 suspected *génocidaires* were imprisoned awaiting trial in national courts (Ingelaere 2016).

Due to severe overcrowding in the prisons and the inability of the national courts to process the high number of cases in a timely manner, the government established *gacaca* courts in 2001 (Ingelaere 2016; Waldorf 2007).[2] Deriving from a precolonial traditional conflict resolution structure, *gacaca* (which means "justice on the grass" in Kinyarwanda) relied on *inyangamugayo*, locally elected judges who did not have legal training, to try genocide suspects. Through a mix of retributive and restorative justice, this home-grown mechanism sought to establish the truth about crimes related to the genocide, accelerate the trials of the accused génocidaires, eradicate impunity, and foster reconciliation and unity among Rwandans (Ingelaere 2016; Republic of Rwanda 2012). Running nationwide in local districts from 2002 to 2012, more than 12,000 local courts tried more than 1 million Hutu in 1,958,634 cases for crimes related to the genocide (Republic of Rwanda 2012). The courts touched the lives of most Rwandans: during the decade of their operation, the *gacaca* courts tried one in every three Hutu who had been adults at the time of the genocide and involved the vast majority of Rwandan adults as judges or witnesses (Chakravarty 2015, 3).

The courts dealt with three categories of cases: category 1 for the planners and organizers of the genocide (and for crimes including rape and sexual torture); category 2 for murderers or accomplices; and category 3 for people who committed crimes that included destruction of property. The vast majority of cases,

67 percent, were related to crimes against property. Category 3 criminals often had to pay fines (in 87 percent of cases). For categories 1 and 2, the *gacaca* courts usually handed down prison sentences (in 93 percent of the cases). If perpetrators confessed their crimes, the length of their sentence could be reduced and incarceration could be replaced with community service (Nyseth Brehm, Uggen, and Gasanabo 2014).

Although some scholars have viewed *gacaca* positively as a new form of localized transitional justice (see Clark 2010; Nyseth Brehm, Uggen, and Gasanabo 2014), other scholars and some international NGOs have criticized the proceedings as a politicized tool of the regime that led to mixed results in achieving reconciliation and justice among the local population (see Chakravarty 2015; Human Rights Watch 2008; Ingelaere 2016; Penal Reform International 2010; Rettig 2008; Thomson and Nagy 2011; Waldorf 2007). Some assessments of *gacaca* have found that the proceedings were more retributive than restorative and that local participation was often coerced rather than voluntary. For instance, in his in-depth ethnographic study of *gacaca* proceedings over several years, Bert Ingelaere (2016) concluded that the *gacaca* courts operated primarily as retributive courts to establish forensic truth rather than to promote restorative justice; drew on accusatory practices rather than confessions; suffered from low levels of participation; and ignored war crimes and revenge killings.

Nonlegal Mechanisms

Complementing judicial mechanisms, the government also established several institutions to teach about the genocide and to foster reconciliation at the societal level. For example, the National Unity and Reconciliation Commission, which was created in 1999, was tasked with promoting national unity and reconciliation through numerous community civic education programs. Likewise, the National Commission for the Fight against Genocide (CNLG) was established to combat "genocide ideology" and to preserve the historical memory of the genocide. Another mechanism that the government has introduced is *ingando* camps ("solidarity camps"), where Rwandans learn about Rwandan identity, culture, and the history of the genocide. Run like military camps and located in different parts of the country, *ingando* camps are mandated for a variety of groups, including secondary school students, teachers, government civil servants, former soldiers and combatants, *génocidaires*, street children, prostitutes, and returned refugees (Mgbako 2005; Purdeková 2011). The camps—which can run from a few days to several weeks—include cultural activities, lectures about Rwandan history, manual labor, and, in some cases, military training. The stated goals of *ingando* camps are to promote reconciliation, unity, and nation building at a local level and to teach about the dangers of genocide ideology (Purdeková 2015). However, some scholars argue that *ingando* camps are concerned less with fostering reconciliation than with disseminating pro-RPF ideology (Mgbako 2005; Purdeková 2015).

Formal Educational Mechanisms

In addition to legal and nonlegal mechanisms, the government has sought to use the country's education system as a tool for peacebuilding and transitional justice. This ambition is aligned with Davies's (2017) conception of "justice-sensitive education" (discussed above), which Davies sees as encompassing three areas: structural reforms, curricular reform, and changes in the institutional culture of schools. In Rwanda, the government has implemented policy changes that affect each of these areas.

POLICY REFORMS. In order to expand access to basic education, the government developed an Education for All plan of action and abolished primary school fees in 2003 (World Bank 2011). A nine-year basic education policy was adopted in 2006, with implementation beginning in 2009. During the election campaign in 2010, President Kagame committed to expanding basic education to twelve years. In 2011, the government began the construction of classrooms in selected schools so that more schools could provide twelve years of basic education. Enrollment rates in primary and secondary schools have increased dramatically since the genocide. In primary schools, the net enrollment rate increased from 79 percent in 1999 to 95 percent in 2015.[3] In secondary schools, the gross enrollment ratio increased from 9 percent in 1999 to 37 percent in 2015.[4] Yet, issues of quality remain a problem, as evidenced by high dropout rates, low transition rates, and low levels of learning outcomes (Williams 2017; World Bank 2018).[5]

Another step the government took toward creating a unified post-genocide state was to change the medium of instruction in schools. Before the genocide, the medium of instruction was Kinyarwanda at the primary level and French at the secondary level (Erny 2003). In 1997, a revised primary and secondary curriculum was implemented with a trilingual policy of instruction (French, English, and Kinyarwanda). In 2008, the government changed the medium of instruction from French to English in all grades; this policy was implemented beginning in 2009. In 2011, the policy was changed so that grades 1 through 3 are now taught in Kinyarwanda, while the other grades are taught in English. The abrupt change in the medium of instruction came as a surprise to many, including the schools and the international donor community, because teachers were not consulted about or trained in the use of English before the switch. The move to English has thus created challenges for both teachers and students and has inevitably privileged Anglophone returnees over other Rwandans (Abbott, Sapsford, and Rwirahira 2015; Pearson 2014; Russell 2015).

The language policy was primarily a political decision that emanated from the Office of the President rather than from the

Ministry of Education; no official policy document was produced. The government joined the East African Community in July 2007 and the British Commonwealth in 2009 and used its membership to justify the change in the language policy (interview with intergovernmental organization, August 2010). Officials also stressed the fact that English is a global language with associated economic benefits (interview with government official, August 2010). However, some people perceived the policy change to be politically motivated because the ruling Tutsi Anglophone elite speak English rather than French, which is spoken by the majority of the educated Hutu population (Samuelson and Freedman 2010).[6] These divisive education policies around language of instruction and expansion of education without attention to quality may in fact undermine broader peacebuilding goals rather than create unity in the long term.

CURRICULUM REFORM. In addition to expanding access to education and shifting the language policy, the government has undertaken reforms to the structure and content of the curriculum and textbooks. One priority for the government in the immediate aftermath of the genocide was to expunge perceived bias in the curriculum associated with the previous regime and to align the curriculum with regional and global standards. To this end, the RPF-led government purged curricular documents, confiscated textbooks, and reconfigured the structure of the Ministry of Education, including its National Curriculum Development Center (NCDC).[7]

The new civics curriculum, developed with the help of UNESCO and UNICEF, was in line with other global civics curricula, focusing on such topics as human rights, citizenship, and reconciliation. Several international organizations and NGOs provided support for the development of teaching materials for civics education. For instance, UNESCO and UNICEF supported a peace education pilot program (Obura 2003). In 1999, a new

curriculum for civics education, referred to as "political education," was introduced for secondary schools. In 2004, the government produced a civics textbook in French and English with
funding from UNICEF. In 2008, the NCDC introduced another
political education curriculum for secondary school (for both the
ordinary level, or O-level, and the advanced level, or A-level).[8] A
two-volume political education textbook in English, aligned with
the 2008 curriculum, was published in 2008 with support from
the International Committee of the Red Cross.

After the genocide, the Ministry of Education placed a
moratorium on the teaching of Rwandan history because there
was no consensus among academics and government officials
about which version of history to teach. In 1999, the ministry
directed schools to begin teaching history again and provided
general guidelines; however, no new textbooks or curricula
were developed (Weinstein, Freedman, and Hughson 2007).
From 2001 through 2006, the ministry collaborated with the
University of California, Berkeley, and the U.S. NGO Facing
History and Ourselves to develop a teacher's guide and an official curriculum for the teaching of Rwandan history. This mul-
tiyear project brought together international experts on Rwanda,
local historians, curriculum developers, and teachers to discuss
content and pedagogy for the new curriculum (Freedman et al.
2008). The University of California published a teacher's guide
to Rwandan history in 2006; however, the government did not
distribute this version of the book due to disagreement around
the content. Rather, the government published its own simpli-
fied and edited version in 2010. The government also developed
a new history curriculum for the O-level in 2008 and for the
A-level in 2010. It was not until 2011, however, that the corresponding history textbooks arrived in schools.[9]

In 2015, the Ministry of Education revised the national curriculum to focus on core competencies. Textbooks for the new

curriculum were published in 2016 and 2017. "Political educa-tion" was renamed "history and citizenship" and is taught at the ordinary level for all students; history continues to be taught at the advanced level for humanities concentrations that include history as a subject. The government announced in 2017 that the Education for Sustainable Peace in Rwanda program would be added to the national curriculum. Despite the emphasis on sus-tainable peace in the newest iteration of reforms, these various curricular and education reforms point to the fragility of the global-local linkage. The government initiates broader compre-hensive reforms to the education system and curriculum in line with broader global trends, which are not always in line with the realities on the ground.

INSTITUTIONAL CULTURE. In addition to reforms to the school system and curriculum, the Ministry of Education has also sought to introduce changes to the pedagogy and school culture from lecture-based to more student-centered methods. The national curriculum and policy documents include language around student-centered pedagogy to reflect this change. For example, the *Educa-tion Sector Strategic Plan, 2010–2015* speaks to the importance of developing "learner-centred methodologies" (18). The 2015 *Rwan-dan Competence-Based Curriculum Framework* also emphasizes the importance of learner-centered curriculum, which "must address learners' individual needs, interests, abilities, and background" (3). However, the implementation of the curriculum in schools has been problematic due to lack of teacher training and delivery of materials (Mushimiyimana 2018).

Similarly, in my interviews with government officials, inter-national organizations, and teachers, I often heard reference to the importance of student-centered pedagogy. However, dur-ing my classroom observations, I primarily observed teacher-centered pedagogy mixed in with occasional small-group discussions, where students were asked to memorize information from the textbooks. Confirming my findings, other studies on education in Rwanda also find that in practice, teacher-centered pedagogy and rote learning persist in most classrooms (Honeyman 2016; Uworwabayeho 2009).

★   ★   ★

AN IMPORTANT PART OF transitional justice, education systems not only engage with future generations in examining a contested past but also endeavor to build a shared future based on common values and a national civic identity. Empirical studies examining the link between education and transitional justice, however, point to the limitations of connecting broader transitional justice processes, including trials and truth commissions, to teaching about these issues in the classroom. For instance, teaching about peace and human rights in schools that reflect social and economic inequalities or unequal educational opportunities does little to alter the underlying structural roots of conflict.

The subsequent chapters demonstrate that despite a determined effort by the Rwandan government to infuse the spirit of peacebuilding in the broader educational reforms and initiatives around citizenship, human rights, reconciliation, and historical memory, when these reforms have been introduced in schools, tensions and contradictions have emerged that have diluted the impact of the government's efforts.

CHAPTER 3

Constructing Citizenship and a Post-Genocide Identity

IN A PRIVATE secondary school on the outskirts of Kigali, Jackson, a civics teacher who grew up in Uganda and returned to Rwanda after 1994, teaches his students about the genocide. He explains that the Belgian colonizers divided the Rwandans into different groups (Hutu and Tutsi), a division that eventually fueled the genocide. But now, in the post-genocide period, "we are fighting against genocide ideology of trying to identify each other as one tribe or another....We are all one, we are all Rwandese." He continues, "I hope you are new Rwandans, that you are new citizens of this country . . . *ikiduhuza kiruta ikidutandukanya* [What unites us is greater than what divides us]" (Classroom observation, School 5, June 2011).

In post-genocide Rwanda, the government has been working to develop and propagate a new sense of national unity and civic identity. This effort has taken many forms, such as the adoption of a new national flag and the introduction of a new national anthem. A key part of the government's strategy is to use schools to construct a new type of Rwandan citizen, one who has a particular civic identity and embraces certain values. The *Education Sector Policy* (2003) proclaims that the government has "decided

55

to rebuild Rwanda as a nation, a nation characterized by values such as: unity, respect for human rights, patriotism and hard work" (5). The primary goal of education and training is to provide all Rwandans with "the necessary skills and values to be good citizens" (Ministry of Education 2003b, 4). Implicit in this notion of good citizenship is a patriotic vision of all Rwandans united by a common culture, language, and history.

This new civic identity, or sense of "being Rwandan," is fundamentally nonethnic in nature. To address the past and to foster unity and reconciliation in a divided society, ethnicity is no longer used as an official form of identity; indeed, ethnic identification is considered taboo and is illegal insofar as it is linked to genocide ideology and divisionism (Buckley-Zistel 2006; Purdeková 2015). The new citizen is, above all, Rwandan, speaks English, and loves the nation, but also has a global orientation.

In this chapter, I first provide an overview of civic identity and nationalism, and then focus on the case of citizenship and ethnicity before and after the genocide. I then explore how the government's citizenship policy has been implemented in Rwandan schools. I discuss the intentions of the Rwandan state, examine the ways in which it deploys education to construct a new national and de-ethnicized identity, and assess the extent to which teachers and students understand and embrace the new civic identity.

Data from surveys of and interviews with students and teachers indicate that the creation of a new civic identity in Rwanda has been largely successful, although instilling a non-ethnic identity has been less straightforward. A uniformly patriotic civic identity that complements a global orientation is evident across schools, regions, and groups. But the data also reveal the persistence of ethnic perspectives and classifications of the self and others. Although the intent of state policy is de-ethnicization and the eradication of the terms "Hutu" and "Tutsi," ideological structures of identity endure, and educational policies and practices at the school level continue to promote divergent identities based on experience and language.

CONCEPTS OF CITIZENSHIP, EDUCATION, AND NATION BUILDING

An education system creates a civic identity by emphasizing a common national history and language (Bendix 1964; Tyack 1966). Thus, education systems contribute to the construction of a "civic culture," or the norms and attitudes of citizens in relation to the government (Almond and Verba 1963). As Will Kymlicka (2001) writes, "Citizenship education is not just a matter of learning the basic facts about institutions and procedures of political life; it also involves acquiring a range of dispositions, virtues, and loyalties" (293).

The conventional notion of civic education, originating in Europe during the eighteenth and nineteenth centuries, inculcates citizens with national values to create a unified nation-state by emphasizing the importance of a common national history, language, and culture (Bendix 1964; Reisner 1922; Tyack 1966; Weber 1976). The creation of a common culture and civic identity based on a "civil religion" of common myths and symbols is institutionalized through mass education and a standardized language (Anthony Smith 1991a, 136). Under this construct, civic education focuses on the rights and duties of a citizen within the territorially bound nation-state while instilling allegiance to the state.

While conventional notions of civic education focus on developing patriotic and nationalist citizens, citizenship education has grown increasingly global in nature and less linked to a nation-state in the past several decades. Civic education now generally incorporates human rights elements (Suárez and Ramírez 2007; Tibbitts 2002), multiculturalism, and diversity (Banks 2004; Kymlicka 2001; Stevick and Levinson 2007), and positions the citizen within a postnational globalized world (Schissler and Soysal 2005; Soysal 1994).

Looking at liberal democracies in a Western context, Kathleen Abowitz and Jason Harnish (2006) explain that citizenship education aims to teach "democratic rights and about the skills and dispositions of cooperation, deliberation, and decision-making" (664). Will Kymlicka (2001) identifies four important elements of citizenship in a liberal democracy: public spiritedness, a sense of justice, civility and tolerance, and a shared sense of solidarity (296).

Anthony Smith (1991b) suggests that two forms of national identities have emerged from the nation-state model. A *civic identity* derives from a common culture and ideology and is based on a liberal and inclusive perspective of citizenship in a Western context; in contrast, an *ethnic identity* derives from an exclusive ascriptive identity based on the notion of common descent. Similarly, Rogers Brubaker (2004) distinguishes between ethnic and civic nationalism: civic nationalism is based on a sense of common citizenship and is "liberal, voluntarist, universalist, and inclusive"; ethnic nationalism is based on a common ethnicity and is "illiberal, ascriptive, particularist, and exclusive" (133). However, the distinction between the two forms of national identity is not mutually exclusive. The Rwandan government draws on a seemingly civic version of national identity that takes the form of a nonethnic but illiberal and exclusive form of nationalism. Andrea Purdeková (2008) argues that this new form of national identity is in fact an ethnic identity in its exclusive framing of a unified "Rwandan" identity.

In his work on nationalism in Sri Lanka and Australia, Bruce Kapferer (1988) talks about the culture of nationalism that derives from myths, legends, customs, language, and tradition. In this sense, nationalism is positioned as a religion: "Nationalism makes the political religious and places the nation above politics. The nation is created as an object of devotion and the political forces which become focused upon it are intensified in their energy and passion" (1). Eric Hobsbawm and Terence Ranger (2012) refer to the nation-state, national culture, and common citizenship as socially constructed cultural artifacts, or the "invention of tradition." In Rwanda, under an increasingly authoritarian state, citizenship education serves the interest of what Rogers Brubaker (2004) refers to as "state-framed nationalism" that is "imbued with a strong cultural content" (145). In this sense, citizenship education contributes to the construction of the new nation, or what Benedict Anderson (2006) terms "an imagined community—and imagined as both inherently limited and sovereign" (6).

Citizenship and the Nation before and after the Genocide

Although citizenship in the post-genocide period is based on "Rwandanness" rather than on ethnic identity, the construction of Rwandan citizenship has evolved over time between ethnic and nonethnic forms. In the early twentieth century, the Belgians propagated the "Hamitic hypothesis," a myth of Tutsi as a separate and distinct race with origins in the Nile. When Rwanda was part of the Belgian colonial state, Hutu were treated as indigenous Rwandan and Tutsi were portrayed as non-Rwandan (Buckley-Zistel 2006; Mamdani 2001). Citizenship was defined in terms of ethnic identity, and "a sense of closure was introduced as to who was inside and who was outside the nation" (Buckley-Zistel 2006, 105). The events of 1959, which Tutsi refer to as a "genocide" and Hutu as a "social revolution," resulted in ethnic violence and the exodus of more than 130,000 Tutsi to neighboring countries.

After independence from Belgium, under the First Republic (1962–1973), citizenship continued to be equated with a Hutu ethnic identity, and Tutsi were portrayed as non-Rwandan foreigners from a distinct racial group. This paradigm shifted during the Second Republic (1973–1990), when Tutsi were reframed as Rwandan under quota policies that allocated access to jobs and education based on ethnic group. Mahmood Mamdani (2001, 138) argues that President Juvénal Habyarimana redefined Tutsi from a nonindigenous "race" to an indigenous "ethnic group." Following the invasion of the northeast of the country by the RPF in 1990, the Habyarimana government shifted toward an ideology of "Hutu power" and protecting a "Hutu nation" based on the idea that Tutsi were an alien race rather than an indigenous ethnic group (Mamdani 2001). The extremist propaganda leading up to the genocide in *Kangura Magazine* portrayed Tutsi as an alien Hamite race, the enemy, and *inyenzi* (cockroaches) (Eltringham 2004).

In the colonial and postcolonial eras, government powers manipulated notions around citizenship and ethnicity to ignite division and violence. However, in the post-genocide period, the construction of a unified and nonethnic identity has been central to the creation of the Rwandan citizen and nation-state. This new national identity is premised on a de-ethnicized vision of "Rwandanness" or "Rwandanicity" known as *ubanyarwanda* or Rwandité (Buckley-Zistel 2006; Purdeková 2015).

The government propagates the notion of the new citizen and the myth of national unity through schools and more widely in society. The official discourse in the post-genocide era promotes the notion of a unified Rwandan citizenry through an emphasis on unity and reconciliation, a common culture, and language (Buckley-Zistel 2006; Longman and Rutagengwa 2004; Purdeková 2015). National laws and policies forbid ethnic identification on public documents or in public spaces (Longman and Rutagengwa 2004; Purdeková 2008). The national development document, *Vision 2020*, proclaims that "since the 11th century, Rwanda existed as a *nation* founded on a common history of its people, shared values, a single language and culture. . . . The unity of the Rwandan nation was also based on the clan groups and common rites with no discrimination based on ethnicity" (Ministry of Finance and Economic Planning 2000, 4; emphasis added).

The government conjures the imagined Rwandan nation as deriving from a shared history, values, and culture, and accentuates the importance of clans rather than ethnic groups as a unifying feature. Johan Pottier (2002) argues that the government presents an idealized representation of the precolonial past based on the historiography of the Belgian colonial anthropologist Jacques Maquet and the court historian for the Tutsi monarchy, Abbé Alexis Kagame, that ignores precolonial social differences. *Amoko*, or ethnic groups (Hutu, Tutsi, Twa), are presented in the official government discourse as an identity that was socially constructed and manipulated by the Belgians during the colonial period.[1] According to the official narrative, before then, these groups existed as "social classes," which were distinguished by socioeconomic status or occupation in terms of those who herded cows (known as Tutsi), farmers (known as Hutu), and hunter-gatherers (known as Twa). Clearly, ethnic terminology did exist in precolonial times and had political and economic as well as ethnic connotations, although the categories were more fluid than they were under the Belgians (Newbury 1988; Pottier 2002; Prunier 1995; Vansina 2004).

The state-led top-down approach to history became entrenched after 2000 with the release of *Vision 2020*, which seeks the "reconstruction of the nation" and the transformation of an agricultural subsistence economy into a "knowledge-based economy" (Ministry of Finance and Economic Planning 2000, 3–9). With *Vision 2020*, the state presents the notion of an "exemplary citizenry" and "governable subjects" (Ansoms and Cioffo 2016; Purdeková 2012) who will execute the process of development and modernization. Bert Ingelaere (2010) documents the state's creation of an image of a modern and developed Rwanda; for example, Rwandans can be fined for not wearing shoes in public or for not having good personal hygiene.

Several civic education programs run by the Rwandan state in the broader community seek not only to promote reconciliation between Hutu and Tutsi but also to impose a new vision of what it means to be Rwandan. The National Unity and Reconciliation Commission (NURC) runs civic education programs such as *itorero, ingando*, and *urgerero*. *Itorero* is a form of moral and political education that teaches civil servants, teachers, and youth about Rwandan nationhood and civic values of national unity and patriotism (Nzahabwanayo, Horsthemke, and Mathebula 2017; Sundberg 2016). *Ingando*, or solidarity camps, teach students, teachers, soldiers, government officials, and returnees about Rwandan identity, history, and culture (Purdeková 2015). Urugerero, a national service program that teaches about the Rwandan state and culture, is required for all high school students. In 2013, the government launched Ndi Umunyarwanda (I Am Rwandan), a national initiative aimed at creating a strong and unified national Rwandan identity through open discussions in the community about identity and ethnicity. The program has three principal goals: to foster *kwiyumvamo ubunyarwanda*, or feeling "Rwandan"; to support the core values of "Rwandanness"; and to avoid taboos in moderated discussions.[2] Although these aforementioned civic education programs and initiatives generally occur outside of formal schooling, many teachers and students have also participated in these programs.

TEACHING ABOUT CIVIC IDENTITY AND THE NATION IN SCHOOLS

In this section, I demonstrate how ideas about citizenship and the nation are taught in the formal Rwandan education system and how teachers and students engage with and deploy these concepts. Students possess overlapping conceptions of citizenship incorporating both the national and the global, suggesting that global constructs of citizenship are filtering down to the school level. However, although civic identity in Rwanda is framed in relation to the global, the emphasis on the national is very strong, with little variation across schools and regions.

Curriculum and Textbooks

Since the 1994 genocide, the Rwandan state has employed formal civics education to build a unified identity and to invoke a global identity tied to human rights discourses, as discussed further in chapter 4. Thus, although promoting a strong sense of Rwandan national identity, the national policy documents, curriculum, and textbooks all incorporate global discourses. For example, the Rwandan *Education Sector Strategic Plan, 2006–2010* (Ministry of Education, 2006) lists one of the main goals of the education sector: "To develop in the Rwandese citizen an autonomy of thought, *patriotic spirit,* a sense of *civic pride,* a love of work well done and *global* awareness" (8; emphasis added).

The government has placed an emphasis on forging a unified Rwandan identity through the revision of the civics and history curriculum and a new English-language policy. At the time of my research in 2011, citizenship education or civics was taught in various forms in the formal education system. At the primary level, elements of civics were included in the social studies curriculum (grades 4–6). At the ordinary level, or lower secondary school (senior 1, 2, 3), civics education was called "political education" and was a compulsory but nonexaminable subject usually taught one hour per week. Although there was a national curriculum and a two-volume textbook for political education, the subject was not prioritized, as indicated by the minimal amount of time allocated to the subject. In 2009, political education for upper secondary school was replaced by "general paper" (GP), an interdisciplinary subject modeled after curriculum in eastern African countries. The curriculum for GP was broadly defined, with topics varying from health, to governance, to transitional justice, to the genocide; there was no textbook for GP. Teachers followed the general curriculum and did not necessarily cover topics on citizenship and human rights. In the 2015 competence-based curriculum, which is still in place, citizenship is taught in social studies at the primary level, and political education is now called "history and citizenship" at the lower secondary level; at the upper secondary (advanced level), GP is now called "general studies." The content around citizenship in the newer curriculum and textbooks is consistent with previous iterations.

The national curriculum and textbooks for civics education and social studies place an emphasis on inculcating national values and patriotism, in addition to providing a global perspective on nationality. The 2004 civics book (National Curriculum Development Center 2004) and the 2008 political education books (National Curriculum Development Center 2008a, 2008b) discuss citizenship, accentuating the nationalistic elements of civic identity. The 2004 civics book devotes one chapter to discussing patriotism and one chapter to the national symbols of Rwanda, including the national flag, anthem, emblem, and motto—"Ubumwe, Umurimo, Gukunda Igihugu" (Unity, Work, and Patriotism)—all of which were re-created in the post-genocide period (National Curriculum Development Center 2004, 8). Volume 1 of the political education book emphasizes the importance of civics education both in developing moral values and for the nation:

> Political Education is very important for young people as they grow up being aware of their role in the development of the country. It is therefore crucial to teach them, as early as possible, about the essential human values so that they may become fair and responsible citizens by the time they mature. To attain this objective, everyone has to know the rights and obligations towards oneself, the family, the society and the nation in general. . . . Civic education plays an important role in changing people's mentalities and in

National symbols

National symbols help to give us a sense of unity. The new coat of arms and national flag were launched on 1 January 2002. These are called **national symbols.** The coat of arms, the motto, the flag and the anthem are symbols of our national unity. This is why the government of national unity decided to give our country new symbols. They wanted us to leave the past and its divisions behind and build our nation in unity.

Our national flag

The coat of arms and the flag

Look at the coat of arms below. On the coat of arms are the words 'Unity, work, patriotism' (Ubumwe, umurimo, gukunda igihugu). This is called a motto. The green ring has a knot tied at the bottom. This ring is a sign of unity. It shows we are working towards a **common aim.** On the flag, the sun and its rays are a symbol of unity because the sun is a light that guides all people.

2. National unity in textbooks. *Source*: Bamusananire et al. 2006c, 112.

building a nation. It is through such an education that citizens develop common moral values considered as either social harmonisation or an evaluation of social vision that accepts modern diversities that are due to a pluralist and democratic society. (National Curriculum Development Center 2008a, 30)

A grade 6 social studies book published in 2006 teaches students about the national symbols for unity. The book asks students to reflect on how the new flag and coat of arms encourage unity (Bamusananire et al. 2006c, 112; see figure 2). The 2016 textbook for history and citizenship for the lower secondary level has a section on citizen duties and responsibilities that includes discussion of the "promotion of peace, national unity and reconciliation," as well as "contribution to national development" (Sebazungu, Okoth, and Agumba 2016, 136).

Civic Identity

Despite the emphasis on citizenship in the school curriculum and textbooks, discussions in the classroom on issues related to citizenship varied by region and by school type.[3] To measure the extent to which students understood and learned about topics related to citizenship and national identity, I conducted a survey of 536 randomly selected secondary students in fifteen schools in three different geographical regions of Rwanda (for more detail on the methods, see appendix A).

In general, students demonstrated a strong sense of Rwandan national identity, as well as a global and regional identity. Most students held strong national, regional, and global civic identities (figure 3). Although students strongly identified as citizens of Rwanda (67.2 percent identified a lot, 23.3 percent identified somewhat), they also identified as part of the broader East African Community (EAC; 63.3 percent identified a lot, 25.8 percent identified somewhat) and as citizens of the world (61 percent identified a lot, 27.4 percent identified somewhat). The data indicate that different conceptions of citizenship—national, regional, and global—are coexisting rather than competing in Rwanda. A student can be both a patriotic Rwandan citizen and identify as a citizen of the region and the world.

Other surveys conducted on a broader scale in Rwanda have found similar results. For example, in the World Values Survey, conducted with a nationally representative sample of Rwandans in 2012, 80.7 percent of respondents reported that they were very proud to be Rwandan, and 57.1 percent strongly agreed that they see themselves as citizens of the world (World Values Survey 2012).[4] A survey conducted by the NURC in 2015 found that 96.7 percent of Rwandans held a "shared sense of national identity and inclusive citizenship" and that 97.3 percent were "proud to be Rwandan" (Republic of Rwanda, National Unity and Reconciliation Commission 2015,

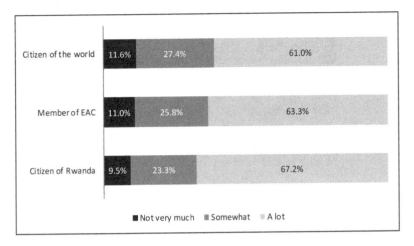

3. Global, regional, and national civic identity.

xvi). However, results from any government survey should be interpreted with caution, given the tendency toward self-censorship.

My survey revealed statistically significant differences in conceptions of national Rwandan identity by type of school. As figure 4 illustrates, students in government and government-aided schools tended to identify as citizens of Rwanda more strongly than did students in private schools. In private schools, 13.5 percent of students reported that they did not identify as citizens of Rwanda very much. The presence of the state narrative around citizenship and national identity is likely stronger in government and government-aided schools than in private schools.

The Relationship between Citizenship and the State

Students in my survey exhibited a strong sense of national identity, with minimal variation across schools or regions or by student characteristics, such as socioeconomic status or gender. When asked about the characteristics of a good citizen (see

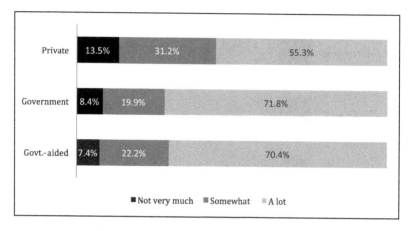

4. Identifying as a citizen of Rwanda by school type.

figure 5), the vast majority of students (84.9 percent) strongly agreed with the statement that people should be loyal and patriotic to their country; 82.4 percent strongly agreed that they should serve in the military; 77.9 percent strongly agreed that a good citizen should obey the law; 76.8 percent strongly agreed that they should participate in community activities; and 67.9 percent strongly agreed that they should work hard. Other questions revealed more variation, such as whether it is important for good citizens to vote in elections or to know the history of their country, which 19.8 percent and 21.5 percent strongly disagreed with, respectively.

In the 2012 Rwandan World Values Survey, respondents had similar responses when asked about what qualities children should be encouraged to learn at home. For example, 62.2 percent mentioned hard work, 72 percent mentioned a feeling of responsibility, 56.4 percent mentioned tolerance and respect, and 60.6 percent mentioned obedience.

Students are expected to adopt "Rwandan values" to become good citizens. Integral to internalizing patriotic Rwandan values is the idea that a citizen should support national policies and

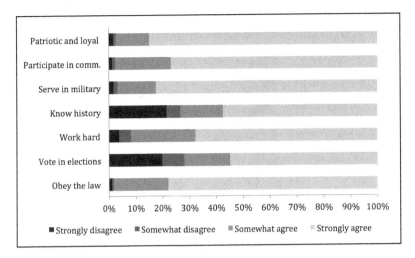

5. Characteristics of a good Rwandan citizen.

politics and demonstrate loyalty to the state. Only 22 percent of students strongly agreed that people could disagree with state leaders. Yet, students also felt that the relationship between the citizen and the state should be reciprocal, with each party having obligations to the other. The majority of students in my survey strongly agreed that the state should not only provide education and health care but also ensure peace and stability and encourage people to be honest and moral (figure 6).

Conceptions of Citizenship Rights

More than three-quarters of the students who participated in my survey indicated that they discussed citizenship rights at least once a week or once a month in class; 11 percent said they never discussed these rights. Discussion of rights differed by region and school type, perhaps due to the relative influence of the state in different regions. Citizenship rights were more commonly discussed in the Eastern and Western Provinces as compared to Kigali, where 18 percent of students said they never

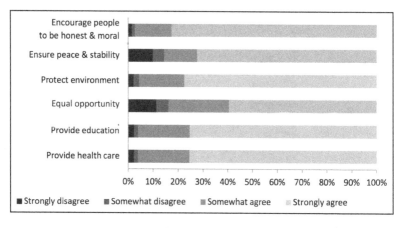

6. The role of the state.

discussed these rights (figure 7). Citizenship was also more frequently discussed in government and government-aided schools,
where the majority of students said they discussed this topic
once a week. In private schools, 17 percent said they never discussed citizenship rights (figure 8).

In classroom observations and interviews with students and
teachers, notions of citizenship and citizenship rights were commonly equated with the right to a nationality and the right to
vote. Olivier, a student in a private school in the Eastern Province, proclaimed that "all Rwandans have the right to citizenship. You have the right to be Rwandan" (Boys' interview, School
3, September 2011). In a group discussion in a government
school in a rural area in the Western Province, Joseph noted that
"a citizen has the right to a nationality and to do what he wants
in his country, but he also must respect the country's laws" (Boys'
interview, School 2, July 2011). Citizenship confers rights but
also responsibilities.

In the classroom, teachers generally taught about the nation
and citizenship in accordance with the national curriculum. Discussions of citizenship were usually in line with what Kymlicka

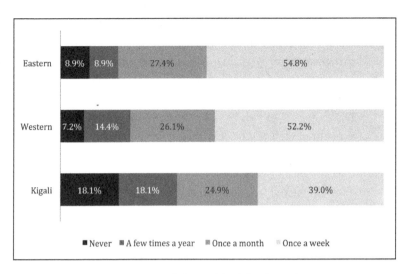

7. Discussion of citizenship rights by region.

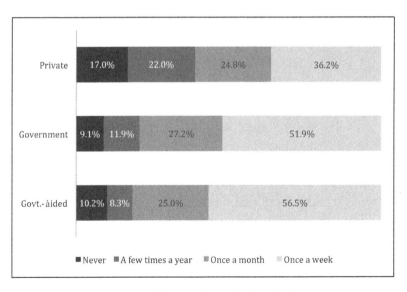

8. Discussion of citizenship rights by school type.

(2001) terms a "minimal" conceptualization of citizenship that emphasizes obedience and respect for laws rather than an active and participatory form of citizenship. Similarly, students generally expressed patriotic and unquestioning outlooks in regard to their civic identity.

Discussions about citizenship were frequently conducted in a rote manner, with the teacher dictating to students prescribed definitions from textbooks. Frank, a Ugandan political education teacher in a government secondary school in the Eastern Province, instructed students about citizenship and the duties of a good citizen:

FRANK: Define citizenship and tell us two types.

BOY: A member of the state ... citizenship by birth and by registration.

FRANK: What are the duties of a good citizen? Name three.

GIRL: Development of country, respect of each other, love and defense of country. (Classroom observation, School 4, June 2011)

TEACHING A NONETHNIC IDENTITY IN SCHOOLS

Central to creating a new Rwandan citizenship is the construction of a nonethnic identity and the promotion of the English language. In this section, I provide an overview of how a unified nonethnic identity is taught in schools and how teachers and students engage with these constructs in practice. Based on my survey and interview data, the goal of a unified and nonethnic identity is illusive. Data reveal the emergence of divergent identities based on one's experience during the genocide, where someone lived before and during the genocide, and language spoken.

Curriculum and Textbooks

National policy documents, the curriculum, and school text-books reinforce the official narrative of a unified identity. Discussion of ethnicity in education policy documents is infrequent (only two of the nine documents analyzed explicitly mention ethnicity) except in reference to the pre-genocide period or to the discussion of a unified Rwandan identity. The main social development policy document—*Rwanda Vision 2020*—explains the government's post-genocide stance on ethnicity, which emphasizes the distortion of ethnic identity under the Belgians: "The colonial power, based on an ideology of racial superiority and in collaboration with some religious organisations, exploited the subtle social differences and institutionalized discrimination. These actions distorted the harmonious social structure, creating a false ethnic division with disastrous consequences" (Ministry of Finance and Economic Planning 2000, 4).

The current government utilizes civics and history education to promote a unified view of identity through the prescribed discussion of ethnic groups, clans, colonization, the genocide, and unity and reconciliation. The 2015 curriculum and textbooks focus on unifying features, including clans, language, and a common culture; the materials emphasize unity and reconciliation and the notion of "one Rwanda." Ethnicity is discussed only within a historical context or in reference to the genocide.

In history textbooks on the precolonial, colonial, and postindependence eras, ethnicity is conveyed as a social construct, initially to indicate social status and later codified and institutionalized by the Belgian colonialists. Textbooks frame ethnicity as an identity externally imposed on Rwandans, rather than as a precolonial characteristic. The origins of ethnic groups are explained in detail in the *New Junior Secondary History Book 2* (Bamusananire and Ntega 2010b) in chapter 2, which details the ethnically discriminatory policies under Belgian colonial rule: "The Europeans therefore decided to categorise the people of Rwanda into different rigid ethnic groups, making the Tutsi superior and the Hutu inferior with the Twa as an insignificant factor. . . . The false racial classification put the Tutsi in the position of being invaders in their own country and exposed them to an eventual ethnic and nationalist backlash from the Hutu who were negatively classified as the aboriginal population of Rwanda" (92).

The history book for Rwandan secondary schools (advanced level) does not mention ethnic groups in the chapter on precolonial Rwanda in the nineteenth century. Instead, when discussing sociocultural organization, the book refers to the "Banyarwanda" (Rwandan people) without distinction among Hutu, Tutsi, or Twa (Bamusananire 2011). The book explains how ethnicity was constructed under the colonial powers: "The Belgian classification of the people of Rwanda made them conceive of themselves as belonging to their different ethnic groups and not to one nation. This led to the break-up of an alliance that was as old as Rwanda's hills and history, and explains the development of ethnic conflicts and lack of true *Rwandan nationalism* which characterized Rwanda's politics for decades" (Bamusananire 2011, 356; emphasis added). Although the history textbooks portray precolonial Rwanda as united, there is evidence of historical, political, social, and economic differences across groups (Newbury 1988; Vansina 2004).

The 2016 history and citizenship book for lower secondary schools includes a unit on "unity" that discusses different identities in Rwanda, including clan identity, national identity, and social identity. The book mentions that "the Government of Rwanda did its best to eradicate divisionism ideology (ethnic identity) sowed by the colonialisms and promoted under the First and Second Republics (1962–1994)" (Sebazungu, Okoth, and Agumba 2016, 150). In this example, "ethnic group" is negatively equated with a rigid racial classification, and "ethnic nationalism" is contrasted with what Brubaker (2004) terms a unified "civic nationalism."

In post-genocide policy and education documents, ethnic groups are referred to as "social groups" or "social classes" to emphasize the socioeconomic aspect of the terminology rather than ethnic distinctions. The official discourse promoting a unified identity suggests that identity derives from clans rather than from ethnic groups.[5] Clans are thus privileged in the post-genocide discourse because a clan may include people from all three social groups (Burnet 2009; Newbury 1988;Vansina 2004). A social studies book for grade 6 explains clans and social classes thus: "It is important to remember that there were no *tribes* in Rwanda. People from every social group belonged to the same *clans*. . . . They shared the same religion and culture. They intermarried with each other. They spoke the same language" (Bamusananire et al. 2006c, 28; emphasis added). This textbook states that in the precolonial era, "tribes" or ethnic groups did not exist; it emphasizes that Rwandans shared the same religion, language, and culture and belonged to the same clans rather than to different ethnic groups, conjuring up the construction of the nation (Hobsbawm and Ranger 2012; Kapferer 1988).

Ethnicity as a form of identity is construed as a historical remnant of the pre-genocide era, except in the particular context of referring to the genocide, as discussed in chapter 5. Identity linked to ethnic groups continues to be invoked in the context of the genocide in educational materials and in the official discourse. Despite the official ban on ethnic identity, the genocide is described in explicitly ethnic terms as a crime committed against a specific group, the Tutsi. While in older textbooks the genocide is referred to as the "1994 genocide," in textbooks published after 2008 the genocide is officially referred to as "the genocide against the Tutsi" or the "1994 Tutsi genocide." The government amended the 2003 Constitution in 2008, officially changing the name to the "genocide against the Tutsi" (Waldorf 2011). This usage in national policy and curricula undermines the policy of a unified identity that the government espouses.

Identity in Schools
Despite the official rhetoric on unity as promoted in national-level policy documents, curriculum, and textbooks, students and teachers continue to classify themselves and others, creating and maintaining groups based on experiences during the genocide, scholarships, participation in clubs, and language. Because ethnicity is no longer a salient marker of identity, at least officially, other markers such as experience during the genocide and language have emerged among students as identifiers. Rather than erasing ethnic identity entirely, students in schools are creating boundaries along language and experience or family history during the genocide. As a consequence, the distinctions between Hutu and Tutsi have expanded into broader categories linked to language and experience during the genocide: Anglophone returnees (*abasaja or abakonyine* from Uganda and TZ from Tanzania); Francophone returnees (*abadubai* from the DRC or *jepe* / GP—Garde Présidentielle from Burundi); genocide survivors (*umucikacumu, abarokotse,* or *abahigwaga*); and those who remained in Rwanda (*sopecya*) or Hutu who are assumed to be complicit in the killings as *génocidaires* or children of *génocidaires*.

Although in the official curriculum and in discussions around ethnicity, students are taught that the Belgians imposed ethnic groups (*amoko*) and that ethnic groups no longer exist in the post-genocide era, students have divergent views on the origin of "social groups."[6] In my survey, the majority of students— 63 percent—appeared to tacitly accept (agree or strongly agree with) the government narrative that there was no conflict among social groups in precolonial times; however, a significant proportion of students, 37 percent, also disagreed or strongly

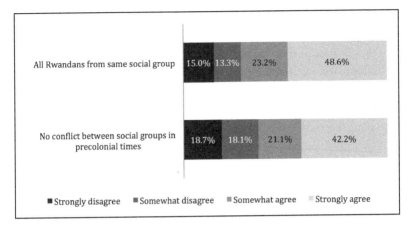

9. Views on social groups in Rwanda.

disagreed with this interpretation. Similarly, whereas the majority agreed with the statement that all Rwandans originate from the same social group, 15 percent strongly disagreed, indicating that a minority of students continued to view social groups as salient (figure 9).

In interviews, students often echoed the sentiment presented in the curriculum and textbooks that emphasizes a narrative of post-genocide unity, whereby all Rwandans are the same. Olivier, a Francophone returnee studying in the Eastern Province, noted: "In Rwanda, all Rwandans are the same; there are no Tutsis, or Hutus, or Twa. We have become one. We are *Abanyarwanda* [Rwandan]" (Student interview, School 3, September 2011). Students repeated this sentiment across schools. In an interview near the capital, Richard explained, "My first wish is to be called *munyarwanda*, because before there were no ethnic groups. Before we did not have ethnicity [*ibintu nk'ibyo by'amoko*], we were all Rwandan" (Student interview, School 5, October 2011). Innocent, a twenty-year-old Hutu student at a Western school, explained that ethnic groups "don't exist here. Many people have already understood that for now there is unity, everyone is Rwandan" (Student interview, School 1, October 2011).

Students and teachers often referred to the avoidance or elimination of ethnic identity. For instance, Fabrice, a student in a government-aided school in Kigali, said, "We can't say that you are Tutsi or that you are Hutu anymore.... We want to eliminate, even erase the genocide ideology" (Student interview, School 7, September 2011). John, a Hutu history teacher at a private school in the Eastern Province, explained that "we would not talk about those tribes now, because we know that here in Rwanda we are *Banyarwanda*, our name Rwandese, there is no other groups of people, we are united" (Teacher interview, School 3, September 2011).

Teachers echoed the mantra of "all Rwandan" expressed by students but also offered critiques of the challenges of teaching the unified vision in their classrooms. Teachers generally followed the official curriculum and tended to avoid controversial topics linked to ethnicity. François, a Francophone Hutu history teacher at a school in the Western Province, mentioned that he avoided discussing the topic of ethnicity: "Those are the things that we avoid in class. We can't talk about ethnicities, or say that this group did that or that the other did that, as we have all become one" (Teacher interview, School 1, October 2011).

Alain, a Hutu political education teacher at a religious semirural school in the Western Province, explained that he teaches students that "we are all Rwandan" in order to avoid provoking conflict: "It's difficult to explain the ethnic divisions [*l'ethnisme*] in Rwanda because what we talk about in class doesn't explain ethnicity. The kids pose a lot of questions about that, but in such a way that you can't necessarily respond.... When you are going to say that there are these races, it's necessary to pay attention: if you say that there were Hutus or even Tutsis, you can provoke a problem that you can't resolve. It's because of that that we must teach the students that *we are all*

Rwandans" (Teacher interview, School 1, October 2011; emphasis added).

Several teachers mentioned their fear of discussing topics linked to ethnicity. Notably, Hutu teachers, except in the Western Province, were less likely to mention ethnicity in interviews, while Tutsi returnees and Ugandan teachers spoke about the topic more openly across regions. Sam, a Ugandan teacher at a private school near the capital, talked about the fear surrounding discussions of ethnicity: "When I am teaching, it becomes hard for me to pronounce the words 'Hutu, Tutsi'" (Teacher interview, School 5, October 2011).

One exception is the discussion of the genocide in explicit ethnic terms, which contradicts the nonethnic narrative, as discussed in chapter 5. Teachers commonly mentioned the tension between teaching about the genocide in ethnic terms and promoting a unified ethnic identity. They spoke of the difficulty in discussing ethnic groups because they "no longer exist" and explaining the genocide, which was committed against a specific ethnic group—the Tutsi. François expressed this widespread sentiment:

> We also don't understand why it is said that there aren't ethnicities in Rwanda, but one says the genocide of the Tutsi. Recently there was a student who asked me this question: "Why is it said that one cannot say Hutu or Tutsi, whereas one can say the genocide of the Tutsi?" It was difficult to respond to this question, but I tried to tell him that the genocide was done against those that were called Tutsis, which is to say, that they were called this in the past, but not now because today there aren't Tutsi or Hutu anymore. (Teacher interview, School 1, October 2011)

Marie, a Hutu political education teacher at a school in the Western Province, also referred to the paradox of discussing the genocide: "In Rwanda, there isn't ethnicity, but we say the

genocide of the Tutsi. I think that could be difficult to explain:
no ethnicity, but the genocide of the Tutsi" (Teacher interview,
School 1, September 2011). Davide, a Tutsi returnee, echoed this
sentiment, explaining: "The students ask me why we talk about
the genocide of the Tutsi, even though you don't want us to talk
about ethnic groups. That's a contradiction" (Teacher interview,
School 7, October 2011).

Covert and Indirect Ethnicity

Although schools do not teach about ethnic identity and using
ethnic identifiers is illegal, the vast majority of teachers in my
interviews, Rwandan and Ugandan alike, commented that students continue to view themselves and others through ethnic
lenses, which they acquire from their families and communities.
Jacques, a Hutu political education teacher in a government-
aided school, explained that ethnic classifications are "still in
people's hearts, just not openly so," and continued, "You can see
that it isn't easy to get rid of [ethnic] identity" (Teacher interview, School 7, October 2011). Davide, a Tutsi returnee teaching
in an urban school, explained how ethnicity persists in students'
minds because students learn about ethnicity at home rather
than at school:

> After everything, the students might not talk about it at
> school, but they definitely discuss it at home. For example, if
> someone is Tutsi, he might tell his son: "Ah son, do you
> know that your uncle or grandfather was killed by the
> Hutu?" And the kid asks: "Who are the Hutu?" The father
> responds: "The *génocidaires*." And the Hutu who tells his son:
> "All of your uncles were killed in the Congo, and the Tutsi
> killed them." Or he might say that today, we aren't as we
> were before because the Tutsi from Uganda are in power.
> There is still this difference, and the students learn that at

home. We can't discuss it at school because if someone hears you, he or she will say that it's ideology. (Teacher interview, School 7, October 2011)

Because schools are largely silent on the topic, students learn about ethnicity or ethnic perspectives from their families and communities. François, a Hutu teacher in a Western school, claimed that students are aware of ethnicity, even if they do not discuss it openly:

Amongst themselves they cannot say that they are from such ethnicities, but on the inside they know it well because at school, there are survivors of the genocide. So for us being teachers, it always seems difficult to talk about that because they well know that each Rwandan belongs to one group or another, even if the kids don't know which groups we, their teachers, belong to. But they know well that we are from a group, and because of that, we try to be neutral, to not involve them in the ethnic conflicts. (Teacher interview, School 1, October 2011)

Students may not directly self-identify as Hutu or Tutsi, but they clearly indicate their ethnic affiliation in the way they reference the other group. Some students indirectly referred to their ethnic identity through reference to the "other" group or in the context of tensions between groups of students. Beatrice, an eighteen-year-old Anglophone returnee from Uganda, spoke about how ethnicity is no longer salient, while at the same time distinguishing between people from her group and those in the "other" group, those who are "called Hutus": "In my opinion, it isn't necessary to say that such and such person is Hutu, Tutsi, or Twa. . . . But for me, I would prefer to marry someone from my group [in the context of ethnic groups]." When asked about tensions at school, Beatrice responded that the cause stems from "ethnic groups": "The cause is a problem with ethnic groups [*amoko*]. You see, the people who are called Hutu, they go there and form a group, even if they don't want to demonstrate that it's a problem. But everyone knows that it's a result of this problem. They sit alone; they study alone" (Student interview, School 4, September 2011).

Despite the acknowledgment of the continued existence of ethnic or social groups, students did not directly self-identify themselves or others as belonging to a specific ethnic group because that would constitute a criminal offense under the genocide ideology law. Benjamin, in a school in the Eastern Province, explained: "It's not authorized to talk about ethnic issues. Even here at school, if they catch you talking about something related to ethnicity, they say that you have genocide ideology, and they imprison you or send you home and tell you to never come to school. So it's difficult to talk about it. In Rwanda, it's taboo to talk about that" (Student interview, School 4, September 2011).

It is clear that ethnic identities persist despite attempts to eradicate ethnic groups as a form of identification (Freedman et al. 2004; Longman and Rutagengwa 2004; McLean Hilker 2009). The Institute for Research and Dialogue for Peace, a government think tank, conducted a study on ethnicity and reconciliation in 2010 and found that "in fact, strictly speaking, the ethnic groups do not exist in Rwanda. However, the social reality of the ethnic group is there and influences life in the society, the political decisions and the quality of social life" (10). In the NURC 2015 Reconciliation Survey, 27.9 percent of respondents said that "there are Rwandans who view themselves, and others, through ethnic lenses" (Republic of Rwanda, National Unity and Reconciliation Commission 2015). Thus, although ethnicity is illegal and does not officially exist, even government-affiliated institutions recognize the continued influence of ethnically based conceptions in society.

Genocide Survivors

Despite the mantra of "one Rwanda" and the taboos around the discussion of ethnic identity, students continued to invoke ethnic classifications indirectly in conversation when discussing the genocide, language, and groups at school. Students were aware of these ethnic proxies and they continued to frame how students understood their own situation. The most common signifier of a distinct identity arose in discussions linked to experience during the genocide. Although one cannot explicitly ask about ethnicity or self-identify as belonging to a particular group, certain markers indicate one's ethnicity, such as whether someone is a returnee or a survivor (referred to as *umucikacumu, abarokotse,* or *abahigwaga*). The way in which one refers to his or her experience during the genocide, as a survivor or as a returnee, often indicates ethnic affiliation. "Survivor" or "returnee" from Uganda, the DRC, or Burundi is code for Tutsi. Tensions and mistrust were also evident between survivors and returnees. Those who remained in Rwanda and are not "survivors" are assumed to be Hutu.[7]

Genocide survivors, normally orphans, generally identified themselves as such and often indicated that they preferred the company of other genocide orphans. Annette explained: "I prefer to befriend other orphans because we have the same life difficulties" (Student interview, School 5, October 2011). Several Hutu students talked about genocide survivors forming groups at school. Lidia, a Hutu at an urban school, explained: "At the beginning of the year, the genocide survivors put themselves together in a group because there was already an association between them, like family united by AERG [Association des Etudiants et Elèves Rescapés du Génocide]. After that, in our class, we were told that it isn't good to put others to the side, that we should all be together in our class without any groups. The survivors understood, and now there aren't groups in our class anymore" (Student interview, School 7, October 2011).

Scholarships and organizations for genocide survivors create tangible boundaries between survivors and nonsurvivors in a resource-scarce environment where many students come from disadvantaged backgrounds and have difficulty paying schooling costs, such as school fees and uniforms (Paxton and Mutesi 2012; Transparency International 2012; Williams, Abbott, and Mupenzi 2015). Students who receive Fond d'Assistance aux Rescapés du Génocide (FARG) funding or participate in the AERG are often signaled out as being different. FARG provides funding for education, health, and other living expenses for students who are classified as genocide orphans or as genocide survivors whose parents have a disability or do not have enough money to pay school fees. FARG pays school fees for secondary school and provides limited funds for university (Interview with FARG, September 2011).[8] Although belonging to the Tutsi ethnic group does not officially constitute a criterion in order to receive a FARG scholarship, because ethnic identity no longer exists officially, it is understood that in order to be a genocide survivor, one must be a Tutsi, because the Tutsi were targeted during the genocide.

The official government discourse around the genocide recognizes Tutsi as genocide survivors, even though moderate Hutu were also killed (Burnet 2009; Eltringham 2004; Vidal 2004). One student explained that FARG supports only "genocide survivors, or as we say in Kinyarwanda 'Abahigwaga'—those who were hunted during the genocide" (Student interview, School 5, October 2011). Fabrice, a Hutu student, used ethnic terms to explain why he did not receive funding, even though his father was killed by the RPF during the war:[9] "I don't receive any aid from FARG. In fact, the primary condition to receive FARG is that you are poor and a Tutsi. This means survivors. So if you are Hutu, you can't receive aid from FARG. But now, we don't talk about different ethnicities" (Student interview, School 7, September 2011). At a private school with a large population of genocide orphans, Richard lamented that although he was an orphan and considered himself to be a genocide survivor, he did not qualify for the scholarship.[10] Although Richard did not explicitly state his ethnic identity and I did not ask him, I assumed that he was likely of mixed heritage because he did not qualify for FARG funding. He felt excluded by other survivors: "Even here at school, there are some students who form groups, for example students supported by the FARG. Sometimes when they see that you are not supported by FARG, they think that you are not a genocide survivor. So when they are in groups, you can't come and share ideas with them. They don't feel at ease with you" (Student interview, School 5, October 2011). Students who did not belong to these groups commented that genocide survivors or FARG students often preferred to associate with each other. Thus, even for students who don't have direct experience or memories of the genocide, the affinity for students who come from families who experienced the genocide remains strong.

Several clubs in the schools aimed at promoting unity and reconciliation are open to all students for participation, such as the Never Again Rwanda (NAR) Club[11] and the Unity and Reconciliation Club. AERG is more exclusive: although it does not explicitly forbid Hutu students from joining, students and teachers understand that the association is for genocide survivors and sympathizers (Tutsi returnees).[12] At club meetings, students are quizzed on their family history and ethnic identity—the only context in which I saw students explicitly self-identify as belonging to a particular ethnic group. In one meeting, members queried students who wished to join the club and asked them to share their personal history in order to determine if they qualified as survivors:

AERG MEMBER: You told us that you never met your father. Was your father a Hutu or a Tutsi?

GIRL: I don't know because I never met him. But I do know that my mother's family is Tutsi and a surviving family, and that's how my life has been oriented.

AERG MEMBER: What makes you think that you are a Tutsi?

BOY: Given my personal history and my parents' identity, I am certain that I am Tutsi. (Field notes, School 7, September 2011)

Ethnic identity in this context is linked to experience during the genocide, so it is not seen as divisive or taboo. This type of ethnic identification is acceptable because it is not expressed in a public context; AERG meetings are private and attended only by members, who are not subject to scrutiny by the school administration.

Returnees

Although genocide survivors are singled out for their difference or for an implicit association with a Tutsi ethnic identity, students also classified themselves and others according to their returnee status. Tutsi Rwandans who returned from Uganda and settled in the Eastern Province are known as *abasaja* or *abakonyine*, while returnees from the DRC are informally called *abadubai*, and those from Burundi are called *jepe* or GP—Garde Présidentielle.[13] Some returnees grew up and studied in another country and consequently may have internalized other cultural norms and languages. Rather than distinguish between Hutu and Tutsi, students invoked returnee status as an identity marker. Students often spoke of these different groups in terms of regional differences. Several students who were returnees from the DRC studying in the Eastern Province, which has a high number of returnees, commented on the returnees from Uganda in a derogatory manner. Some students spoke of cultural differences and stereotypes around *abaokyines*, such as that *abaokyines* live in the forest alone raising cows and speak Kinyarwanda with a distinct accent.

Samuel, a twenty-year-old returnee from the DRC, said: "People from Uganda [*abakonyine*], you may find that many of them are rigid. You find them in the market, where they go to sell cows. When they drink alcohol, they start fighting because of their culture. But people from the Congo [Rwandan returnees], they don't do that" (Student interview, School 4, September 2011). Samuel positions himself as a returnee from the Congo in contrast to returnees from Uganda, even though they are both Tutsi. In this context, regional differences are more important than ethnic identity. In a different school, Olivier, a nineteen-year-old student and also a returnee from the DRC, talked about the groups students form at school based on returnee status:

GARNETT: At school, is there still tension between groups of people?

OLIVIER: Not tribes, there aren't tribes. But that [formation of groups] happens here. . . . People who came from Uganda who are Rwandan are called *abakonyine*. Sometimes they make their groups. When they make their groups, you can't come from elsewhere . . . they are so close.

GARNETT: What about people who lived in the Congo or Burundi?

OLIVIER: There are a lot of Francophones [at school] but they don't do that. They are popular among everyone. They are social. I like Francophones. They don't say, "I'm Anglophone" to complicate themselves, they are free [open-minded]. (Student interview, School 3, September 2011)

Language as Identity

As Olivier points out, boundaries emerge in terms of experience as a returnee from a bordering country and also from language—Anglophones are positioned in contrast to Francophones. The official language policy has played an important role in constructing the new Rwandan citizen.

In 2008, the government abruptly changed the medium of instruction from French to English in all grades; this policy was implemented in 2009. This change was presented by the government in practical and nonpolitical terms, namely, for integration into the EAC and the global economy. However, some teachers and students perceived the policy change as political and as benefiting the Anglophone Tutsi returnees associated with the ruling class (Samuelson and Freedman 2010). With the shift in the medium of instruction, the distinction between Anglophones and Francophones has heightened, and Anglophone returnees have been privileged over other Rwandans (Abbott, Sapsford, and Rwirahira 2015; Pearson 2014; Russell 2015). For many students and teachers, the policy change has had a deleterious impact: the quality of education has been sacrificed for political ends.

Language differences vary by region. Although all Rwandans speak Kinyarwanda, the mother tongue, most also speak French or English depending on their education and background. The Eastern Province is predominantly Anglophone due to its proximity to Uganda and to the influx of returnees from Uganda, whereas the Western Province tends to be Francophone due to its proximity to the DRC. Two schools from the regions illustrate the sharp differences in the implementation of English as the medium of instruction.

A government school in the Eastern Province strongly promoted the use of English: the staff were generally Anglophone, comprising returnee Tutsi from Uganda and Ugandan teachers; the students spoke more English compared to students at schools in Kigali or in the west. The signage at the school underscored the prevalence of English: "English must be used at all times in the school." The English-only policy was strictly enforced. In contrast, a school in the Western Province continued to rely on French informally; signs around the school were in French, despite the fact that the curriculum and medium of instruction were in English. Although some of the staff members at this school were bilingual, they often felt more comfortable conversing with me in French; some of the teachers were purely Francophone. The older students preferred French to English, depending on their personal background or experience. In Kigali, teachers and students generally spoke English well due to their exposure to the language from living in an urban area or in Anglophone countries.

Many of the students in my interviews had been exposed to other languages through their own experience or their families' experiences living in other countries: about half reported that their parents had lived in a country other than Rwanda, including Uganda (21 percent), the DRC (24 percent), and Burundi (5 percent); 10 percent of the students had attended school in another country (Uganda and the DRC, among others).[14] The majority of students said that they spoke Kinyarwanda at home (93 percent), although some also spoke English (39 percent), French (13 percent), and Swahili (11 percent) at home, reflecting diverse experiences across the population. Eighty-six percent of students reported speaking English in class, while 57 percent said they spoke Kinyarwanda, and 18 percent spoke French. So even though English was the official medium of instruction, students and teachers still relied on Kinyarwanda or French to explain topics, a finding that was confirmed by teachers and students in interviews and through classroom observation.

I observed that the Rwandan teachers often switched to Kinyarwanda, or occasionally to French, to explain complicated concepts, especially at schools in the Western Province and in Kigali, less so in the more Anglophone schools in the Eastern Province. Alain, a Francophone teacher at a school in the Western Province, explained the rationale for the use of multiple languages while teaching: "Sometimes we also use Kinyarwanda to foster understanding of the subject matter because the students studied in French in primary school. Even for us teachers,

when we teach in English there are some expressions that don't
go over very well. That's why we are obligated to use French or
even Kinyarwanda to facilitate understanding" (Teacher interview, School 1, October 2011).

The vast majority of teachers were educated in French and
are Francophone, but they were all required to teach in English
(except for language courses).[15] Some teachers already spoke
English well, such as the Anglophones (returnees from Uganda
or Tanzania) and those from Uganda and Kenya. Others, such as
Francophone returnees from Burundi or the DRC and those
who had remained in Rwanda during the genocide (Hutu or
Tutsi survivors), tended to be Francophone. With the students,
language depended on a variety of factors, including age and
background. Children of returnees who had lived or studied in
another country spoke French or English more fluently than the
average Rwandan student; students who had studied only in
Rwanda spoke French or English well if they had studied in a
high-quality primary school in an urban area. In the schools
where I conducted research, the vast majority of students in the
rural areas and in basic education schools, particularly in the
Western Province, did not speak French or English well enough
to hold a conversation. However, the majority of students surveyed reported that they understood somewhat when classes
were taught in English (73 percent); 26 percent said they com-
pletely understood.

Despite the numerous challenges of the language policy
articulated by teachers and students in interviews, the majority
of students said that they liked that classes were taught in English
(97 percent) and they thought the change from French to
English was a good one (92 percent). Students generally viewed
English as an important language for communicating with
people from other countries and for procuring good jobs.
The strong support for the language policy may also reflect
self-censorship or fears associated with outwardly criticizing

government policies, even in anonymous surveys. Students generally expressed that learning in English was easier than learning in French, although Francophone students were more critical of the change and of the difficulties they faced. Juliet, an eighteen-year-old Francophone returnee, said: "It's important to know English. But it would have been good to also reinforce English without losing French. That was a big problem, changing suddenly from French to English. For instance, second-year students had to study in English even though they had studied in French in their first year [of secondary school]. It was very difficult for them to understand, very difficult" (Mixed group interview, School 1, September 2011).

Juliet expressed the sentiment held by many Francophone students: that they should be learning in French and English rather than only in English. Further, she echoed the sentiment often expressed by Francophones who believe that English is privileging the Anglophones in school and employment: "Students who have been in school these past three years have already missed out" (Mixed group interview, School 1, September 2011). Both Anglophone and Francophone students appeared to be aware of the difficulties for Francophone students. Janet, an Anglophone, mentioned the difficulties faced by her Francophone classmates: "It was a big change. There were some students who started to fail when they switched from French to English, even if they did well in the past. It was difficult for them because they didn't understand very well" (Girls' group interview, School 4, September 2011).

Even though the majority of students perceived the benefits of learning English and expressed a preference for studying English over French, subtle tensions emerged between the Francophone and Anglophone students. The majority of Francophone students generally felt that they were disadvantaged by the change for the benefit of the elite class of Anglophone returnees, who dominated positions in government and university; researchers have uncovered similar sentiments (see Reyntjens 2004; Samuelson and Freedman 2010). Although younger students were less affected because they switched to English at a younger age, many older students in the upper levels had to take their exams in English after studying in French throughout their schooling. Francophone students and teachers frequently mentioned the difficulty of switching from French to English without preparation, saying that they felt like they were at a disadvantage. Benjamin, an Anglophone student, explained the discrepancy:

> In my opinion, I find that the change from French to English has affected a lot of students. But for me, it hasn't affected me because I studied in English. But for my class-mates who studied in French, it's difficult for them. For example, in my senior 5 class, when a teacher is in class, he poses questions to the students about what he is in the process of teaching. But some students aren't able to respond because they can't express themselves in English. Or the student might explain a topic in class. If a student doesn't understand the explanations very well, he can't ask questions because he doesn't know how to pose them in English. In this case, he remains with his question, or he might prefer to ask the question to one of his classmates when the teacher has left the classroom. (Boys' group interview, School 4, September 2011)

Anglophone students expressed more confidence in the class-room and were more likely to speak out and talk. Benjamin opined: "There are some people here who were affected by the change in language. For example, when there are conferences, debates, or speeches here, generally the students who studied in the Anglophone system participate the most. And when they deliver their points, they dominate the others who studied in French. They become isolated. And they are afraid of sharing their problems with the administration, like the headmaster" (Boys' group interview, School 4, September 2011).

During my classroom observations as well as in group interviews, Anglophone students often spoke, whereas Francophones were timid or incapable of contributing to the discussion, presumably due to a lack of comprehension or lack of confidence.

Language also serves as a dividing factor linked to identity— Francophone students commonly referred to Anglophones as a distinct group or spoke about cultural differences between groups, expressing preference for people who spoke French or were similar to themselves. Teachers commented on the boundaries maintained by students. Karen, a Ugandan history teacher in a private school near the capital, described the groups that formed in class when she assigned group work: "So when you are grouping them you're sort of mixing them. You mix the Francophones and the Anglophones. Obviously, when you tell them to group themselves, the Anglophones will all sit together because they know each other. . . . When you tell them to sit in a group of ten, you will find ten Anglophones sitting around one table" (Teacher interview, School 5, October 2011).

The language change was most difficult for teachers, most of whom were not trained in English or consulted prior to the change (Williams 2017). Most teachers referred to the change as "sudden" or "abrupt"; one teacher said he learned about the change on the radio (Field notes, School 1, September 2011). Jean Paul, a Francophone student in a school in the Western Province, explained the challenges for the teachers:

> I can say that the problem was one of forcing English, while certain teachers weren't capable of teaching or giving the courses in English. They studied in French, but they were forced to teach in English and they didn't receive a serious training in this language. That's where it was a problem for the students who had been taught by the teachers who don't

really know English, just like them. It would have been better if the teachers had first been trained, and after having mastered the language, then changing the system because teaching things in a language that you don't know is difficult. (Mixed group interview, School 1, September 2011)

George, a Ugandan teacher, summed up the challenges of the new language policy: "First, most of the teachers cannot teach in English, and they're not supposed to teach in French, so the only option is to use Kinyarwanda. Second, students' performances, especially those who were in the upper classes, suffered because of language. So students in previous year[s] tended to study subjects like math and physics, since they could not study subjects like history and literature, which require more explanation" (Teacher interview, School 4, November 2011).

Davide, a Francophone returnee teacher, explained the negative consequences of the language change on the quality of education and learning outcomes:

Regarding the change from French to English, we think that it was a reform that wasn't well studied. Perhaps there were political reasons, but they must consult those who are involved in education because these changes might have consequences. . . . Education [quality] has really declined, especially with language and understanding. . . . They shouldn't make sudden changes. They should tell us in advance. I saw that when they made the change from French to English, they said: you are going to start to teach in English without even being trained. That's when the students don't know what to do, or the teachers. It's now three years after the change that they are saying that they will have an English training for the teachers. Just imagine. How are the students really going to learn? They always start where we should be finishing. They should first train the

teachers, and after that, introduce the change. But they
introduced the change without a training. It's really a shame.
(Teacher interview, School 7, October 2011)

In addition to privileging Anglophone over Francophone
students in the classroom, the language policy has had negative
implications in terms of teachers' and students' abilities to engage
in active and critical discussion of topics, because their capacities
for comprehension and personal expression are constrained.

For Pierre Bourdieu (1991), language exemplifies "relations
of symbolic power in which the power relations between speak-
ers or their respective groups are actualized" (37). The Rwandan
language policy, although seemingly apolitical, in fact reinforces
symbolic boundaries and privileges one group over another,
fostering divergent identities (Bourdieu 1991; Carter 2012).
Through the language policy, the power of the Anglophone
Tutsi elite is represented in the classroom as well as at the political level. However, the government justifies the switch to English
because English is the global lingua franca (Cha 2007).

CONCLUSIONS

The Rwandan state uses education to promote a national identity that is at the same time global and patriotic and is putatively
delinked from ethnicity. The message of citizenship in Rwanda
corresponds with broader global norms while espousing scripted
national values such as loyalty and patriotism. Norms around
global citizenship are inherently in opposition to the nationalistic
and traditional cultural values that the curriculum promotes;
nonetheless, the two coexist at the policy and the classroom level.

Evidence gathered from interviews with and surveys of students and teachers suggests that although the promotion of a
strong Rwandan civic identity has been largely successful, the
state has been able to eliminate only the public expression of

ethnic identity, not the sense of identity itself. The official government narrative underscores a de-ethnicized identity of one Rwanda based on a shared language and culture, but many individuals continue to view themselves and others in ethnic terms. Teachers and older students are more aware of ethnic identity, and ethnic identity is less salient among younger students, although ethnic perspectives do persist. For most students, the configuration of ethnic identity is no longer constrained to a simple Hutu-Tutsi dichotomy but is linked to experience during the genocide and to language, both of which serve as proxies to cognitively define identity. The significance of identity is strongly linked to individual and family experience during the civil war and genocide.

The official government narrative, which asserts that ethnicity is a socially constructed phenomenon linked to beliefs about groups based on physical phenotypes, cannot efface deeply ingrained beliefs and perspectives. Although boundaries between groups have become more fluid and have shifted in Rwanda, a cognitive view on ethnicity persists, meaning that identity markers exist in individuals' thought processes and perspectives on the world and in their everyday interactions (Brubaker 2004). This development has implications for the meaning of a new civic identity in post-genocide Rwanda.

Although education policies and practices promote reconciliation and integration to some degree, they also foster ethnic perspectives and reinforce boundaries among groups. The civics and history curriculum focuses on a singular narrative about the genocide, yet special financial assistance is made available to genocide survivors (e.g., through FARG) and clubs exist specifically for genocide survivors and sympathizers (AERG), and the language policy favors Anglophone over Francophone students. Boundaries based on new markers, such as language, experience during the genocide (i.e., returnee, survivor), participation in clubs, and scholarships, have replaced the notion of three exclusively and rigidly defined groups (Hutu, Tutsi, and Twa). Language coupled with experience during the genocide has created a new identity that is inherently more complex than the Hutu-Tutsi dichotomy.

Distinctions and boundaries among groups manifest at the school level, challenging notions of unity and one Rwanda. A policy of not explicitly addressing ethnicity or race, which has been described as "color mute" (Pollock 2004) in the U.S. context, does not necessarily eradicate ethnic identity but merely shifts the focus to other cultural markers and signifiers. Openly acknowledging and discussing the cognitive construction and perceptions of ethnic identity may have important implications for long-term reconciliation and peacebuilding. For example, Northern Ireland's history curriculum draws on primary sources to provide a balanced rendition of historical events from both the Catholic and the Protestant perspectives in order to foster dialogue and reconciliation in the classroom (Kitson 2007; Terra 2013). Such an approach raises the question of whether it is better to ignore ethnic constructions or to address them directly and face the consequences of reconciliation and peacebuilding head on.

As the situation in Rwanda demonstrates, eliminating ethnic terms from the public discourse does not necessarily eliminate them in people's cognitive perceptions. Structures of identity endure and are manifested through language, experience, and everyday interactions. Ethnicity, regardless of whether or not it is merely a social construction, continues to exist with real consequences, even when the government does not officially sanction its existence. Perhaps it would be better to address the topic of ethnicity openly in schools, as Davide, a Tutsi returnee, affirmed: "We must talk about ethnicity, we must talk about Hutu and Tutsi. . . . The fact that we are different doesn't mean that we must reject one another. Rather, we must accept one another and be proud of our identities" (Teacher 7a, School

7, October 2011). While some postconflict countries have embraced the notions of diversity and multiculturalism by directly
discussing intergroup differences (Kitson 2007; Kruss 2001), in
Rwanda, the government has implemented the opposite approach,
which may have negative consequences for long-term peacebuilding and for building a strong civic identity. By suppressing
discussion of identity and denying the existence of cognitive
notions of ethnicity identity, the government may be undermining long-term sustainable peace.

CHAPTER 4

Using and Abusing Human Rights Norms

As I PREPARED for my first field visit to Rwanda in 2010, I was advised by several colleagues, both academics and those from nongovernmental organizations, about the perils of doing research in Rwanda under the current regime. One colleague advised that I not mention the term "human rights" or discuss ethnicity. Although discussing ethnic identity was and still is taboo in public spaces (see chapter 3), I was surprised to discover human rights language in Ministry of Education policy documents, curricula, and textbooks. Teachers explicitly taught about human rights in class. Human rights language came up often in my discussions and interviews with teachers and students.

I soon realized that human rights terms were invoked regularly in both national policy documents and in schools; however, the notion of human rights had a different meaning in the local context than in the official context. Rather than discussing alleged violations of human rights being committed by the Rwandan Patriotic Front (RPF) across the border in the Democratic Republic of Congo (DRC)—violations that, at the time of my research, were receiving attention in the international media and were well documented by Human Rights Watch (2012) and Amnesty International (2012)—teachers and students talked about human rights terms symbolically, mentioning the United Nations or the genocide, but without real consideration of their own rights or the current state of human rights in Rwanda. When pressed about the meaning of human rights in their daily lives, many teachers and students grew uncomfortable, and discussions became strained. Many of the teachers and students whom I interviewed sought to portray life in post-genocide Rwanda as idyllic, celebrating the achievements of the government and the vast improvements in the quality of life and the extent of unity among Rwandans. However, some of my respondents did openly critique the government for repressing freedom of speech and for favoring Tutsi genocide survivors and returnees over Hutu.

The tension I found illustrates a paradox of the relationship between the Rwandan state and human rights: while the government employs human rights language in national policy documents, it represses rights in certain contexts. In the post-genocide era, the Rwandan government's selective use of human rights discourse plays an integral role in the broader peacebuilding project, which seeks to foster reconciliation and a new civic identity and to preserve the memory of the genocide. This chapter demonstrates how the Rwandan government uses a human rights discourse strategically and selectively as part of the wider peacebuilding project and to garner international legitimacy. In the curriculum and the classroom, the government promotes some human rights, particularly those around gender equality and children's rights, but it silences discussions of violations of political and civil rights and recent human rights abuses.

The Rise of Global Human Rights and Human Rights Education

Although discussions of global human rights first emerged during the drafting of the Covenant for the League of Nations after World War I (Lauren 2011), human rights were not institutionalized until after World War II. In response to the mass violations of rights per-petrated by the Nazi regime, the international community envi-sioned the inclusion of human rights language as part of a broader transitional justice and peacebuilding process. The term "human rights" appeared for the first time in the 1945 UN Charter and was codified in the Universal Declaration of Human Rights in 1948 (Donnelly 2013; Stacy 2009). The International Covenant on Civil and Political Rights (ICCPR) and the International Covenant on Economic, Social, and Cultural Rights (ICESCR) were signed in 1966 and formed the foundation for international human rights law. These two covenants are accepted by the majority of coun-tries: by 2017, 169 countries had acceded to the ICCPR and 165 countries had acceded to the ICESCR (Office of the High Com-missioner for Human Rights 2017).

Empirical studies have documented the rise in global human rights discourse in the post–World War II era (Keck and Sikkink 1998; Tsutsui and Wotipka 2004). A global human rights dis-course has been increasingly institutionalized, as evidenced by an increase in international human rights instruments (Elliott 2007), references to human rights in national constitutions (Beck, Drori, and Meyer 2012), the proliferation of national human rights bodies (Koo and Ramirez 2009), and the inclusion of human rights in textbooks (Meyer, Bromley, and Ramirez 2010). Neoinstitutional sociologists describe the emergence of global human rights norms as linked to a broader shift in a "world culture" that shapes national-level policies, curriculum, and textbooks (Meyer 2010; Meyer, Boli, et al. 1997). Construc-tivist political scientists explain the spread and adaption of global human rights norms as part of a "norm cascade" through which norms are adopted and internalized by different actors on the ground (Finnemore and Sikkink 1998; Keck and Sikkink 1998; Risse-Kappen, Ropp, and Sikkink 1999).

To advance knowledge and awareness of international human rights treaties and conventions, the United Nations has promoted human rights education (HRE). HRE is defined by the UN World Programme for Human Rights Education (2014) as all forms of learning, education, training, or information that is directed toward developing a universal human rights culture. The definition of HRE encompasses not only teaching *about* human rights, but also teaching *for* human rights and *through* human rights (Bajaj 2011a; Tibbitts 2002). The global rise and institutionalization of HRE is linked to globalization, the expansion of mass education, and the spread of the global human rights movement (Ramírez, Suárez, and Meyer 2007; Russell and Suárez 2017).

Several studies have shown the extent to which a global HRE discourse has expanded across diverse regions and countries, influencing policy, curriculum, textbooks, and classroom discussions. Francisco Ramírez and his colleagues (2007) note a rise in HRE publications and organizations after 2000. In a cross-national study of textbooks, John Meyer, Bromley, and Ramirez (2010) find an increase in the discussion of human rights after 1995 in civics and social studies books. A related study demonstrates an increase in discussions of human rights in textbooks in the post-1990 period across several dimensions of human rights in both Western and non-Western countries (Russell and Suárez 2017). An analysis of the 2009 International Civic and Citizenship Education Study data finds that human rights were discussed in classrooms in the thirty-eight participating countries (Schulz et al. 2010). Other studies illustrate how HRE is understood among students in India, Colombia, and Northern Ireland (Bajaj 2011b; Barton 2015; Wahl 2017).

Although many countries sign and ratify international human rights covenants, in practice, they do not always enforce them, indicating "loose coupling" between intention and action. Studies provide empirical evidence of how countries sign on to human rights treaties in order to deflect international criticism of human rights abuses (Clark 2010; W. Cole 2005; Hafner-Burton and Tsutsui 2005, 2007). Emilie Hafner-Burton and Kiyoteru Tsutsui (2005) find evidence that countries that sign on to human rights treaties are not more likely to protect human rights in practice. Similarly, Wade Cole (2005) demonstrates that the costs associated with treaty ratification are more important than the content in predicting whether a country accedes to a treaty.

In contrast to macrolevel sociological and political science research that notes the rise in human rights globally, anthropological perspectives on human rights emphasize the ways in which local actors engage with and adapt global rights discourse. The notion of "vernacularization" explores the translation and contextualization of human rights for the local context (Goodale 2009; Goodale and Merry 2007; Merry 2006). Several empirical studies have explored how local actors engage with global human rights discourse. Sharon Abramowitz and Mary Moran (2012) use ethnographic data to show how Liberians frame discussions around gender-based violence and human rights in local cultural contexts, finding that the discourse is bidirectional. Sealing Cheng (2011) presents the contradictory effects of vernacularization through an ethnography of antiprostitution efforts in South Korea. She argues that localizing women's human rights perpetuates a gendered notion of the nation.

Steve Stern and Scott Straus (2014) refer to this disconnect between the global and the local as the human rights paradox: "There can be no human rights without a claim to the universal, to the transnational, and to transcendent principle. But there can also be no human rights without locality, politics, history, and actors" (9). In an effort to bridge the global and the local binary, Mark Goodale (2007) argues for an approach that locates how human rights discourse is applied in practice. In the following section, I present evidence from Rwanda to understand how global human rights discourses are understood and constituted by nonelite actors—namely, teachers and students—in local contexts.

HUMAN RIGHTS DISCOURSE IN
POST-GENOCIDE RWANDA

Rwanda is a signatory to the majority of the eighteen international human rights treaties and conventions (Office of the High Commissioner for Human Rights 2017). The pre-genocide Rwandan government signed on to most of these treaties before 1994, yet the Hutu-dominated Habyarimana regime flagrantly violated human rights during the genocide (the genocide is considered one of the most egregious mass violations of human rights in history). However, the post-genocide government, dominated by the RPF, has also opted to protect only limited rights, focusing on upholding social and economic rights over civil and political rights.

Since coming to power in 1994, the RPF-led government has consistently invoked a human rights discourse to varying degrees. The government has not only signed on to international conventions but has also integrated human rights discourse in national policy documents. *Rwanda Vision 2020*, the main policy document guiding national development, refers explicitly to human rights, noting that the state will be "respectful of democratic structures and processes and committed to the rule of law and the *protection of human rights* in particular" (Ministry of Finance and Economic Planning 2000, 12; emphasis added). This sentiment is echoed in the Ministry of Education's *Economic Development and Poverty Reduction Strategy (PSRP), 2008–2012* (2007) and the *Education Sector Strategic Plan, 2006–2010* (2006). In the *Education Sector Strategic Plan*, the objective of the education sector is framed specifically in human rights terms: "To promote an integral, comprehensive education oriented toward the *respect of human rights* and adapted to the present situation of the country" (Ministry of Education 2006, 8; emphasis added). The Rwanda Ministry of Justice's (2017)

National Human Rights Action Plan proclaims the government's "commitment to its international human rights obligations, and the Government's desire to improve both the promotion and protection of human rights" (Republic of Rwanda, Ministry of Justice 2017, i). Yet, there is little discussion of the definition of human rights or of what they mean in the Rwandan context.

Human rights are often mentioned in conjunction with gender equality, with a strong focus on promoting gender equality and women's rights. In the *Education Sector Strategic Plan, 2006–2010*, the stated goal of education is to promote both "respect for human rights" and "gender equality" (Ministry of Education 2006, 8). Gender is prioritized as a crosscutting issue within the main education and national development policies (i.e., Vision 2020 and the Poverty Reduction Strategy Paper) from 2000 to 2010. The Rwandan *National Gender Policy* (Republic of Rwanda, Ministry of Gender and Family Promotion, 2010) and the *Girls' Education Policy* (Ministry of Education, 2008b) are devoted entirely to the promotion of gender issues at the national level and in the education sector, respectively. In a related analysis across eight Rwandan national policy documents, I find references to gender equality more numerous than mentions of human rights: "gender" is mentioned 196 times in all eight documents, whereas "human rights" is mentioned twenty-two times across five documents (Russell 2015).

Although the Rwandan government employs global human rights language in policy documents, it takes a selective approach to the rights that it chooses to secure in practice. The government has expanded social and economic rights while limiting civil and political rights. For example, the government made strides in achieving the Millennium Development Goals, including the expansion of access to twelve years of basic education and community-based health care, and in promoting gender equality (Abbott, Sapsford, and Binagwaho 2017; Abbott,

Sapsford, and Rwirahira 2015; UNDP Rwanda 2014). The Rwandan government has also been successful in promoting gender equality in terms of increased representation of females in government: Rwanda has the highest percentage of women in parliament in the world (Inter-Parliamentary Union 2016).[1] The 2003 Constitution requires that women hold at least 30 percent of positions in "decision-making organs" (Republic of Rwanda 2003, Article 9.4), and the government has passed several important laws in favor of women's rights. The 1999 Inheritance Law mandates equal inheritance for women and men; the 2008 Gender-Based Violence Law protects women's rights and criminalizes gender-based violence, including domestic violence and conjugal rape (Republic of Rwanda 1999, 2008b).

Some scholars have argued that the post-genocide government has focused on gender equality to enhance its legitimacy within the international community and to detract from ethnic tensions (Hogg 2013) and from other forms of human rights violations (Russell 2015). Gender equality is viewed positively by Western donors and, in general, is considered less politically sensitive than political or civil rights violations or interethnic tensions (Burnet 2008; Longman 2006; Russell 2015). Focusing on gender equality at the level of national policy has been not only economically practical but politically strategic. Programs in Rwanda that promote gender equality garner considerable support and donor funding from the international community (Burnet 2008; Longman 2006; Straus and Waldorf 2011). The Rwandan government continues to strategically employ a focus on gender equality as a means to further economic and social development and to promote societal reconciliation in the post-genocide era. A concerted government focus on gender in human rights terms is intended to deflect attention from a contentious past—namely, the genocide and the legacy of intergroup tensions.

Many observers see the regime's public commitment to human rights as cynical and hypocritical, given accusations that the regime has in fact committed numerous human rights violations and abuses. International human rights organizations (such as Human Rights Watch) have been restricted in Rwanda, and the government has been criticized internationally for human rights violations in eastern DRC (Amnesty International 2012; Human Rights Watch 2012). One contentious issue concerns the killing of innocent civilians by the RPF leading up to and in the aftermath of the genocide. The RPF waged a war from 1997 to 1999, known as the war against the "infiltrators" (*abacengezi*)—the former Interahamwe who fled to the DRC after the genocide—where innocent civilians were often caught in the cross fire (Burnet 2009; Stearns and Borello 2011). A former Human Rights Watch researcher, Allison Des Forges, estimates that the RPF killed between 25,000 and 45,000 Hutu, both innocent civilians and suspected *génocidaires*, during and after the genocide (Des Forges 1999, 18). In addition, the Rwandan government has been accused of committing human rights violations and of supporting the abusive M23 rebel group in the DRC (Amnesty International 2012; Human Rights Watch 2012).[2] These violations of human rights have never been officially acknowledged by the current government; rather, the mention of these violations is taboo and amounts to genocide ideology.

The government of Rwanda has been criticized by international human rights organizations for a lack of freedom of expression and free press, for the repression of political opposition, and for torture and unlawful military detention (Amnesty International 2017; Human Rights Watch 2012, 2017b; Melvin 2010). In the 2017 presidential election, which resulted in a landslide victory for Paul Kagame, opposition candidates were intimidated (Amnesty International 2017; Human Rights Watch

2017a). Freedom House, an independent organization that monitors political rights and civil liberties, has ranked Rwanda as "not free," with a score of only 24 out of a possible 100 due to the suppression of political dissent and freedom of expression (Freedom House 2017).

TEACHING ABOUT HUMAN RIGHTS IN SCHOOLS

In addition to the inclusion of human rights discourse in national policy documents, school curricula and textbooks also cover the subject. I also observed classes where teachers taught about human rights, and students mentioned learning about human rights on the survey and in interviews.

Curriculum and Textbooks

Human rights discourse is evident in the national curriculum and textbooks, with a greater emphasis in more recent iterations. The national curriculum frameworks for political education and citizenship education, social studies, and history all mention human rights. In particular, the political education and social studies curricula include in-depth content on human rights. The 2008 political education curriculum for the ordinary level presents citizenship in terms of the "rights and obligations of a citizen" and mentions the importance of playing "an active role in the promotion and protection of human rights" (National Curriculum Development Center 2008d, 9–23). The 2015 history and citizenship curriculum includes a subtopic on "human rights, citizen duties and responsibilities," with the stated expectation that students will be able to "explain the concept of human rights, citizen duties and responsibilities, and suggest ways of preventing human rights violations" (Rwanda Education Board 2015, 6).

The textbooks for political education, social studies, and history and citizenship education all devote at least one section to human rights, which are generally linked to children's rights. In older books, the discussion of human rights is focused on international legal mechanisms and treaties to protect human rights, rather than on human rights as applied to the Rwandan context or to students' lives in a relevant, student-centered manner. The 2008 political education book for the lower secondary level and the chapters on human rights in the 2006 social studies books for the primary level encompass topics on types of rights and violations of rights. The 2006 grade 6 social studies book includes a subsection on "rights and responsibilities" that explains and enumerates the main human rights in connection with the United Nations. The 2008 political education book defines human rights as "the rights and freedom inherent to every human individual" (National Curriculum Development Center 2008a, 71). The chapter discusses the history of human rights, including various UN treaties, and the principles and characteristics of human rights. However, the material is presented in a very technical and non-child-friendly manner, and human rights are enumerated rather than applied to a locally relevant context. The 2006 social studies books for grades 4 and 5 each have a chapter on children's rights (Bamusananire et al. 2006a, 2007b). The 2004 civic education book also has a chapter devoted to "child and human rights."

The newer textbooks attempt to relate human rights to the local context by asking students to relate them to their own life. For example, the 2017 social studies book contains a section on human rights that lists important human rights and asks students to discuss whether these rights are being implemented in their province (see figure 10).

This example emphasizes social and economic rights, such as the right to education and shelter, over more contested civil and political rights. The 2016 history and citizenship book has a chapter on "human rights, citizen duties, and responsibilities"

2.3 Human Rights

 Check yourself 2.2

Identify five things that a person must have in order to live in dignity.
Share what you have identified with the class members.

Human rights are those things that a person must have in order to lead a normal life. They are basic standards which people live in dignity.

Some of the rights are:
- Right to life
- Right to clean water
- Right to clothing
- Right medical care
- Right to identity

- Right to education
- Right to a balanced diet
- Right to shelter
- Right to safe and clean environment

Do research on the above human rights. Discuss whether these rights are being implemented in our province.

10. Human rights in textbooks. *Source*: Munezero et al. 2017, 19.

in which human rights are defined and discussed in relation to the United Nations and the National Commission for Human Rights of Rwanda (Sebazungu, Okoth, and Agumba 2016, 132).

Student Conceptions of Human Rights

In my survey of more than 500 secondary students across sixteen schools in 2011 (see appendix A for more details on the methodology), students reported that human rights were discussed frequently in their political education class: 62 percent said they discussed human rights at least once a week, and 20 percent said they talked about human rights at least once a month; only 7 percent said that human rights were never mentioned in class. There was statistically significant variation by region and type of

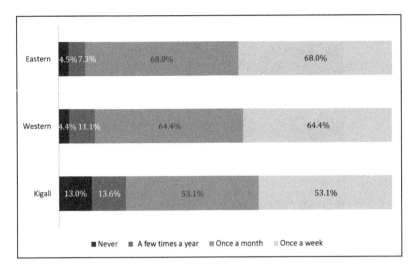

11. Discussion of human rights by province.

school, which is similar to statistics reported on the discussion of citizenship rights (see chapter 3). According to the students, human rights were discussed most frequently in the schools in the Eastern Province, followed by schools in the Western Province and Kigali, where 13 percent of students said they never discussed human rights in class (see figure 11).

Government-aided (generally religious) schools tended to emphasize human rights to a greater extent than private schools, with government schools falling in the middle. Figure 12 shows that 74 percent of students reported discussing human rights at least once a week in government-aided schools; nearly 15 percent of students at private schools said they never discussed human rights.

Despite the frequency of discussion of human rights in the classroom, students did not seem to grasp the significance and application of human rights for their daily lives. When asked about the meaning of human rights, students generally discussed human rights in abstract terms. In one group discussion, John, an

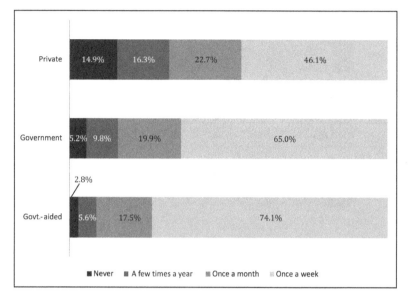

12. Discussion of human rights by type of school.

eighteen-year-old student in a rural private school in the Eastern Province, said that "human rights are how people respect
freedom and the duties of being a human being" (Mixed group
interview, School 3, September 2011). In a discussion at a school
in the capital, Kevin, age seventeen, articulated his belief that
"human rights are the rights that each human should have, like
the right to life, the right to education, right to shelter" (Boys'
group interview, School 6, August 2011). Richard, a twenty-
three-year-old accounting student in a semiurban private school,
echoed this sentiment: "When we learn about human rights, we
are told that it's something very important that everyone needs
all over the world and in everyday life. Since each human being
holds a certain value, each . . . should be viewed as a creature of
God, whether a Black man or a White man. When we study

human rights, we study our rights and the laws that protect us" (Boys group interview, School 5, October 2011).

A majority of respondents (56 percent) felt strongly that people should participate in activities to promote human rights. However, students rarely mentioned concrete activities to promote human rights during interviews or in class.

Economic and Social Rights over Civil and Political Rights

Rather than associating human rights with a more applied context relevant to their daily lives, students framed rights in global and abstract terms and tended to emphasize economic and social rights over civil and political rights. Whereas the textbooks generally provide an overview of human rights and present civil and political rights (first-generation rights) and social and economic rights (second-generation rights) as indivisible, in the classroom, teachers and students tended to emphasize second-generation rights, such as education and shelter, over more contested first-generation rights due to political sensitivities surrounding political and civil rights in Rwanda. The focus on social and economic rights over civil and political rights is common throughout sub-Saharan Africa, where economic and social development are seen as priorities. For instance, the main human rights document for the continent, the African Charter on Human and Peoples' Rights (1981), emphasizes economic and social rights, the needs of the community, and a humanistic orientation, or *ubuntu* (Stacy 2009).

Several examples illustrate how economic and social rights tend to be prioritized in the classroom. In a political education class in a semiurban private school outside of Kigali, the teacher discussed human rights in the context of citizenship (Classroom observation, School 5, August 2011). The teacher wrote "Citizen's Rights and Human Rights" on the blackboard and asked, "Who can tell us in your language what is the meaning of human rights?" Several girls called out the term in Kinyarwanda: *Uburenganzira bwa muntu* (human rights). The teacher then talked about Rwanda joining the United Nations and asked students to name "some human rights in Rwanda." The students called out answers, such as the "right to education" and the "right to medical services," and the teacher wrote what students said on the blackboard. Students tended to define human rights in terms of fundamental human rights (right to life, freedom from torture) and social and economic rights (such as the right to education), rather than emphasizing civil and political rights such as freedom of expression and the right to vote:

BENJAMIN: Human rights are the basic needs or the human pursuit to live.

JAQUES: In my opinion, human rights are the essential needs that a human being should receive or be granted by other human beings. For example, each human being has the right to live. If you kill another person, that means that you don't respect his/her rights. Another thing that I can say: each person has the right to have a place to live. For example, in our country, there are a lot of children who don't have a place to live. That shows that their rights aren't respected.

MAXIMILIAN: In my opinion, human rights are everything that a man needs to live. If you don't find them, that means that his rights aren't respected. For example, the right to eat and the right to study. But unfortunately, I see that people don't have all of that. That means that they don't have all of their rights. (Boys' group interview, School 4, September 2011)

As the example above illustrates, some students were clearly aware of the disjuncture between what they learned in school about human rights and what rights they were entitled to in practice, mentioning the examples of housing, food, and education as rights that were not always realized. Josef, a twenty-one-year-old accounting returnee from Uganda, talked about the right to education and about how education in Rwanda is inherently unequal: "There is an article that says that all kids have the same right to education, but in Rwanda this isn't the case. The means and capacities of the families are different: some can afford to send their kids to boarding school, while others don't have the means to put them in boarding school" (Boys' group interview, School 5, October 2011). Nonetheless, few students discussed this discrepancy in regard to political and civil rights, perhaps due to fear of political repercussions. For example, when students were asked questions in class such as "Do you have freedom of speech?," they always responded affirmatively (Classroom observation, School 5, August 2011). However, during one-on-one interviews, some students were more critical of the regime. Juliet, an eighteen-year-old Francophone returnee in a government-aided school in the Western Province, commented that although she thought that rights were generally respected in Rwanda, the right to freedom of expression is not always realized, a fact that she viewed as a restriction on human rights: "I believe that *human rights* are somewhat respected, but here in Rwanda not everyone has the right to express himself/herself because there are moments when you can say something and go directly to prison for twenty-five years; there are things that we cannot say above all about our history, about the genocide. It's necessary to be prudent" (Student interview, School 1, October 2011; emphasis added). These examples point to the tenuous nature of teaching about civil and political rights in a postconflict authoritarian context, where students may question what is taught in schools in contrast to their lived reality but are not encouraged to ask their questions in the classroom.

Avoiding Sensitive Topics

Although national educational documents include global rights discourses, they use vague language rather than specific examples of human rights issues and violations in recent history and the present day. Nor do they offer much detail as to how human rights should be protected or realized on the ground. Similarly, teachers and students focused on noncontroversial aspects of the human rights discourse linked to global bodies, other countries, or the Rwandan genocide, rather than confronting instances of recent or current human rights violations. The avoidance of discussion of challenging issues in the classroom also undermines the goal of achieving meaningful reconciliation.

When asked during interviews what topics they covered in class, the majority of political education and general paper teachers said that they taught human rights. However, due to time restrictions, some teachers said they avoided topics that were controversial, sensitive, or outside their area of expertise. A political education teacher from a school in the Western Province explained that she does not teach about human rights, gender, or the genocide, even though these topics are in the textbooks and the curriculum. She said that there is not sufficient time to cover all the topics in the curriculum, so she focuses on economics, her area of expertise (Teacher interview, School 1, September 2011). When asked about subjects that are difficult to teach, Paul, a general paper teacher in a religious school in the Western Province, noted that certain topics are easier to address when talking about human rights:

> With the older students, there aren't any problems but with the younger students it's difficult to address any subject. For example, for the fourth-year students, we prefer to teach them about human rights, protection of the person, humanitarian law, the Red Cross intervention during the war, and

also a little about the genocide. For the fifth year, it's more about debates and the opportunity to exchange ideas and to help the students to work on their ideas. We professors play the role of mediators in guiding the students and *keeping the students on track, to correct their ideas*, and to summarize these ideas so that they can grasp the general ideas of the subject. In fact, that's the pedagogy that we use. (Teacher interview, School 1, October 2011; emphasis added)

Human rights were generally taught in the context of international legal conventions on human rights and framed as a concept emanating from the United Nations. Teachers did not necessarily perceive the discussion of human rights to be controversial because they followed the national curriculum, which presents human rights within a legalistic framework rather than as an approach seeking to empower students. In a political education class, Sam, a Ugandan teacher, wrote key phrases from the textbook on the blackboard while explaining: "The constitution gives citizens of Rwanda rights; many of these rights are based on the human rights listed by the United Nations. The government must respect and protect these rights" (Classroom observation, School 5, September 2011). He then asked students to name human rights but did not discuss the lack of human rights or other sensitive topics. George, a Ugandan teacher at a government school in the Eastern Province, explained: "When I teach about human rights, basically you refer to the UN, it's what we use. The UN human rights charter, basically we teach this content" (Teacher interview, School 4, September 2011).

Although teachers incorporated human rights into their courses in the classroom, they did so in a way that avoided discussion of contentious topics. Discussions of human rights violations in the local context might involve talking about human rights violations during the genocide and current violations perpetrated by the government. However, the restrictions on free speech and political activity imposed by the all-encompassing Genocide Ideology Law (2008) hamper the open discussion of civil and political rights.[3] Thus, teachers tended to follow the curriculum and textbooks closely, especially when teaching about human rights, framing discussions in global and abstract terms. Teachers generally copied definitions verbatim from the textbooks onto the blackboard.

The practice of copying from the textbooks was pervasive in courses with politically sensitive topics, such as history and political education, as well as in other types of courses. In one political education class in an urban, government-aided religious school, the teacher taught about the "notion of human rights and international humanitarian law," following the topics exactly as they appeared in the political education textbook (National Curriculum Development Center 2008a).

TEACHER: Who are the people who have to be protected by international humanitarian law? [*elaborates in Kinyarwanda*]
STUDENTS: Citizens.
TEACHER: Who can give me an example of the violation of international humanitarian law?
STUDENTS: Gadhafi, Bashir, Al-Shabaab. (Classroom observation, School 7, August 2011)

This example, among others, illustrates the extent to which students are focused on global definitions of human rights and human rights violations in other countries, such as Libya, Syria, or Somalia, rather than on human rights violations in Rwanda. The difficulty and fear of discussing the current political situation or past human rights violations in Rwanda encourage teachers to focus on human rights violations in other contexts.

For example, during a political education class in a private religious school in a rural area of the Eastern Province, the teacher taught about different forms of government. He wrote "Dictatorship" on the board, explained that it means "no freedom of speech, press, choice, or liberty," and then asked students for characteristics of this type of government. A boy said, "They don't have human rights." The teacher pressed, asking "For instance?" The student responded, "Freedom of speech." However, neither the teacher nor the students in the class connected this conversation to their lived reality in Rwanda (Classroom observation, School 3, June 2011).

When human rights violations were mentioned in the Rwandan context, they were usually presented in reference to the 1994 genocide. Flora, a Francophone returnee in an urban school, said, "I think that in Rwanda, during the *genocide* of 1994, *human rights* weren't respected, meaning that these rights that had been established in 1945 were flouted because people endured torture and violence" (Girls' group interview, School 7, August 2011; emphasis added). Marie similarly compared human rights violations to the lack of respect during the genocide (Girls' group interview, School 4, July 2011). Paul, a teacher in a religious school in the Western Province, explained the connection: "When we talk about human rights, we also talk about the genocide, also because we see directly how human rights were violated during the period of the genocide, and also before the genocide" (Teacher interview, School 1, October 2011). George equated human rights with the Rwandan genocide: "After teaching *human rights*, then we talk about *human rights violations*, then we arrive at *genocide*" (Teacher interview, School 4, September 2011; emphasis added). However, the extrajudicial revenge killings of suspected Hutu *génocidaires* by the RPF regime after the genocide, military involvement in the DRC, and present violations were almost always strictly off limits (see, for example, Des Forges 1999). When the subject of killings by the RFP did occasionally come up, human rights were not invoked. For instance, when asked about the consequences of the genocide, Fabrice explained that his father was killed by the RPF during the period following the genocide but avoided framing it as a human rights violation:

GARNETT: What are the consequences of the genocide?

FABRICE: There are a lot. For example, there was the war in 1997, when the Interahamwe wanted to re-enter the country by force. It was also during this period that my father was assassinated by the RPF. So at the time, the Interahamwe attacked the Rwandans without a military uniform, so they had infiltrated the population, and it was difficult for the RPF soldiers to recognize them, because they had already blended in with the population. (Student interview, School 7, September 2011)[4]

In spite of discourse around "student-centered learning" and critical thinking in policy documents, based on my observations, classroom activities did not appear to foster the critical thinking or open discussion necessary for the implementation of HRE. Only 34 percent of students surveyed said that they often expressed opinions that differed from those of their teachers; students in government-aided (religious) schools were more likely than their peers in other government schools or private schools to express their own opinions. Nonetheless, more than half of the sample reported that they worked in groups in class and posed questions. Classroom observations revealed a mix of teacher-centered and student-centered techniques.

Although the most common method of instruction consisted of the teacher writing on the board and students copying notes into their notebooks, several teachers attempted to incorporate student-centered learning through group work and student presentations and by posing questions to the class. However, questions and discussions were constrained to safe and non-controversial topics and did not transcend the bounds of the curricular framework. Several teachers mentioned that they do not like to "veer off course" for fear of encountering difficult questions (Teacher, School 1; Teacher, School 7). Teachers perceived the implementation of student-centered learning, such as group work, as less controversial than allowing students to ask critical questions.

HUMAN RIGHTS AS WOMEN'S RIGHTS: TEACHING ABOUT GENDER EQUALITY IN SCHOOLS

Although human rights terms are often framed in economic and social rights or in relation to children's rights, they are also explicitly linked in both curricular documents and in the classroom to gender equality and women's rights.

Curriculum and Textbooks

Gender equality is an important topic in political education, history, and social studies curriculums and textbooks. Both the social studies books for the primary level and the political education books for the secondary level devote entire chapters to the topic of gender. Volume one of the political education book discusses gender in the context of armed conflict, education, and social discrimination, specifically referring to the terms "gender discrimination" and "gender promotion" (National Curriculum Development Center 2008a). Volume two devotes a chapter to "gender and development" (National Curriculum Development Center 2008b).

National policy documents frame gender explicitly in human rights terms, within the context of gender inequality or gender discrimination, as well as in regard to equal access to education for boys and girls. The discussion of education is focused on the issue of gender disparities in terms of access and achievement in education and employment: "Gender is one of the most obvious areas where there is likely to be inequality in education. The inequality that exists between the sexes becomes more pronounced as the level of education gets higher. This tendency is reinforced in education management and administration positions where there are many more men than women in decision-making roles. This simply reflects the lack of opportunity women have to reach the higher levels of education, which would give them the qualifications to reach higher positions in employment" (Ministry of Education 2003b, 15).

Education is also presented as playing a key role in promoting gender equality through economic and social development. The *Education Sector Strategic Plan, 2010–2015* states, "The Government is committed to ensuring that women are also well skilled beyond the basic level to contribute positively to *economic and social development*" (Ministry of Education 2010, 17; emphasis added). Providing equal opportunities to males and females and remedying disparities within the educational system and society is thus considered crucial to national development.

Discussions of gender equality are couched in human rights and development language in educational texts. Volume one of the political education textbook presents gender equality in rights and development terminology and as part of a larger national project for reconciliation and unity:

> This [gender] promotion aims at giving to men and women the same rights in the economic, political and social domains. In order to achieve this, it is necessary to reconsider the current status of the Rwandan woman, who seems to be kept in dependence that handicaps her from contributing valuable participation in all domains of national life. The participation of the women in the development of the country and in the process of decision-making from her current status of just another mother is necessary to consolidate unity and reconciliation of Rwandans and to promote the spirit of tolerance, peace and love. (National Curriculum Development Center 2008a, 160)

Student Views of Gender Equality

While women had limited access to social, political, and economic power in the postindependence period leading up to the genocide, the post-genocide government has made a concerted effort to include women in the public sphere and to promote women's rights (Longman 2006). Since coming to power in 1994, the RPF-led government has established the Ministry of Gender, created women's councils, and implemented gender quotas in the national parliament (Burnet 2008). While some studies have found evidence of a positive shift in women's attitudes and perceptions about equality (Burnet 2011), other studies point to continued challenges in changing cultural norms and practices (Berry 2015; Debusscher and Ansoms 2013; Russell 2016).

Student survey data from my study illustrate high levels of support for gender equality and equal rights for women and men across different types of schools and regions. The majority of students agreed or strongly agreed with the statements that "the state should provide equal opportunities to men and women," "women should participate in politics," "men and women should have the same rights," and "boys and girls should be treated the same in school" (see figure 13).

Interview data from students similarly revealed a high level of awareness and support of the concepts of "gender balance" and "gender equality" across boys and girls, in urban and rural areas, and in different types of schools. In Rwanda, the term "gender balance" is often used in reference to gender equality, indicating a focus on equal numbers of men and women rather than a critique of gendered and unequal societal structures.

Students across a variety of schools, including private and religious schools, demonstrated similar understandings of gender equality or gender balance as equalizing rights and opportunities for women and men rather than as an effort to dismantle

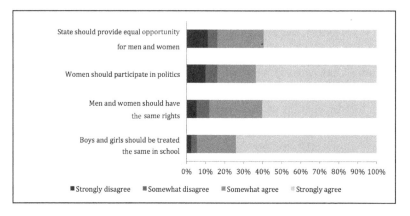

13. Views of gender equality.

structural inequalities. In an interview in a rural religious high-achieving school, students discussed the meaning of equality in terms of equal treatment and respect:

GARNETT: What is equality between women and men? What does it mean to you?

CLAUDE: *Gender balance* between men and women is to treat both the same, to respect everyone. (Mixed group interview, School 1, September 2011; emphasis added)

Similarly, in a rural private school of average quality, students in an interview equated notions of gender equality with providing equal opportunities for both men and women.

GARNETT: Now I want to ask you about what equality between men and women and boys and girls means to you.

PATRICK: According to how people in Rwanda give meaning to this term, *gender equality* means *equalizing* people, especially men and women, and even children. That's to protect the feminine gender against any sort of abuse with tasks and work. And everyone should understand that what a man can do, a woman can do, as well. It also means equalizing work opportunities. (Mixed group interview, School 3, September 2011; emphasis added)

Rights Discourse: Women's Rights as Human Rights

A rights-based discourse was prevalent in the discussions of gender at the school level. When asked about human rights, students frequently mentioned women's rights as an example of human rights. Patrick, a twenty-year-old studying computer science in senior 4 at a private school in the Eastern Province, said, "When people say human rights, I immediately think of children's rights and *women's rights* because they are the most vulnerable categories" (Mixed group interview, School 3, September 2011; emphasis added). Janet, in an urban school in the same province, stated: "When we are talking about human rights, we learn about all kinds of human rights. For example, we talk about the rights of children and the *rights of women*" (Girls' group interview, School 4, July 2011; emphasis added).

In a discussion with a group of girls in a rural public school about the meaning of human rights, students mentioned gender equality and women's rights as examples of human rights, explicitly couching gender equality in rights terms:

GARNETT: So I want to ask you about some topics that you might learn here at school or at home. So my question is, what does the term "human rights" mean to you?

BEATRICE: Let's take for example what happened before. In the past, it was said that the woman didn't have the *rights* of a man, like talking before the authorities or even in society. She was always at home. She didn't study. She didn't benefit from all of the *rights* of a man, but now she is at the same level as the man. There are the same *rights* for everyone.

GARNETT: In terms of the example that you just gave, that shows equality between the woman and the man. What is this term called?

AIMEE: It's *uburinganire hagati y'umugabo n'umugabo* [gender equality]. This means that there is complete equality between the woman and the man.

GARNETT: Do you think that gender equality is also a human right?

JOSELINE: Yes, it's a *human right* because the woman is also a person. Before women were poorly treated, and their *rights* were not respected. For example, there were times when the man beat his wife and the woman didn't even have the right to complain. But now, the woman has all of the *rights*. In promoting woman's freedom, with *women's rights*, the right to life is expected, which is among human rights. (Girls' group interview, School 2, September 2011; emphasis added)

Similarly, in a high-achieving urban public school, when students were asked about the meaning of human rights, gender equality was mentioned:

GARNETT: What does the term "human rights" mean to you? Can you give me an example?

ANNA: The rights to have the same *rights* as a girl or a boy. *Gender equality*.

GARNETT: So do you think that gender equality is a human right?

GIRLS: Yes.

GARNETT: So what is gender equality?

FIONA: Because the same *rights* aren't given to girls and boys. Now, everyone is benefiting from the same *rights*; for example, in terms of work, gender isn't considered. Merit is considered, for those who are capable. But knowing that it was the men who had the opportunities to have everything like the best jobs and positions. (Girls' group interview, School 6, September 2011; emphasis added)

The issue of gender equality, or women's rights, is often mentioned by students as an example of human rights because gender equality is a noncontroversial aspect of human rights (Russell 2015). Compared to other more contested rights, such as civil and political rights, women's rights in post-genocide Rwanda are concrete and therefore easy to discuss openly in schools.

Post-Genocide Nation Building

Students viewed the promotion of gender equality and equal rights as a project of the post-1994 government and as part of the larger nation-building effort. Students often explained gender progress in reference to the post-genocide period and the RPF-led government. In a mixed-gender group discussion in a rural basic education school in the Western Province, both girls and boys framed gender in rights terms and in reference to the genocide:

GARNETT: What does the term "gender equality" mean to you?

MARCEL: Having *equal rights* between a boy and a girl, or between a woman and a man.

SILVIE: *Before the genocide* [*jenocide*], girls didn't have the same *rights* to go to school as boys. But now, the girls study and they have the same opportunities as boys at school and at work. I also feel *capable* of being one of the country's authorities. I am *capable* of leading like the others can do. Before the genocide, I thought that it was impossible. But now, I understand that I can also do it. Before, women didn't have *rights* to do everything, but now they have all of the same *rights*, so they can access everything.

MARCEL: Usually gender includes everything that happens within the family. Before 1994 [*the genocide*], a girl didn't have the right to an inheritance from her father. It was said that she would be given to another family. And her father could marry her to a boy that she didn't even know, even without the girl wanting to do so or without knowing. But now, a girl has the right to inheritance and she can marry whomever she wishes. (Mixed interview, School 2, July 2011; emphasis added)

Students believed that gender equality meant equal rights for men and women and equal access to education, opportunities, and inheritance, as well as equal treatment before the law. In an interview, Emmanuel explained: "Before [the] *1994 genocide* the girls were inferior, they weren't treated the same as the boys. The boys were superior and girls were inferior. They had no rights, so now they try to treat them the same way" (Mixed interview, School 1, September 2011; emphasis added).

In a discussion in a high-quality school in an urban area, students recognized the meaning of gender equality and framed the discussion in reference to the genocide: "Before [*the genocide*], the girls were ignored in society. There were *rights* that the girls didn't benefit from, like the right to education and the right to run the country. But now, there is equality between women and men. For example, if there is an opportunity for academic scholarships, this opportunity is given to everyone, regardless of whether you are a boy or a girl. You just need to fulfill the criteria to get it" (Mixed group interview, School 7, June 2011; emphasis added). Hence, students were aware of the government's national policies for the promotion of gender equality and framed these policies as the starting point for gender equality in the Rwandan context. Furthermore, gender equality was conflated with a postconflict focus on development and human rights.

CONCLUSIONS

In post-genocide Rwanda, the state uses human rights discourse as part of the peacebuilding and nation-building project and to build legitimacy with donors and the broader international community (Russell 2015). Although national policy and curricular documents incorporate a global rights discourse, these rights are not protected in practice (Melvin 2010). The Rwandan government utilizes a rights discourse as a means to garner legitimacy with the international community or as a form of "window dressing"—a public but insincere expression of a commitment to protect or promote human rights (Hafner-Burton and Tsutsui 2005; Russell 2015). Certain types of rights, such as women's rights and gender equality, are privileged, whereas discussions of recent human rights violations or the limits imposed by the regime on civil and political rights are avoided. This discrepancy has led to a focus on gender equality at the expense of considering other social inequities (e.g., those related to ethnicity) that negatively impact the goals of reconciliation and peacebuilding.

Even though the national curricula include lessons on human rights, in practice, teachers de-emphasize controversial subjects such as local human rights violations in favor of abstract discussions and a technical enumeration of rights as presented in UN documents due to the restrictive political space. When students do study human rights, they spend little time on politically sensitive topics such as the oppression of political and civil rights, and focus instead on progress in ensuring women's rights. This incongruity illustrates the dilemma of implementing "universal" human rights in a context in which the government explicitly prioritizes social and economic rights at the expense of civil and political rights (Donnelly 2013). Wielenga (2012) finds that "the government can thus believe itself to be aligned with a culture of human rights (socioeconomic rights), whereas many Rwandans may feel human rights (civil and political rights) are undermined by the government" (271). This government-ordained emphasis on social and economic rights may be due in part to the regime's authoritarian inclinations and readiness to restrict political and civil rights.

The avoidance of discussion about contentious local human rights violations points to the difficulty of addressing local realities and contested versions of the recent past. My observations confirmed that it is easier for teachers to discuss sensitive topics related to human rights in abstract terms or in relation to other countries than in the context of Rwanda. Implementing semblances of student-centered learning, such as group work, is safer than allowing students to ask critical questions or openly debate ideas. This practice may be due to the sensitive nature of discussing rights in the local context, as well as the deeply entrenched culture of teacher-centered learning, and indeed, studies have found the lack of student-centered pedagogy to be a prevalent issue in Rwandan schools (Honeyman 2016; Rubagiza, Were, and Sutherland 2011; Uworwabayeho 2009). The difficulty in addressing sensitive topics around human rights violations is further exacerbated by the lack of professional development for teachers around contentious issues.

The teaching of rights is also restricted by limited space for discussion, critical thinking, and active learning. The transmission of global and national models is thus modified in the application in the classroom context, highlighting the limitations of teaching about global human rights through a student-centered approach in a restrictive political context (Russell and Quaynor 2016; Tibbitts and Fernekes 2011). The undemocratic polity limits the extent to which global models can be incorporated into civics education. The authoritarian government, which does not guarantee freedom of expression, fosters a fear of discussing rights issues openly in the classroom.

The inherent tension between the government's effort to incorporate rights language as part of a nation-building project and the government's violation of rights in practice points to the contested nature of adopting global frameworks, particularly in fragile and conflict-affected states. The way in which Rwanda has embraced norms linked to human rights and gender equality helps connect the country to the broader world but does not encourage critical discussion within Rwandan schools of contested issues of the past. In order for Rwanda to reap the benefits of HRE to address past and present human rights violations and to contribute to sustainable peace, the political context will have to change to allow for more open dialogue and dissension.

CHAPTER 5

Addressing the Genocide and Promoting Reconciliation

Education at all levels ... is an important means of addressing issues of peace and reconciliation in the context of Rwanda post-1994.

—Ministry of Education 2006, 19

As THE RWANDAN state seeks to transmit an official version of memory and truth around the genocide, how the historical narrative is taught in schools is crucial to the wider aim of societal reconciliation. In the quotation above, from the *Rwandan Education Sector Strategic Plan, 2006–2010*, education is presented as playing an integral role in addressing broader societal issues of peace and reconciliation.

The Rwandan state draws on the education system not only to forge a new national unified "Rwandan" identity, as discussed in chapter 3, but also as part of the broader transitional justice project that relies on diverse institutions and sites to memorialize the genocide and to promote social cohesion and reconciliation (see chapter 2). The notion of *kwibuka*, the Kinyarwanda word for "remember," is linked to the preservation of the memory of the atrocities that happened during the genocide and is used by the state to try to avert a future genocide.

In this chapter, I draw on survey and interview data from students and teachers in fifteen schools across three provinces to investigate the following questions: How does education contribute to constructing an official collective memory and reconciliation? How do schools in Rwanda teach about the genocide? How do teachers and students understand the genocide and the notion of reconciliation? I present data on the kind of reconciliation and unity the regime seeks to promote, how students are taught about the genocide, and how teachers and students actually engage with the genocide and reconciliation in school.

In the first section, I provide an overview of the aims of transitional justice in fostering reconciliation and collective memory and discuss Rwanda specifically. Next, I present data from surveys and interviews about how genocide and reconciliation are taught in schools. I examine both the intended curriculum, as envisioned in the textbooks, and what actually occurs in class. I base my conclusions on surveys and interviews with students and teachers, as well as on classroom observations. At the end of the chapter, I discuss the extent to which the state has been successful in teaching about the genocide and how perceptions of the genocide relate to promoting broader societal reconciliation.

Transitional Justice, Reconciliation, and Collective Memory

In the aftermath of intergroup conflict or collective violence, governments draw on official and unofficial transitional justice mechanisms to address human rights abuses and to achieve societal reconciliation. Global models of transitional justice and reconciliation influence the way in which state actors address past conflicts. A report from the UN secretary-general defines transitional justice as "the full range of processes and mechanisms associated with a society's attempts to come to terms with a legacy of large-scale past abuses, in order to ensure accountability, service justice and achieve reconciliation" (United Nations 2004, 4). These processes include both judicial and nonjudicial mechanisms that encompass national and international trials, truth and reconciliation commissions, reparations, memorial sites, and education reforms (see chapter 2 for more details on transitional justice mechanisms). Transitional justice mechanisms and processes have a variety of aims, including holding individual perpetrators accountable for past crimes, publicly documenting the truth and recognizing past injustices, and encouraging civic trust and reconciliation (De Greiff 2012; Hayner 2011; Jelin 2003; Minow 1998; Roht-Arriaza and Mariezcurrena 2006).

Reconciliation is often considered a main goal of transitional justice. Reconciliation is the process by which societies that have undergone violent conflict seek to address the past and to develop shared values and a common identity. In their edited volume on transitional justice, Eric Stover and Harvey Weinstein (2004) define reconciliation as "the reconfiguring of identity, the revisiting of prior social roles, the search for common identifications, agreement about unifying memories if not myths, and the development of collaborative relationships that allow for difference" (18). In a restorative justice model, the main aim is to construct a history of past abuses and to create reconciliation between victims and perpetrators; in a retributive justice model, the intent is to hold individuals accountable for past crimes through legal mechanisms (Stover and Weinstein 2004; Teitel 2003).

Related to constructing a record of past events is the way in which historical or collective memory is maintained by the state. "Collective memory" generally refers to memories constructed within society by individuals or among particular groups. Maurice Halbwachs (1992) defines collective memory as emerging from socially constructed frameworks: "There exists a collective memory and social frameworks for memory; it is to the degree that our individual thought places itself in these frameworks and participates in this memory that is capable of the act of recollection" (38). Collective memory develops not only from the memories of individuals but also from broader cultural memories.

In writing about the children of Holocaust survivors, Aleida Assman (2012) explores the idea of second-generation or intergenerational memory passed down through family, as well as transgenerational political and cultural memory. Similarly, Daniela Jara (2016) extends these notions to understand intergenerational narratives and memories of children of the post-Pinochet dictatorship in Chile. Marianne Hirsch (2008) writes about the notion of "postmemory" or "the relationship of the second generation to powerful, often traumatic, experiences that preceded their births but that were nevertheless transmitted to them so deeply as to seem to constitute memories in their own right" (103).

In the case of authoritarian governments, states produce official collective memories. James Wertsch (2002) documents how the Soviet state used educational texts to disseminate an official account of history, or an "official collective memory," aimed at imposing an official version of the past on the national collective memory (72). In his book on memory, history, and forgetting, Paul Ricoeur (2004) talks about how memory can be "forced" or "manipulated" (69). The Rwandan government has produced an official collective memory around the genocide that may be interpreted by some as forced or manipulated to serve the interests of the state. As Pierre Nora (1989) asserts, "Memory is blind to all but the group it binds" (9). In Rwanda, the official "enforced memory" excludes memories of Hutu victims from the dominant Tutsi memory (Lemarchand 2009, 105).

Although most postconflict countries focus on trials or truth commissions to address past human rights violations, education is also an important component of transitional justice that can be used to promote intergroup reconciliation in the aftermath of violent conflict (Bekerman and Zembylas 2011; Bellino, Paulson, and Worden 2017; E. Cole 2007a, 2007b; Minow 2002; Stover and Weinstein 2004). In particular, history education plays an integral role in how countries address past events. Reforms in history education, or discussions about how to teach about the violent past, particularly the recent past, are usually contentious in a postconflict context. History education serves multiple purposes that are often in conflict with one another: to transmit notions of citizenship and a positive narrative of the nation; to promote reconciliation and truth-telling; to commemorate past events to establish a collective memory; and to promote a more democratic culture through debate about the past (E. Cole 2007b; Paulson 2015). There is a tension between history education for the promotion of national identity and unity and a critical historiography that encourages students to investigate past events from multiple perspectives (Wertsch 2002).

The ways in which governments strategically use historical or collective memory to address issues of truth and justice and to teach about the past have important implications for peacebuilding, reconciliation, and how youth learn about recent histories, both in and out of school. As Alexandra Barahona De Brito and her colleagues contend, "control over the narrative of the past means control over the construction of narratives for an imagined future. What and how societies choose to remember and forget largely determines their future options" (Barahona De Brito, Gonzalez Enriquez, and Aguilar 2001, 38). Furthermore, youth play an active role as social agents in how memories about the historical past are remembered (Bellino 2014).

In a postconflict or authoritarian context, governments may choose not to teach about the past or to teach a redacted version of the past (E. Cole 2007a) to conform to a "state-approved civic truth" (Tyack 1999, 922) written by the victors of the conflict and thereby excluding many perspectives. Controversial issues are often avoided or revised in history textbooks (Avery and Simmons 2001). Writers of textbooks create national myths and symbols to overcome historical divisions and controversies (Moreau 2003). Although history education is critical for societies dealing with past atrocities and for promoting social reconciliation, a certain level of reconciliation must be reached before history books and curricula can be revised in a way that will be broadly accepted by teachers and students (E. Cole 2007a). Contested historical narratives can render the teaching of history problematic in postconflict countries, especially in those with nondemocratic governments (E. Cole 2007a; Freedman et al. 2008).

The Wider Reconciliation Project in Rwanda

To memorialize an official collective memory or historical truth about the genocide and to promote societal reconciliation, the Rwandan government has implemented various transitional justice mechanisms, including criminal trials, local *gacaca* trials, memorial sites, and government initiatives for reconciliation (see chapter 2 for more detail). Some of these mechanisms draw from traditional Rwandan forms of justice, while others are inspired by global models. The regime has not been eager to acknowledge this global influence, its reluctance stemming from resentment at what it sees as Western interference even though an estimated 30 to 40 percent of the national budget comes from foreign donors (World Bank 2017). For instance, although the government presented *gacaca* as a local initiative, the courts were dependent on funding from international donors.[1] But the global influence is evident, with international organizations, such as UNESCO and UNICEF, and international consultants playing a key role in developing Rwandan policy documents, curricula, and textbooks in line with global models.

The Rwandan government has sought to address the legacy of the genocide through international and national trials, as well as through various other local initiatives. As discussed in chapter 2, the International Criminal Tribunal for Rwanda (ICTR), established in 1995 by the UN Security Council, tried leaders of the genocide. Additionally, national courts began prosecutions of accused *génocidaires* in 1996. However, due to the severe overcrowding of the prisons and lack of capacity of the national courts to process the high number of cases efficiently, the government established *gacaca* courts in 2001 (Ingelaere 2016; Waldorf 2007). Modeled on a precolonial conflict resolution structure, *gacaca*, or "justice on the grass," aimed to establish a record about crimes related to the genocide, hasten the trials of the accused *génocidaires*, eliminate a culture of impunity, and foster reconciliation and unity among Rwandans (Ingelaere 2016; Republic of Rwanda 2012).

In addition to international and local trials, the state has preserved the official memory of the genocide through memorial sites and various government programs aimed at instilling unity and reconciliation. The state propagates a physical display of the official collective memory of the genocide through what Nora (1989) terms *lieux de mémoire*, or sites of memories. In Rwanda, the government established six national memorials—Bisesero, Kigali, Murambi, Mtarama, Nyamta, and Nyarabuye—to commemorate the genocide, thereby influencing legitimate discourse around the genocide (Meierhenrich 2011). There are hundreds of unofficial and informal memorials of the events of 1994 in churches and villages around Rwanda.[2] Some memorial sites, such as Murambi, strategically use the display of human remains—skulls and bones of the victims—to enforce the official collective memory of the state.

On the grounds of the largest of the memorials, the Kigali Genocide Memorial, are mass graves containing the remains of more than 250,000 victims. The memorial, which also hosts three permanent exhibits that document and teach about the genocide, is run by Aegis Trust, an NGO based in the United Kingdom, in collaboration with the National Commission for the Fight against Genocide (in French, La Commission National pour la Lutte contre le Génocide, hence the acronym, CNLG), which the government created in 2007. Aegis also offers education programs on the genocide and peace education for students and teachers, as well as a mobile exhibit for schools. In 2009, Aegis launched Learning from the Past and Building the Future, a pilot program for secondary students in five districts. In 2013, the program was expanded and established as the Rwanda Peace Education Program; it was integrated into the national curriculum in 2014. In 2015, Aegis provided training for teachers in how to deliver the new peace education in a learner-centered fashion.

The government has established several institutions to teach about the genocide and foster reconciliation at the societal level. For example, the National Unity and Reconciliation Commission (NURC), which was created in 1999, is tasked with promoting national unity and reconciliation through numerous community civic education programs. Another mechanism for educating Rwandans is the use of *ingando* camps, or solidarity camps, where students, teachers, government officials, and returnees learn about Rwandan identity and culture and the history of the genocide. The goal of *ingando* camps is to promote reconciliation, unity, and nation building at a local level and to teach about the dangers of "genocide ideology" (Purdeková 2015). NURC also runs *itorero*, a mandatory civic education program for students, teachers, and civil servants to transmit

Rwandan culture and values (Nzahabwanayo, Horsthemke, and Mathebula 2017; Sundberg 2016) Likewise, the CNLG was established in 2007 with the purpose of fighting against genocide ideology and preserving the historical memory of the genocide through advocacy, research, and documentation.[3]

As part of memorializing the past, the state puts forth an official collective memory about the genocide. This official version of the genocide portrays the past from a singular perspective told from the point of view of the victors of the civil war and the ruling party. The official narrative memorializes the genocide against the Tutsi with the Tutsi as victims and the Hutu as the perpetrators (Burnet 2009; Eltringham 2004; Vidal 2004). In doing so, this narrative also reinstates a victor/perpetrator narrative perpetuating an "antagonistic" mode of remembering that reifies good and evil in binary terms (Bull and Hansen 2016). The most pervasive official memorialization of the genocide is the annual commemoration and period of remembrance, Kwibuka, which starts on April 7 and lasts for one hundred days (Vidal 2004). The officially stated goal of the Kwibuka commemoration is to remember, unite, and renew.[4]

Another example of state control over the official collective memory is the terminology around the genocide. The official name of the genocide has shifted since 1994. In the years following the genocide, people generally referred to it as "the genocide," "the war," or the "events of 1994," whereas the government officially called it *itsebatsemba n'itsembabwoko*, or the massacres and the genocide, meaning that Hutu were killed in massacres and Tutsi were killed in a genocide (Burnet 2009). After 2000, the term *jenocide*, appropriated from the French, came into use; this term subsequently evolved into the "genocide of the Tutsi" and the "genocide against the Tutsi." The latter term was officially codified in 2008 with an amendment to the 2003 Constitution (Burnet 2009; Waldorf 2009). The current appellation around the genocide unambiguously constructs the Tutsi as the sole victims of the genocide rather than allowing for a more nuanced portrayal of the events around the genocide and civil war, which included deaths of Hutu.

Teaching about the Genocide in Schools

What students are taught in schools plays a role in the broader societal initiative aimed at preserving the memory of the genocide and fostering reconciliation. In this section, I discuss how the state seeks to teach about the genocide in schools, how teachers and students understand the genocide, and the tensions that ensue when what is taught does not neatly align with the perceptions and memories of teachers and students.

Genocide in the National Curriculum and Textbooks

Students learn about the events of the genocide and reconciliation in the formal primary and secondary education system. All schools, including private and religious ones, are mandated to follow the national curriculum. In the 2008 social studies curriculum for primary school, genocide is not introduced until grade 6. At the secondary level, the 2008 national curriculum for history highlights the genocide as a main topic for the third year of Rwandan history for ordinary-level students and in the sixth year for advanced-level students. The genocide is also covered briefly in the 2008 political education curriculum for ordinary-level students and in the 2010 advanced-level general paper curriculum. The competence-based curriculum introduced in 2015 for the primary and secondary levels includes genocide as a crosscutting topic across social studies, history and citizenship, and general studies, following the general direction of the previous curriculum.

Despite the incorporation of the topic of the genocide at the curricular level, little time is actually devoted to teaching this sensitive subject in class, and teachers receive very little training on how to teach it. In 2011, ordinary-level students studied history just two hours each week, and the genocide was one of many topics to be covered in that time. Political education was allotted one hour a week and was nonexaminable; consequently, teachers and students did not prioritize this subject. All advanced-level students, regardless of their concentration, had to take the general paper interdisciplinary course for two hours a week, during which time the genocide appeared as a topic of discussion only in the last year of upper secondary school (senior 4) in the unit on peace and conflict. Only students in a humanities concentration were required to take a history class at the advanced level. History and political education teachers normally spent only one or two classes discussing the genocide and reconciliation; some teachers avoided the topic altogether. Far more time was spent studying STEM subjects (science, technology, engineering, and mathematics), because they are seen as the pathway to economic development (Russell 2015). There is no doubt that the state regards the history of the genocide as important, but it sees the development of the skills that can give Rwanda a brighter economic future as even more important.

As of 2011, the Ministry of Education did not provide any special training for history or civics teachers on how to address the genocide and reconciliation. Several teachers I interviewed mentioned that they had attended government civic education workshops—*itorero* or *ingando*—where they learned about the official version of the events, but they did not receive any training in how to teach students about the genocide. The only training available seems to have been provided by international NGOs. In 2015, for instance, Aegis provided training for teachers on how to deliver the new peace education in a learner-centered fashion.

In textbooks, the genocide is taught according to the official government narrative, which emphasizes the role of the colonialists in creating ethnic groups and ethnic division and the role of the Habyarimana government in planning and carrying out the genocide. The grade 6 social studies book devotes a section to explaining the causes and consequences of the "genocide" (Bamusananire et al. 2006c), which is largely attributed to the colonialists who divided the Tutsi and Hutu into separate "races" rather than social classes and to the "bad leadership" and "bad governance" of the governments that ruled after independence (64). History books, as compared to civics and social studies books, tend to provide more discussion of the genocide, which receives greater attention in the upper levels of curriculum.

At the secondary level, political education and history books allocate entire sections to discussing the causes and consequences of the genocide. For instance, volume 1 of the political education textbook devotes a subsection of the chapter "Unity and Reconciliation" to discussing the historical causes of the "1994 genocide," its consequences, and strategies to prevent genocide (NCDC 2008a, 156–157). Volume 2 includes two pages on the political and social impact of the genocide (NCDC 2008b). Both volumes contain a section on unity and reconciliation following the discussion of the genocide.

The 2010 and 2011 history books include a chapter that discusses the "1994 genocide against the Tutsi" (Bamusananire and Ntege 2010c; Bamusananire 2011). The teacher's guide—*The History of Rwanda*—devotes one chapter to the "Liberation War 1990–1994" and the "genocide against the Tutsi" (NCDC 2010a). Locating the roots of the genocide in the colonial period, when Belgians grouped the Hutu and Tutsi into distinct "ethnic groups," *The History of Rwanda* presents the massacres against the Tutsi that occurred following independence in 1962 (144). The book blames the genocide on ethnic and regional discrimination and bad governance, with the crash of the plane carrying President Habyarimana being the spark that ignited the killing (145). Both the 2010 and 2011 history books for the advanced

and ordinary levels cover the "Tutsi genocide" in a chapter
drawing on the same narrative presented in *The History of
Rwanda* (Bamusananire 2011; Bamusananire and Ntege 2010c).
In the book for the ordinary level, the term "genocide" is
explained as the planned annihilation of a specific "national,
ethnic, racial or religious group" (Bamusananire and Ntege
2010c, 112). "The 1994 Tutsi genocide," write the authors, "was a
carefully planned and executed exercise to annihilate Rwanda's
Tutsi population and moderate Hutu who did not agree with
the prevailing extremist politics of the time" (112).

In curricular documents and textbooks published before
2008, the genocide is referred to as the "1994 genocide." However, in official policy documents and textbooks produced after
2008, the genocide is called the "genocide against the Tutsi" or
the "1994 Tutsi genocide." In fact, the terminology around the
genocide is so sensitive that general studies textbooks that were
introduced into schools in 2016 for the new competence-based
curriculum were recalled due to their incorrect reference to the
genocide as a "civil war" rather than as the genocide against the
Tutsi (Tumwebaze 2017).

Discussion of the Genocide in Schools

To gauge how students understand and learn about topics related
to the genocide and reconciliation, I conducted a survey of 536
randomly selected secondary students in fifteen schools in three
regions of Rwanda (for more details on the methods, see appendix A). More than half of the students said that they often discussed the genocide in school (55.7 percent) and at home
(51.9 percent); 39.1 percent said they sometimes discussed the
genocide in school, and 44.2 percent said they sometimes discussed it at home (see figure 14). Only a small percentage said
they never discussed the genocide at school (5.2 percent) or at
home (3.9 percent), implying that the genocide was an important topic of conversation in and outside of school. However,

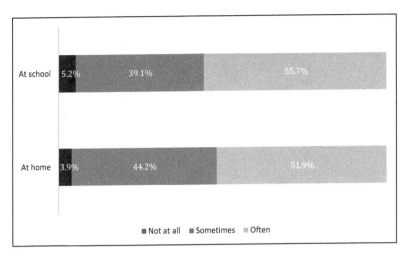

At school   5.2%   39.1%   55.7%

At home   3.9%   44.2%   51.9%

■ Not at all   ■ Sometimes   ■ Often

14. Discussion of the genocide at school and at home.

the results also indicate that a sizable proportion of students did not discuss the genocide in class or at home despite the inclusion of the topic in the national curricular mandates. The survey data also reveal statistically significant variation across regions and schools. For instance, students in schools in the Western and Eastern Provinces reported discussing the genocide more than students in Kigali, where about 10 percent of respondents said they did not discuss the genocide at all in school. Students were more likely to discuss the genocide in government and government-aided schools as compared to private schools; in private schools, 11 percent of students reported that they did not discuss the genocide at all, compared to only about 3 percent in government and government-aided schools. Students spoke about learning about the genocide during the official government commemoration period and through activities and events organized by local government officials.

When asked what they considered the most important cause of the genocide to be, the majority of students cited bad government (53.5 percent), as well as ethnic hatred (30.6 percent),

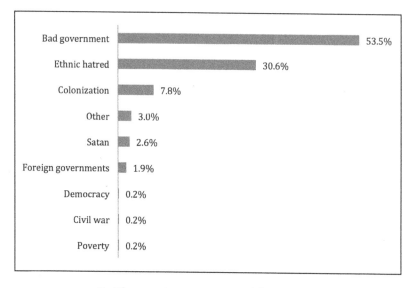

15. The most important cause of the genocide.

colonization (7.8 percent), and Satan (2.6 percent); hardly any students selected civil war, democracy, or poverty as a main cause (see figure 15). Even though the official narrative in the curriculum and textbooks emphasizes the role of colonizers in provoking the genocide, students viewed bad government and ethnic hatred to be the most important causes.

When asked about the causes of the genocide in interviews, students and teachers echoed what was highlighted in the national curriculum and textbooks and what was mentioned in the survey. Most mentioned bad government, colonizers who divided the people, ethnic conflict, or ignorance. Several also mentioned the plane crash of President Habyarimana as a trigger of the genocide. Importantly, ethnic conflict was always attributed to the colonizers rather than to internal factors. In one representative interview with a group of boys in a semiurban private school, the boys discussed what they had learned about the causes of the genocide:

RICHARD: According to what we study in history, the Rwandan genocide [*jenoside y'urwanda*] was caused by colonization. The colonizers came to Rwanda, and they divided the population into three ethnicities: Hutu, Twa, and Tutsi. Before that, the Rwandans were the same; there weren't divisions. The colonizers named the Hutus the farmers, the Tutsis the cattle farmers, and the Twa the potters. That's when the divisions started. And that created the genocide.

JOSEF: For me, the cause of the genocide was the ignorance of the people. (Boys' group interview, School 5, July 2011)

Very few interviewees cited opinions that diverged from the official narrative. However, in a few cases, interviewees had opinions of the causes that did not align with the official government narrative. For example, Sam, a history teacher from Uganda, explained how he was reprimanded by a student for talking about a taboo cause of the genocide: "I had tried to talk about the situation where, maybe the attack of the RPF could also have triggered some stuff . . . and the kid said 'no you can't say that' and a student telling me what I should say and shouldn't say" (Teacher interview, School 6, October 2011).

Some students said that they had considered the causes of the genocide independently of the government narrative and had developed their own assessments. Innocent, a twenty-year-old Hutu boy in a Western Province school, explained his perspective on the causes of the genocide, questioning the official narrative of precolonial unity:

In fact, many people said a lot about the genocide and regarding what I studied and also what I heard spoken about, the teachers tell us that it is colonization and also bad governance. In fact, regarding colonization we talk a lot about a lot of things related to that; as an educated person, I took the time to analyze all of that, and I sorted out what is necessary. I think that above all it was the ignorance of the had government; it's not only the colonizers because even before that, there were these social classes where if someone had a lot of cows, he was a Tutsi. If he had less, he was a Hutu; and if he didn't have any, he was a Twa. All of that existed even before the colonizers arrived; so if the Rwandans had been strong and united, the colonizers would not have been able to divide them. (Boys' group interview, School 1, September 2011)

Terminology around the Genocide

The government version of the historical events surrounding the causes and consequences of the genocide is tightly controlled, and the way in which the genocide itself is discussed is regulated by the state. During interviews and informal conversations across different types of schools and regions, students and teachers generally referred to the genocide simply as "the genocide" or "the 1994 genocide," although some people—across different types of schools and regions—called it the "Tutsi genocide."

I observed several classes in which the teacher was lecturing on the genocide or mentioned the genocide in the context of the discussion. These teachers generally followed the official textbooks and curriculum when discussing the "Tutsi genocide." For example, in a history class in a government-supported school in the Western Province, the teacher was lecturing on the "Liberation War of 1990–1994." One student called out "Tutsi massacre" in reference to the genocide. The teacher, a Hutu, asked the class: "Is this correct? No, the word is 'Tutsi genocide'" (Classroom observation, School 1, September 2011). Jackson, an Anglophone Tutsi returnee in a private school, lectured on the topic of the genocide for a general paper course without referring to the official curriculum or textbook and incorporated outside material and his own impressions from the perspective of someone who had returned after the genocide (Classroom observation, School 5, July 2011). However, in government and government-supported schools, teachers, especially Hutu teachers, generally followed the official curriculum and textbooks and were careful not to allow for the discussion of controversial topics, such as ethnicity or alternative narratives of the genocide. In particular, Hutu students and teachers were more likely to refer to the genocide by its official name due to the fear of being accused of divisionism or genocide ideology.

In a government-aided religious school, Davide, a Tutsi returnee, explained that the government changed the official name of the genocide to emphasize the fact that the genocide was committed against a specific group—the Tutsi, rather than the Hutu:

DAVIDE: So the students ask me why we talk about the genocide of the Tutsi, even though you don't want us to talk about ethnic groups. That's a contradiction. In fact, before we discussed just the genocide. This term, genocide against the Tutsi, was added two years ago. . . . It's *genocide yakorewe abatutsi* [genocide against the Tutsi], whereas before it was *itsembabwoko ni tsembatsemba* [the extermination of the ethnic group (Tutsi) and the massacres (of the Hutu)]. Later they changed it in 2008.

GARNETT: Why did they change the name?

DAVIDE: I'm not sure. Before, I even asked myself this question, but I think that for the moderate Hutus that were killed, it's not a genocide, it was a massacre. For the genocide, one has to specify that it was committed against the Tutsis because they wanted to exterminate this race. (Teacher interview, School 7, October 2011)

Contested Narratives of the Past

Although students and teachers in the classroom generally repeated the official line when discussing the terminology around genocide, aligned with the "public transcripts" about the genocide (Scott 1990; Zorbas 2009), in private discussions or at home, they might discuss other ideas or versions of past events that conflicted with the official narrative.

In my interviews with teachers, the majority expressed that they could teach only what is in the official curriculum and could not discuss what they considered to be the "real history" or refer to their personal experiences or opinions regarding the genocide. Paul, a Hutu general paper teacher in a government-supported school in the Western Province who had been imprisoned during the insurgency following the genocide, explained that teachers had to follow the national program, or the "official" version of history, in the classroom: "We must follow the official narrative, we can't diverge from the program because we can't lose time. And also, with the history of Rwanda, which is controversial, we must know how to best address it" (Teacher interview, School 1, October 2011).

Jacques, a Hutu political education teacher at a government-supported school in the capital, underscored the need to follow the national program to avoid questions that students might have about what they learn at home, saying, "We always try to remain on the periphery of the issues so that the students can't ask questions out of curiosity based on what they might have heard at home" (Teacher interview, School 7, October 2011). What is learned at home may contradict the official narrative of events and thus lead to dangerous territory for teachers.

François, a Hutu history teacher in a government-supported Western Province school, lamented the lack of books on the Rwandan genocide that discuss the "real history": "There are not a lot [of books] here. There is also a book from Human Rights Watch discussing the genocide and the war of the infiltrators, but we can't use that, it's forbidden. But this book has the *real history*. There are examples that are given in these books that are real, that we ourselves have even experienced, but we can't teach those because they aren't in the program [official curriculum]" (Teacher interview, School 1, October 2011; emphasis added).

In general, I found that Tutsi teachers tended to have more freedom to discuss the genocide due to their position as the "victims" of the genocide and because they are currently in power, although, as discussed below, there was also a difference in how survivors and returnees addressed the topic. In contrast, Hutu teachers were more cautious because of the collective Hutu guilt, whereby all Hutu are linked to the *génocidaires*. Teachers in the Western Province tended to be more critical of the official government narrative than teachers in the Eastern Province or in the capital, perhaps due to their proximity to the violence following the genocide.

Personal narratives of the genocide often differed from the official version. Several teachers in the Western Province spoke in interviews of the violence that occurred after the genocide, known as the insurgency (1997–1999) and the war against the infiltrators (*abacengezi*)—the former Interahamwe who fled to the Congo after the genocide (Burnet 2009; Stearns and Borello 2011). However, they also cautioned that they would never mention these events in the classroom; as Davide, a returnee, put it bluntly, "You won't find a reference to a double genocide in this book" (Teacher interview, School 7, October 2011). Alain, a Hutu political education teacher at a religious school in the Western Province, explained that he would not mention the insurgency in the classroom: "If it's not in the program, we can't talk about it. . . . When we talk about the genocide, we go from 1990 until July of 1994, and then we stop there. We don't talk about everything that has happened after this period" (Teacher interview, School 1, October 2011).

Similarly, François explained that he would never teach about the 1997 war against the *abacengezi* in class: "We don't talk about that, because if we talk about that, it's as if you want to say that the Hutu were also killed, and there you insinuate the *double genocide*, whereas it's forbidden to mention this. And if a student talks about that [the double genocide], it's necessary to tell him that those who died there were people who wanted to help the infiltrators and that it was also to assure security, and that it wasn't to aim at a group of people" (Teacher interview, School 1, October 2011; emphasis added).

A minority of teachers and students referred to the "double genocide," or the systematic killings of Hutu by the RPF, which took place during the civil war from 1990 to 1993 and after the genocide (Des Forges 1999). The atrocities committed by the RPF are not taught in the official curriculum or included in the official historical narrative of the genocide because they are considered taboo. One Hutu boy, Fabrice, spoke of losing his father to the indiscriminate killings by RPF soldiers during the war against the infiltrators (Individual boy, School 7, September 2011). A Hutu girl referred to the double genocide as a sensitive topic: "For example, like that it's the RPF that orchestrated Habyarimana's crash. If you insist on that, that might create a problem for you. And also the subject of double genocide, saying that the Hutus also died during the genocide" (Individual girl, School 7, October 2011).

Genocide Ideology

Discussions of double genocide or other forbidden topics publicly constitute acts of genocide ideology. The reluctance to veer away from the state-sanctioned narrative is tied to the threat of being accused of genocide ideology, accusations of which are punishable with a prison term of ten to twenty-five years and a fine. Children as young as twelve may be tried for the crime of genocide ideology (Republic of Rwanda 2008a, Article 9).[5] A parliamentary report released in 2004 accused several national and international NGOs, as well as schools, of genocide ideology;

subsequently, the Ministry of Education suspended thirty-seven teachers and twenty-seven students in 2004 on accusations of genocide ideology (Amnesty International 2010; Longman 2011; Waldorf 2009). A senate commission on genocide produced a report in 2007 that found incidents of genocide ideology in twenty-six schools (Human Rights Watch 2008; Waldorf 2009).

In interviews, students and teachers were aware of the consequences of being accused of espousing "ideology," and concepts of "genocide ideology" and "divisionism" permeated discussion of the genocide and reconciliation. Students generally understood genocide ideology as the discussion of ethnicity with the intent of inciting ethnic conflict and genocide. Fabrice, an eighteen-year-old Hutu boy in an urban school, explained the term:

GARNETT: What is genocide ideology?

FABRICE: When someone wants to sow conflict among the Rwandans and instill ideas showing that they aren't the same, that they are from different groups or ethnicities. For example, I get a microphone, I go to the stadium, and I start to tell people: "The Tutsi aren't good" or even start to say bad things about ethnicity. That's the ideology of the genocide, which could incite further genocide.

GARNETT: What are the consequences?

FABRICE: You could be put in prison. (Student interview, School 7, September 2011)

Some students spoke of the grave consequences of inciting genocide ideology. Benjamin, an eighteen-year-old returnee from Uganda in a government school in the Eastern Province, said: "No, it's not authorized to talk about ethnic issues. Even here at school, if they catch you talking about something related to ethnicity, they say that you have *genocide ideology*, and they imprison you or send you home and tell you never come to school. So it's difficult to talk about it. In Rwanda, it's taboo to talk about that" (Boys' group interview, School 4, September 2011; emphasis added).

Although the genocide features prominently in the history and political education curricular documents and is an important topic in class, teachers and students described the difficulty they faced when discussing the genocide either due to the fear of being of accused of ideology or to painful memories. Although most students in my survey and interviews were very young or not yet born when the genocide took place in 1994, many had lost family or friends or had suffered in other ways, such as their parents being imprisoned. Although students generally viewed the genocide as an event of the past, they also felt connected to the genocide based on what their families had experienced or through intergenerational memories. In one group discussion in a Western Province school, students were asked if they discuss the genocide at home. One of the students, Clemetine, a seventeen-year-old female genocide survivor, talked about the effects of the genocide on her family: "Yes, for example my mother is disabled due to the genocide; there are moments when I ask my mother why she is disabled, and she says that she was healthy before [*yarameze neza*]. Also, I never knew my father because of the genocide. My mother says that my father was killed during the genocide and that she became disabled because they wanted to kill her, but luckily God protected her" (Girls group interview, School 1, September 2011).

Teachers spoke of the difficulty and fear of teaching about a topic that is inherently controversial and fraught with tension and contradictions. A program officer from the Kigali Genocide Memorial explained the challenges teachers face when teaching about the genocide: "The national curriculum teaches about the genocide but is not adequate.... Teachers don't have the confidence to talk about the genocide and sensitive issues.... They mostly teach about the causes and the consequences, but they avoid certain topics and they don't let students ask questions" (Interview, September 2012).

Identity influences the way in which students and teachers talk about the genocide. Of the teachers I interviewed, the majority of Ugandans and Rwandan returnees talked about the genocide in a detached, open manner, whereas Tutsi survivors of the genocide spoke with more reserve about their traumatic experiences. Rwandans who were in the country during the genocide (generally Hutu) were even more cautious when discussing the genocide and were always careful to refer to it as the "Tutsi genocide."

Alain, a Hutu teacher in a Western Province religious school, talked about the difficulties inherent in teaching about the genocide:

> When we talk about the genocide, we say that it was the Hutu who killed the Tutsi. It was written [like that] at the memorial sites, and after we finish [talking about that], we talk about unity and reconciliation ... [and] after that we say that in Rwanda there isn't a difference; that's when it becomes a problem and where we say that there was a group that killed another group. And in Rwanda there isn't a difference; that's where it becomes a problem to say that there is segregation of Tutsi and Hutu. That's when they start to ask questions if these people [Hutu and Tutsi] exist today. (Teacher interview, School 1, September 2011)

Jackson, an Anglophone returnee, spoke of the difficulty of explaining to his Hutu students that the Hutu had perpetrated the genocide against the Tutsi (Teacher interview, School 5, October 2011). François, a Hutu teacher, mentioned the challenges in answering questions about the genocide that could lead to accusations of genocide ideology and imprisonment:

We teach only what is in the programs, but there are times
when a student interferes and asks a question or even gives
a response that brings us to sensitive subjects, and that
becomes a problem for us teachers to explain. Being teachers who already know the consequences of ethnic divisions
like the trauma in the homes of certain students, we are
called upon to moderate the students around topics that will
not lead them to the division of groups. . . . Regarding this,
our role is to moderate, but also to remove [certain infor-
mation], because if you [are] teaching things that aren't in
the program and that sow division, you can be put in prison.
(Teacher interview, School 1, October 2011)

Davide, a Tutsi returnee teacher, talked about the sensitivities around teaching the genocide:

I, personally, always said that the genocide was aimed at the
Tutsis, but there were also moderate Hutus who were killed.
But we can't say: "Oh yeah, there was a genocide of the Tutsis, but there were also Hutus who were killed in the DRC."
That's like accusing the RPF. And if you were to teach that
in class, in which a colonel's student hears that and goes to
tell his/her father, who is the general of the RPF: "Ah, father,
you also committed genocide in the Congo, you killed
Hutus there. Our teacher told us that." And you create problems like that. We teach that there was a genocide of Tutsis
and moderate Hutus because that's clear, since we can't say
everything. For example, when we are in the Facing History
Club, the students ask me questions: "The government
doesn't want us to talk about Hutu and Tutsi, but when we
talk about the genocide, we say the genocide against the
Tutsi." (Teacher interview, School 7, October 2011)

Teachers talked about the emphasis on unity and reconciliation in the curriculum, as well as about the challenges in

teaching to a mixed group of students that includes survivors and children of perpetrators. Even students who were born after the genocide or who were too young to remember the events carry with them a "postmemory" (Hirsch 2008) or intergenerational memory passed down from their families and communities (Assman 2012; Jara 2016).

Emmanuel, a Tutsi genocide survivor in an urban school, discussed the difficulty of teaching his students, a group who encompassed "survivors of the genocide" (Tutsi) and "survivors of the war" (Hutu): "So to talk about the genocide, we can't concentrate on one side, saying that the Tutsi are dead, the Hutu killed. If you mention the words Hutu or Tutsi, that can bring back division. We must be neutral, even if it's difficult" (Teacher interview, School 6, October 2011).

This example points to the difficulty of discussing the genocide and civil war without mentioning the conflict between the two ethnic groups, even while teachers are mandated to refer to the "Tutsi genocide." Even the Ugandan teachers, such as George, who were generally detached from the subject of the genocide, discussed the sensitivities surrounding the topic: "We don't go too deep because it will be hard for some students [survivors] and they will respond badly because they were also victims" (Teacher interview, School 4, October 2011).

Teaching about Reconciliation in Schools

Intimately tied to the narrative of the genocide is the narrative of the future: a unified Rwandan identity and a focus on *ubumwe n'ubwiyunge*, unity and reconciliation. As I discuss in this section, teaching about the genocide is considered integral to teaching about reconciliation. Although teaching about the genocide is often framed as a historical event tied to a particular official narrative, the reconciliation project is framed as a civic endeavor necessary for the new Rwandan nation. This section reviews how the broader reconciliation project is implemented in schools, with a focus on how reconciliation is taught and understood by students as well as on the differences and tensions across groups and continuing challenges in realizing the reconciliation project.

Reconciliation in the National Curriculum and Textbooks
There is a strong emphasis on the notion of unity and reconciliation in education sector policy documents and in the primary and secondary curricula and textbooks. In addition, various activities and clubs, such as the Never Again Rwanda Club, are organized around the genocide; unity and reconciliation clubs sponsor activities during the annual commemoration period. The current emphasis on the values of reconciliation and unity in educational documents is a contrast to pre-genocide textbooks, which emphasized divisions between groups and propagated negative stereotypes (Gasanabo 2006; Rutayisire, Kabano, and Rubagiza 2004). For example, a pre-genocide history textbook explains the social groups: "The Rwandan population . . . is divided socially into three groups that are dominated by hierarchy. There are the Batwa, the Bahutu, and the Batutusi" (Direction des Programmes de l'Enseignement Secondaire 1989, 68).[6]

Primary students are taught about reconciliation in simple terms. A 2006 fourth-grade social studies book provides an example of a quarrel between two neighbors in which one neighbor's goats escape and destroy the other neighbor's garden (see figure 16). The idea of reconciliation is explained in the context of solving the conflict by seeking help from the village elder (Bamusananire et al. 2006a, 63).

The 2008 political education book for secondary ordinary-level classes stresses the importance of education in fostering unity and reconciliation: "Civil education has a significant meaning in a bid to change this negative mentality and rebuild our nation. Our country has launched a rehabilitation program that gives people hope of a durable peace once and for all, after

Quarrels between neighbouring families

Case study

Neighbours quarrel

Two families quarrel because goats escape and eat the neighbour's vegetables. The two farmers argue and hit each other. Some of the goats are killed. The two families become very angry with each other and there seems no chance of peace.

Reconciliation

A member of one family goes to a village elder to ask for help. A meeting of elders is called to hear both families. One person from each family speaks to the meeting.

The elders leave the room to discuss what they have heard. They return and ask further questions:
- Were the goats let out on purpose? They hear it was an accident.
- How much were the vegetables worth?
- How much were the goats worth?

16. Reconciliation as portrayed in one textbook. *Source*: Bamusananire et al. 2006a, 63.

many years of unending wars that culminated in a genocide that destroyed people and the national economy. It is through the policy of *unity and reconciliation* as well as sharing values that a national reconstruction will be attained" (NCDC 2008a, 23; emphasis added).

This textbook has an entire chapter on unity and reconciliation, including a discussion of national cohesion—clans and a common culture and language—and ethnic divisions. The book explains the terms "unity" and "reconciliation": "With national unity, the citizens of the same country live like brothers and sisters, in perfect harmony, because they share a common heritage—the country. By *reconciliation*, it is necessary to pay attention to the restoration of broken relations or the unification of people who were separated because of a conflict" (NCDC 2008a, 151; emphasis added).

The 2011 advanced-level history book and the 2010 teacher's guide for history both have a section on unity and reconciliation that explains the work that the Government of National Unity and the NURC have done to counter "division" caused by the colonial past and by the former Hutu governments (NCDC 2010a, 151; Bamusananire 2011, 429). Both books discuss the *gacaca* trials as part of the reconciliation process.

Students' Conceptions of Reconciliation

The broader state project of reconciliation takes place in a variety of venues, including schools, the community, and the family. Within schools, students mentioned clubs, dormitories, and classrooms as sites of interacting with students from different backgrounds.

Along with the genocide, reconciliation is a common topic discussed in school and at home: 47.1 percent and 51.9 percent of students reported that they often discussed reconciliation at school and at home, respectively; about 44 percent said they discussed reconciliation sometimes at school and home (see figure 17). Only 9.2 percent said they never discussed reconciliation at school, and 4.5 percent said they never discussed it at home. These results indicate that the state-sponsored discourse around reconciliation is pervasive both in schools and within the privacy of homes. Similar to discussions around the genocide,

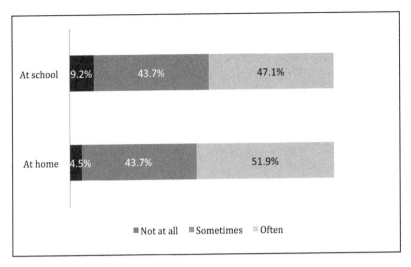

17. Discussion of reconciliation at school and at home.

discussions of reconciliation are more common in government and government-supported schools and in the Eastern Province.

In interviews, students generally spoke positively about the progress toward reconciliation. When queried, most students said that "it's already attained" or mostly achieved. However, some students also mentioned challenges to achieving reconciliation, such as the relatively short time that had passed since the genocide and continuing tensions among groups, manifesting in de facto segregation in school. During the interviews, students equated "reconciliation" with forgiveness, unity, seeking the truth, learning to live together, and the absence of ethnic groups—with being "all Rwandan." Students believed that reconciliation had emerged as a response to the genocide. In an interview with a group of boys in a school in Kigali, Fabrice, an eighteen-year-old Hutu, explained what the term "reconciliation" meant to him: "Reconciliation means that before the conflict, there were two groups here in Rwanda, Hutu and Tutsi.

And after that, they can reconcile. There is no reconciliation without the conflict. Reconciliation comes after forgiving each other. After taking the time to think about what happened during the conflict, then there is reconciliation and unity" (Boys' group interview, School 7, July 2011).

Reconciliation was also viewed as a means of remembering the past, or as enforcing the collective memory. Later in that discussion, Ignace, an eighteen-year-old, explained: "Remembering is focusing on the past. When you do not want to seek revenge for yourself, but to focus on the past to preserve your future. Because when you reconcile, that's the source of development for our country" (Boys' group interview, School 7, July 2011).

To Ignace, reconciliation was part of remembering the past but was also future-oriented and necessary for the development of the country. In contrast, others in that discussion believed that reconciliation involved forgetting the past. Jackson explained that remembering is also associated with holding grudges, *kubika inzika et kwibuka*. Derick said, "But if they continue with these mentalities, it will take twenty years to achieve reconciliation. There is something people do not consider: we have to forgive and forget" (Boys' interview, School 7, July 2011). He later said that reconciliation "is for your heart [*umutima*] to know," a concept found in studies on notions of reconciliation in Rwanda. Bert Ingelaere (2016) distinguishes between "thin" reconciliation or "living with" (*kubana*) versus "thick" reconciliation, *ubwiyunge*, or reconnecting from the heart (89). Although most of the students spoke of reconciliation in broad terms as getting along with different groups, some referred to it as a deeper notion emerging from the heart.

At a meeting held by the Association des Etudiants et Elèves Rescapés du Génocide (AERG) for genocide survivors and supporters, one boy expressed his views on the ideas of unity and reconciliation and noted the difficulties: "In my opinion, unity and reconciliation mean pardoning, reconciling, and supporting unity. But I think that there will always be an obstacle to achieving these things because we can't change history. People still carry the pain of the genocide" (AERG meeting, September 2011).

Most students thought that relations between groups had improved compared with five years previously. Beatrice, an Anglophone returnee, stated, "There are still some problems, but reconciliation will be achieved" (Girls' interview, School 4, September 2011).

Gacaca and the ICTR

The survey results indicate that there is not much emphasis in the classroom on learning about the different transitional justice mechanisms, such as *gacaca* and the ICTR. For example, only 25.2 percent of students said they discussed *gacaca* often at school; 32.9 percent said they discussed it often at home; the majority reported discussing *gacaca* sometimes at school (50.7 percent) and at home (53.6 percent; see figure 18). A fair amount of students never discussed *gacaca* at school (24.1 percent) or at home (13.5 percent). Yet, the vast majority of students strongly agreed (70.5 percent) or agreed (23.9 percent) that the *gacaca* trials punished those who committed crimes during the genocide; only 5 percent disagreed with this statement.

Although students seemed to be generally aware of *gacaca*, as evidenced in the survey and interviews, there was less discussion of the ICTR. Whereas 69 percent of students knew that *gacaca* is a traditional form of justice in the community, close to 43 percent said they did not know where the ICTR trials were held (they were held in Arusha, Tanzania).

In interviews with students, the discussion of reconciliation was often linked to *gacaca*. Students commonly mentioned *gacaca* as a means of achieving reconciliation and uncovering the truth about crimes committed during the genocide. Janet, nineteen, explained:

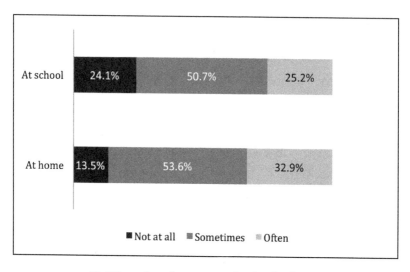

18. Discussion of *gacaca* at school and at home.

Gacaca and reconciliation go together. *Gacaca* was established to reestablish good relations. *Gacaca* reunited the
people. During *gacaca,* people revealed the truth about what
happened during the genocide. With this truth, they discov-
ered where many of the corpses of genocide victims were
buried, so then memorial sites were erected to honor the
victims and to serve as a symbol of the Rwandan genocide.
As a result, no one can deny that the genocide [*jenoside*]
happened in Rwanda. It's like proof of the genocide and a
symbol of reconciliation. That's the importance of *gacaca*, as
well. . . . Those who had offended others asked for forgiveness . . . . Even if *gacaca* has ended, the process continues.
There is hope that reconciliation will be achieved. (Girls'
group interview, School 4, September 2011)

Students across schools supported the idea that *gacaca* contributes to reconciliation and unity. For instance, Joshua, an
eighteen-year-old student at a rural government school in the

Western Province said: "I have thought about *gacaca. Gacaca* has created a certain unity among Rwandans. It helped them to take the same direction and to join forces to build their country. For the criminals, it was time to ask for forgiveness" (Mixed interview, School 2, September 2011). Jessica, an eighteen-year-old student at an urban government school in the capital, explained: "*Gacaca* has helped a lot because it unites the Rwandans. There aren't problems anymore of Hutus or Tutsis. That helps to achieve reconciliation" (Girls' group interview, School 6, October 2011). Frederic, a seventeen-year-old at the same school remarked: "I think that it [reconciliation] has already been achieved because of the success of *gacaca*, which has really helped to achieve reconciliation. *Gacaca* judged those that killed [others] during the genocide, and required that they provide information. After that, the *génocidaires* were punished or had to work for TIG [Travaux à l'Intérêt Général, a work program for prisoners]" (Boys' group interview, School 6, August 2011).

Compared to *gacaca*, the ICTR was less known among the students; students in urban and higher-quality schools knew more about the tribunal as compared to students in rural schools, who often had never heard of it. The ICTR was perceived to be less effective than it could be because it was located in Tanzania rather than Rwanda. Furthermore, the ICTR was associated with the United Nations and with external factors, whereas *gacaca* was seen as a form of justice rooted in local traditions. Patrick, a twenty-year-old student at a rural school in the Western Province, compared the two forms of justice: "*Gacaca* is the solution for Rwanda because it has been conceived by Rwandans for themselves to resolve their problems. But with ICTR, not everything about it is good; it delays the trials. *Gacaca* tried many criminals in a short period of time, while ICTR tries a small number of them over many years" (Mixed group interview, School 2, September 2011).

Several national surveys conducted during the *gacaca* trials revealed that the population generally viewed the trials as a more relevant approach to seeking justice and reconciliation than the ICTR. For instance, in a representative survey of adults in four communes in Rwanda in 2002, Phuong Pham and his colleagues found respondents to be more supportive of the *gacaca* trials (90.8 percent) and national trials (67.8 percent) when compared with the ICTR (42.1 percent) (Pham, Weinstein, and Longman 2004). A 2010 government survey reported that the vast majority of respondents (93.7 percent) believed that *gacaca* revealed the truth about the genocide (Republic of Rwanda, National Unity and Reconciliation Commission 2010). A survey conducted in 2011 found that respondents generally thought positively about *gacaca* but expressed some concerns. For instance, more than 90 percent of respondents agreed that *gacaca* had functioned well, but a majority of respondents also mentioned issues with victimization of witnesses and false testimonies (Pozen, Neugebauer, and Ntaganira 2014).

Challenges to Achieving Reconciliation
Despite the general acceptance of the official narrative of reconciliation and unity and support for *gacaca*, students across different types of schools and regions conceded that challenges and tensions among groups continued to exist. For instance, Kevin, a seventeen-year-old student in an urban government school, disagreed with another student that reconciliation had been fully achieved and listed continuing challenges:

> There are still things that hinder the achievement of reconciliation, because if we say reconciliation, that means convening the people who committed the genocide and those who lost their loved ones during the genocide and uniting them. And if they accept to be together and united, it's a good thing, but I would say that reconciliation hasn't yet been achieved at a higher level. I don't know if you remember; it was during the commemoration of

the genocide. There was a person who gave a testimonial at the memorial site in Gisozi about what happened during the genocide. But a few days later, he was found dead. So there are still challenges. (Boys' group interview, School 6, August 2011)

In spite of supporting the official narrative of unity and reconciliation, genocide survivors and those who had lost family in the genocide often found it difficult to forgive the perpetrators. Noella, a seventeen-year-old genocide survivor in an urban school, explained why achieving reconciliation is important but difficult to attain: "For example, with me: the man who killed my father. If he asked me to pardon him, it would not be easy to pardon him; because I lost something that my father would have done for me, it's too difficult. For example, my father had the means (wealth), and now since he [my father] isn't alive anymore, my family became poor" (Student interview, School 6, October 2011). David, a boy in an urban school, said: "In my opinion, reconciliation is very hard to achieve in our country. Sometimes, people might be pardoned, but it's very difficult to forget because when you are facing someone who killed members of your family, you can't ever forget what happened. Perhaps with time, we might achieve real reconciliation. Like they say in French: '*Le temps guérit tout*' [time heals everything]" (Mixed group interview, School 7, July 2011).

The main challenge to achieving reconciliation that students mentioned was time. Claude, an eighteen-year-old Hutu student, explained how it takes time for people to change their mentalities: "Reconciliation will not come quickly; it will take a long time. Just like how the Hutu learned to hate the Tutsi—this took a long time from 1959 to 1994. So it was a long trajectory, and that will also be something that reconciliation will take a long time to overcome. That can't be overcome easily; this past is still in people's heads" (Boys' group interview, School 1, September 2011).

Survey and interview data indicate that although progress has been made in promoting the reconciliation narrative at the school level, challenges in fostering societal reconstruction persist. Although students supported the notion of reconciliation and unity, they were also cautious about discussing the past. For instance, in the survey, 36 percent of students continued to believe that what happened in the past should *not* be openly debated in schools. Thus, reconciliation is portrayed as consisting of forgiveness and accepting the official narrative of de-ethnicized unity. Sharing individual experiences and views on the past or diverse collective memories has a less prominent role in the Rwandan government's approach to reconciliation. Even though students seemed to openly discuss and accept the official narrative of reconciliation and unity, reconciliation or forgiveness at the individual level was more difficult and was not addressed within the school curriculum due to the lack of time and the constrained political environment.

Survey and interview data also indicate indirect levels of reconciliation as measured by trust. For instance, levels of societal trust were low: 78 percent of students agreed or strongly agreed that most people could *not* be trusted, with little variation across students or schools. Other surveys have found low levels of trust among the general population in Rwanda (Paluck and Green 2009; World Values Survey 2007). Using a nationally representative sample of Rwandans, the 2007 World Values Survey found that only 5 percent of the population agreed with the statement "Most people can be trusted" (World Values Survey 2007). The World Values Survey is a cross-national survey conducted in a large number of countries on political and social attitudes. In 2000–2007 data, Rwanda had the lowest level of social trust of the eighty-eight countries where a World Values Survey was conducted. By 2012, however, levels of trust had improved, rising to 17 percent (World Values Survey 2012).[7] This trend may indicate that an understandably low level of trust following the genocide is climbing due to the passage of time and to reconciliation efforts.

In my survey, 84 percent of students strongly disagreed or disagreed with the statement "There will always be conflict among different social groups," pointing to a tendency toward reconciliation. However, in my interviews, some students mentioned that students continued to gather in groups according to social background. Silvie, a Hutu girl, explained: "When we started secondary school, we didn't know each other, so the students formed groups, for example the survivors of the genocide" (Individual girl, School 2, July 2011). Although students generally viewed relations between students as having improved during the previous few years, some discussed continuing tensions among students. Beatrice, an eighteen-year-old Tutsi returnee, talked about past and current tensions between groups:

GARNETT: So do you think that, in general, people at school usually get along?

BEATRICE: Yes, now they get along, in a way. But sometimes when we are in class, you might see that some students form a separate group, so other students form another group elsewhere. There are some people who don't feel at ease with us [returnees or Tutsi]. Some have their mentalities, and the others don't care.

GARNETT: And have things changed? How was it five years ago, or one year go?

BEATRICE: Yes, there is a change. Because five years ago, people feared one another. Before, in the evening, you might see someone encounter another person and run away in fear that he/she might be killed. There was something called *"guhotora"* [killing someone during the night by choking him or her]. There were a lot of people killed during this time. People named each other: "You there are Bahutu (Hutu), you there are Batutsi [Tutsi]." But we don't live in fear anymore.

GARNETT: What about here at school?

BEATRICE: There haven't been problems with the ethnic groups [*amoko*] here at school. But in past years, we heard that that happened at other schools, which had a lot of problems caused by the ethnic groups. People wrote pamphlets and posted them on the door of the headmaster's office. For example, if the headmaster were Tutsi, they wrote: "You are going to kill us, we are going to exterminate you." So there were tensions. (Student interview, School 4, September 2011)

Despite the sense that reconciliation had been achieved, as this quote illustrates, tensions between groups and distrust persisted in some schools, particularly among survivors and returnees (Tutsi) and the children of perpetrators (Hutu).

Degree of Reconciliation

Measuring the degree to which reconciliation has taken place in the aftermath of a conflict is a difficult and perhaps impossible task. Some studies have indicated the challenges in measuring the notion of reconciliation in the Rwandan context due to the restrictive political and social milieu (see, for example, Pozen, Neugebauer, and Ntaganira 2014). Moreover, given low levels of trust and high levels of self-censorship in Rwanda, data from surveys, particularly government-conducted surveys, may not be entirely reliable. In 2002, Pham and his colleagues found that the majority of the population surveyed expressed a positive view of reconciliation, with 67.5 percent supporting interdependence with other ethnic groups and 63.6 percent supporting social justice (Pham, Weinstein, and Longman 2004). Several national government surveys have attempted to measure the level of reconciliation in Rwanda at different periods following the genocide. The 2010 Rwanda Reconciliation Barometer Survey, a nationally representative survey conducted by NURC periodically, reported that the vast majority of respondents, nearly 90 percent, said they had forgiven those who hurt others in the past (Republic of Rwanda, National Unity and Reconciliation Commission 2010). A follow-up survey conducted in 2015 reported that national reconciliation, as measured by questions about understanding the past, citizenship and identity, political culture, security, justice and rights, and social cohesion, had improved from 82.3 percent in 2010 to 92.5 percent in 2015 (Republic of Rwanda, National Unity and Reconciliation Commission 2015).

Although it is difficult to measure the degree to which students are actually reconciled, I constructed a scale as a proxy for reconciliation, measuring the level of discussion and acceptance of an official government narrative around reconciliation. The index is more a measure of acceptance of the official reconciliation narrative than of actual reconciliation. In my survey, I defined "reconciliation" as a proxy for the official discourse on unity and reconciliation, drawing on several items, including discussion of reconciliation, the genocide, and *gacaca* in school and at home; perception of lack of conflict among social groups; and perception that people generally got along.[8] To control for the influence of other student and school factors, I ran a multiple regression analysis to explain the variation in the reconciliation scale across different predictor variables.[9] Based on this index, I created a scale of low, medium, and high levels of reconciliation and ran a multinomial regression model; I then calculated predicted probabilities across the three levels of reconciliation (see appendix A for additional details of analysis). In this section, I discuss the predicted probabilities for statistically significant differences in reconciliation levels across student and school characteristics.

While individual characteristics such as ethnicity and gender, as well as attitudes about citizenship and trust, were statistically significantly related to degree of reconciliation, other characteristics, such as socioeconomic background, were not important in predicting differences in reconciliation. I found that those in positions of political power or in more advantageous positions within the education system (i.e., returnees or survivors) were more likely to have positive views on reconciliation. Students who identified as genocide survivors or returnees (Tutsi) demonstrated more support of reconciliation compared to Hutu students, a finding that may be due in part to the fact that Tutsi are more likely to support the government narrative of unity and reconciliation relative to the Hutu population (Paluck and Green 2009). Figure 19 depicts differences in levels of reconciliation by ethnic group: 39.3 percent of Tutsi reported high levels of reconciliation, compared to 31.5 percent of Hutu, whereas only 29.4 percent of Tutsi had low levels of reconciliation compared to 34.8 percent of Hutu.

Although Tutsi students reported significantly higher levels of agreement with the official reconciliation discourse as measured on the survey, during group and individual interviews, Tutsi (both survivors and returnees) were more likely to mention the challenges of achieving reconciliation and the difficulties of reconciliation at an individual level. Thus, it appears that whereas Tutsi students generally support the official government discourse on reconciliation, they were also more likely to raise questions or to be critical of the reconciliation process relative to Hutu students, a perception that speaks to the relative levels of fear across the groups surrounding discussion of the genocide and ethnicity. Students who identified as survivors or returnees were less likely to fear accusations of divisionism or genocide ideology relative to the majority Hutu population by virtue of their identity.

Figure 20 shows that levels of reconciliation also differ by gender, with girls exhibiting higher levels of reconciliation (35.6 percent) compared to boys (30.3 percent). Reconciliation levels were higher for girls than boys, possibly because they felt

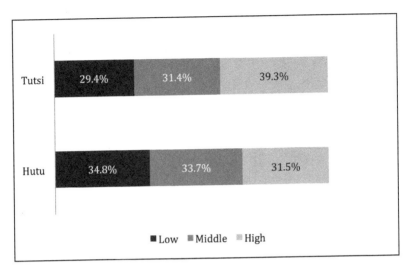

19. Level of reconciliation by ethnicity. *Note*: Figure is based on predicted probabilities from a multinomial logistic regression (see appendix A for more details).

they had benefited from the RPF's post-genocide policies for gender equality favoring girls and women (Russell 2016).

Students who reported higher levels of trust and a stronger national civic identity had higher levels of reconciliation. Students who strongly identified with being a citizen of Rwanda also had higher levels of reconciliation (36.5 percent) compared to students who said they only somewhat identified (28.9 percent) or did not identify as citizens of Rwanda (18 percent) (see figure 21). In contrast, those who did not strongly identify as citizens had lower levels of reconciliation (50 percent) compared to those who only somewhat identified (38.4 percent) or strongly identified (29.7 percent).

Levels of trust were related to degree of reconciliation. Figure 22 shows that students who strongly disagreed that they could trust their neighbors were more likely to have a lower level of support for reconciliation (47.2 percent); only

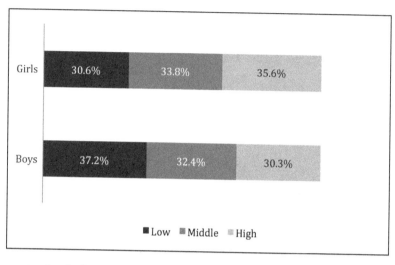

20. Level of reconciliation by gender. *Note*: Figure is based on predicted probabilities from a multinomial logistic regression (see appendix A for more details).

20.2 percent of students who strongly agreed with the statement had a low level of reconciliation. Conversely, students who strongly felt that they could trust their neighbors also had higher levels of reconciliation (45.4 percent).

Differences in notions of reconciliation also emerged across different types of schools and regions. Students in government and government-aided schools scored higher on the reconciliation index, as did students in the Eastern Province, where there is a higher proportion of Tutsi returnees from Uganda. Figure 23 illustrates that students in government schools (34.6 percent) and government-aided schools (34.7 percent) were more likely to have high levels of reconciliation compared to those in private schools (28.3 percent). Those in private schools (40.8 percent) were more likely to fall into the low-reconciliation category compared to those in government schools (31.2 percent) or government-aided (31.4 percent) schools.

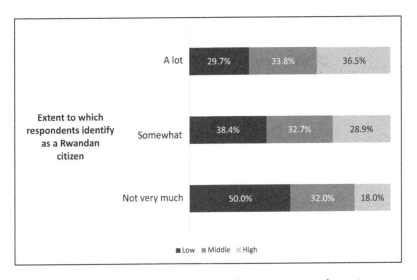

21. Level of reconciliation by views on identity as a Rwandan citizen. *Note*: Figure is based on predicted probabilities from a multinomial logistic regression (see appendix A for more details).

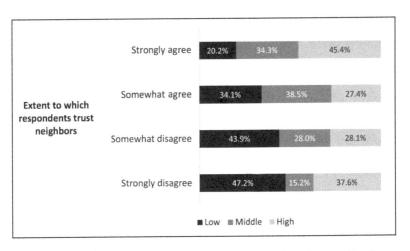

22. Level of reconciliation by trust. *Note*: Figure is based on predicted probabilities from a multinomial logistic regression (see appendix A for more details).

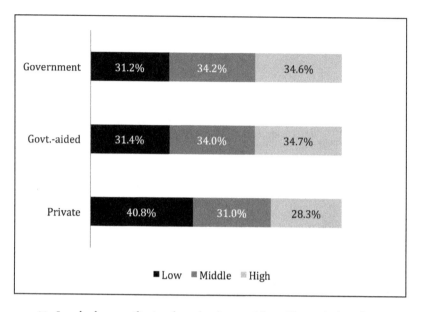

23. Level of reconciliation by school type. *Note*: Figure is based on predicted probabilities from a multinomial logistic regression (see appendix A for more details).

Figure 24 shows that students in the Eastern Province (38.7 percent) were more likely to have higher levels of reconciliation compared to those in Kigali (33.1 percent) or the Western Province (27.3 percent), whereas those in Kigali (39.6 percent) and the Western Province (32 percent) had lower levels of reconciliation compared to those in the Eastern Province (30.1 percent).

The survey results indicate that the official narrative is stronger in government schools and government-aided schools compared to private schools, which are less dependent on government resources and thus may be more independent in terms of what they teach students. Nonetheless, private schools are constrained by the official curriculum, which they are required to follow. Students in the Eastern Province exhibited higher levels on the reconciliation index, mirroring political trends in that

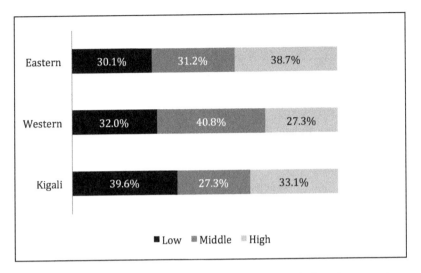

24. Level of reconciliation by region. *Note*: Figure is based on predicted probabilities from a multinomial logistic regression (see appendix A for more details).

region, which is populated by high numbers of Anglophone returnees, who tend to be more supportive of the current regime relative to people in Kigali and the Western Province.

CONCLUSIONS

As this chapter shows, the Rwandan state's ambitions to use the education system to teach the "truth" about the genocide and to foster intergroup reconciliation have been undercut, in part, by the incompatibility of those goals and by the way in which they have been pursued. Not surprisingly, students have found it hard to understand how the genocide was ethnically motivated even though the ongoing process of reconciliation denies the salience of ethnic differences. To complicate matters, the manner in which the history of the genocide is taught and reconciliation is encouraged in schools hinders discussion about the past and creates fear rather than social cohesion, impeding the progress of the regime's peacebuilding project. Moreover, the goals of the broader peacebuilding project are decoupled from the lived realities of students and teachers in schools.

The official curriculum presents a "forced memory" (Ricoeur 2004), or singular narrative, of the genocide that conflicts with private perspectives and individual or family memories of the recent past. Public discussion of these topics is strictly forbidden under the genocide ideology law; however, outside of the classroom or in private, individuals continue to form their own narratives and interpretations, or "hidden transcripts," of the past (Scott 1990; Zorbas 2009). Despite the monumental efforts of the government to re-create an imagined narrative of the genocide while wielding the threat of imprisonment for genocide ideology, collective memories, intergenerational memories, and counternarratives live on in the minds of students and teachers.

Because it does not allow for the incorporation of divergent narratives and memories of the past, the manner in which the genocide is taught in schools encourages only partial, or thin, reconciliation. Education is used to inculcate an "official collective memory" of the genocide and to promote a narrative of unity and reconciliation rather than to foster critical debate and discussion about past events. An inconsistency arises between history as supporting the present official narrative and history as lived accounts of memories across disparate groups. René Lemarchand (2009) asserts: "Enforced memory in today's Rwanda does more than suppress ethnic identities, it rules out 'recognition' and makes the search for a 'critical memory' an exercise likely to be denounced as a source of 'divisionism'" (108).

In a similar vein, Lars Waldorf (2009) spotlights the regime's incompatible goals: "There has always been an inherent tension between the government's forward-looking reconciliation narrative, which seeks to erase ethnicity, and its backwards-looking genocide narrative, which inevitably emphasizes ethnicity"

(104). As I discuss in chapter 3, the government promotes a nonethnic national identity but at the same time mandates that schools teach about the "Tutsi" genocide.

The difficulty of teaching sensitive topics linked to the genocide is amplified by a lack of pedagogical training for teachers on how to teach about the genocide and other sensitive topics. Although official policy documents refer to the importance of fostering critical thinking skills in the classroom, in practice the government neglects to give teachers the training they need to develop critical thinking skills, foster open discussion and empathy among students, and develop democratically engaged students (E. Cole 2007b). The regime's sincerity about wanting to encourage critical thinking is also open to doubt. Teachers noted difficulty in teaching about the genocide due to the fear of being charged with genocide ideology, a fear that limits in-class discussion and the promotion of student-centered and active learning. In addition, teachers' abilities to discuss events surrounding the genocide and reconciliation are linked to their identities and personal experiences, with Tutsi returnees and survivors more likely than Hutus to speak openly. Teachers are afraid to field questions from students for fear that the conversation could stray away from the official version of events.

Consequently, the official narrative around the genocide constrains an open discussion about the past that would incorporate multiple narratives from different groups, in turn constraining efforts at societal reconciliation. Although students know a lot about reconciliation in theoretical terms and generally regard themselves and their fellow students as unified and reconciled, or as moving in that direction, the microlevel views of individuals and groups continue to be shaped by their own and their families' and communities' views on identity and by an overall lack of trust between groups. Hence, there is an inherent contradiction between the larger metanarrative of reconciliation and unity, which is derived from global models, and the micro-level processes of reconciliation and memory-making, which are influenced by individual and local factors.

Although references to reconciliation are linked to broader global norms on reconciliation and transitional justice mechanisms, the implementation of reconciliation in Rwanda at the local level is constrained by the political environment. This version of reconciliation is more akin to thin reconciliation (*kubona*), which involves only coexistence, rather than to a thick reconciliation process that involves true introspection and forgiveness.

To be sure, some degree of reconciliation seems to be occurring. That, at least, is what the results of my assessment of "proxy" reconciliation suggest, although the survey results also point toward significant differences in the degree of reconciliation felt by various groups. The government's own national surveys also show that the population is increasingly reconciled—but some skepticism of those surveys is warranted. Even so, reconciliation would likely have progressed more swiftly and effectively if the official narratives of reconciliation and the genocide did not present teachers and students with contradictions while also threatening dire consequences for those who point out those contradictions.

CHAPTER 6

The Potential
and Limitations of
Education for Peacebuilding

AT THE GLOBAL level, the notion of "sustaining peace" has gained traction as part of the larger 2030 Agenda for Sustainable Development. The United Nations designated 2018 as the "Year of Sustaining Peace," as evidenced by the release in January 2018 of *Peacebuilding and Sustaining Peace: Report of the Secretary-General*, followed by a UN General Assembly high-level meeting in April 2018. Security Council Resolution 2282 (2016) describes "sustaining peace" as including "activities aimed at preventing the outbreak, escalation, continuation and recurrence of conflict, addressing root causes, assisting parties to conflict to end hostilities, ensuring national reconciliation, and moving towards recovery, reconstruction and development" (1–2). In this definition, the emphasis is not only on ending conflict but also on addressing root causes and building a foundation for long-term reconciliation, reconstruction, and development. In addition, this new approach emphasizes the nexus across development, peacebuilding, and human rights. The notion of sustaining peace seeks to expand the peacebuilding agenda to include reconstruction after conflict and to draw attention to underlying institutions, norms, and attitudes that influence the construction of peace (Mahmoud and Makoond 2017).

In the same vein, the Rwandan Ministry of Education is aligning the education sector with the global sustainable peace and development agenda, which views education as preventive of future conflict and linked to national development. In February 2017, the Ministry of Education formally launched a new sustainable peace program, funded by international donors, in conjunction with Aegis Trust. The stated goal of the new program is to foster "constructive exchange on genocide and peacebuilding, thus helping to promote social cohesion and *sustainable peace* in Rwanda" (Aegis Trust 2017, 2; emphasis added). The new program, which will be implemented in "Peace Schools" across the country, complements and builds on the introduction of "peace and values" as a crosscutting topic in all subjects in the 2015 curriculum.

Whether this realignment of Rwanda's education policy will proceed smoothly remains to be seen. In the past, as this book has chronicled, the government has sought to link its education policy to global initiatives around citizenship, human rights, and reconciliation, and in doing so has encountered a variety of problems.

Despite the considerable challenges that have emerged in the post-genocide peacebuilding project, many of the teachers and students with whom I spoke were optimistic about the future. During a visit to a school in the Western Province, set against the background of the lush, green landscape and distant volcanoes, I spoke with Innocent, a twenty-year-old Francophone from the local area who was studying literature. Nearing the end of our discussion in an empty, drafty classroom, I asked Innocent how he imagined Rwanda would be in ten years' time. He spoke of the possibilities for peace: "For now there is *peace* [*amahoro*], but in ten years it will be even better than today because the whole world aims at *development*, and Rwanda will be much more developed than today. The future is so bright" (Student interview, School 1, October 2011; emphasis added). When pressed about whether conflict might reignite in the future, he replied, "I don't think that there will be conflict, but one never knows; and above all, we can't know what each person thinks because we can't look into the heart [*umutima*] of each person" (Student interview, School 1, October 2011).

In this exchange, Innocent highlighted the power of development to build peace and prevent future conflict; he did not mention initiatives aimed at promoting intergroup reconciliation. In doing so, he was echoing the government's stance, which since the genocide has promoted a developmental discourse that sees poverty reduction and socioeconomic development as the foundation for long-term peace. However, other scholars have found evidence indicating that focusing on economic development might not necessarily lead to peace, but could exacerbate underlying structural inequalities that might trigger conflict (Purdeková 2015; Uvin 1998). For instance, in his work investigating Rwanda leading up to the genocide, Peter Uvin (1998) explored precisely how the development aid enterprise indirectly laid the structural conditions that facilitated the genocide.

In the quarter of a century since the genocide in Rwanda, the government has used the education system in an attempt to spur development and peacebuilding through various reforms and strategies, drawing on global models. However, while national policy documents and education materials have sought to neatly integrate global frameworks around citizenship, human rights, and reconciliation into the education sector, implementing these models in schools has been difficult and has exposed inherent tensions in the policies themselves and between the policies and the lived experiences of students and teachers. Education reforms in the post-genocide era have served as a means to concentrate on the future and to deflect discussion of a contested version of the past. In other words, a discourse on peacebuilding and development has been promoted in order to avoid confronting difficult aspects of the conflict. Rather than encouraging open discussion around ethnicity and human rights violations, the state has addressed its troubled history in a ritualized way through stylized nation building, promoting an official reconciliation discourse and emphasizing gender equality at the expense of other human rights.

GLOBAL NORMS, EDUCATION, AND PEACEBUILDING

This book shows the extent to which the Rwandan government draws on global models centered around citizenship, human rights, and reconciliation for the purpose of the government's national peacebuilding project. However, it also demonstrates that implementing selective versions of these global constructs at the local level produces unintended consequences and complications among teachers and students. The data I collected in Rwanda illuminate not only how the Rwandan government uses global norms for peacebuilding, but also how these ideas play out in practice and the contradictions that emerge between the intentions of the policy makers and the reality in schools.

One contradiction centers on citizenship. While the Rwandan state aims to produce a new generation of globally oriented and English-speaking citizens who disregard ethnic differences and focus on national unity, the education system has in fact nurtured nationalistic and obedient citizens who are afraid to question or critique the regime or to speak openly about the past. Rather than encourage the development of active and engaged citizens who can help sustain peace over the longer term, the government's narrow vision of citizenship produces patriotic but unquestioning citizens who fear the consequences of dissent. In chapter 3, I demonstrate how the Rwandan government deploys global norms around citizenship but at the same time enforces a patriotic and nonethnic, unified Rwandan identity. While the government appears to have had success in promoting this new identity, it has been less successful in eradicating ethnic identity. As the evidence shows, rather than efface ethnic cleavages, this approach has generated new conflicts across social groups linked to language and experience during the genocide, and these strains threaten to weaken the wider peacebuilding project.

Another contradiction centers on the use of human rights norms and discourses. Paradoxically, the Rwandan Patriotic Front (RPF)–led government—which is viewed as repressive by many Rwandans and international observers—promotes a story of human rights discourse in national policy documents while simultaneously limiting and violating rights in practice. Chapter 4 illustrates the extent to which the Rwandan government incorporates human rights discourse in national policy documents, and how these discourses are taken up by students and teachers. I show that although human rights language is included in national documents, the government engages in a selective and strategic use of human rights. For instance, the government emphasizes gender equality while failing to uphold other human rights. The government promotes socioeconomic rights at the expense of civil and political rights and ignores violations of political and civil rights. While aiming to foster reconciliation and unity, the government forbids discussion of past injustices and human rights violations, mandating that citizens forget what is outside the official narrative of the recent past. Human rights discourses are showcased in certain instances and muted in others.

A related tension concerns the nexus between genocide, reconciliation, and ethnic identity. In post-genocide Rwanda, the state has sought to use education to build a new national and de-ethnicized identity, disconnected from the very ethnic identities that led to the genocide. However, while the government

draws on global discourses around human rights and reconciliation, it does so in a way that suppresses candid discussion of the
genocide, thereby limiting efforts at reconciliation and peacebuilding. The state seeks to elevate a nonethnic national identity
devoid of any mention of Hutu or Tutsi identity, yet the education system invokes ethnic identity in the official discourse
around the 1994 genocide and in reference to scholarships and
clubs for genocide survivors. While the state promotes an official
narrative around the genocide and reconciliation, this tightly
controlled project of peacebuilding actually undermines genuine discussion around past experiences. As discussed in chapter 5, the data from teachers and students reveal that the tightly
controlled official narrative around the genocide and reconciliation excludes counternarratives and makes students and teachers
fearful of speaking openly about events surrounding the genocide, in case they are accused of disseminating "genocide ideology." As a consequence, reconciliation is superficial, or "thin,"
across different groups.

Although the RPF regime has attempted to engineer a new
Rwandan civic identity and to control the national narrative
around the genocide and reconciliation, the regime has not been
able to eradicate counternarratives and to control notions of identity. Governments and policy makers often regard education as a
powerful tool for addressing past conflict and rebuilding a nation;
however, evidence presented in this book demonstrates that education is in fact a weaker tool for shaping minds and controlling
the narratives of the past than many politicians and bureaucrats
believe and is often vulnerable to political influences.

DECOUPLING AND UNINTENDED
CONSEQUENCES

This book expands upon neoinstitutional sociological work to
ascertain how global models are diffused to the national and
school levels and translated by local actors. While previous

empirical work has noted the diffusion of global models and scripts linked to human rights, global citizenship, and women's rights cross-nationally (Buckner and Russell 2013; Meyer, Bromley, and Ramirez 2010; Nakagawa and Wotipka 2016), this book explores how these global models are implemented and interpreted among students and teachers in a postconflict context.

Numerous studies have demonstrated decoupling between global and national levels in the realms of human rights and citizenship (W. Cole and Ramírez 2013; Hafner-Burton and Tsutsui 2005; Joppke 2007; Soysal 2000), but few have examined the mechanisms of decoupling at subnational levels and among local actors. The evidence presented in this book illuminates the intricacies of implementing global models across different national and local contexts and the decoupling that results between what is intended and what actually occurs in terms of identity formation and reconciliation. Although the government incorporates global norms into national policy documents, these ideas are reshaped and reinterpreted by teachers and students in classrooms.

Findings from this book also highlight the difficulties of implementing global models in a postconflict context. For instance, a global concept of reconciliation, modeled on the South African Truth and Reconciliation Commission, seeks to bring about transparency and reconciliation between different groups in society. But in Rwanda, global discourse around reconciliation signifies acceptance of an officially mandated ideal of reconciliation rather than open discussion among individuals. This inability to openly discuss and confront deeply entrenched inequalities and grievances in society perpetuates differences and inequalities rather than resolving underlying antagonisms. The prohibition on discussing ethnic identity may lead to more problems in the long term, because identity is intimately linked to other status markers and access to resources. As demonstrated in chapter 3, Anglophone returnee students and "survivors" are privileged over Francophone students, or "Hutu," through the language of instruction, scholarship, and clubs. Avoiding candid and critical conversations about the past and the sensitivities around ethnic identity may undermine the project of reconciliation in schools (as discussed in chapter 5).

The findings from this book also point to the complexities of relying on education to promote reconciliation, nation building, and sustainable peace. An oppressive political climate is always likely to hamper genuine discussion in the classroom. The authoritarian political environment in Rwanda (Straus and Waldorf 2011), for instance, makes candid discussion about past and present human rights violations unrealistic. Thus, although a country's education system has the potential to play an important role in postconflict peacebuilding (Bush and Saltarelli 2000; Novelli, Lopes Cardozo, and Smith 2017), this book shows that education may not be as effective at changing deeply embedded attitudes or in fostering genuine reconciliation as many scholars (and politicians) assume, particularly in politically restrictive environments. Moreover, the introduction of new policies, such as changing the medium of instruction or prioritizing access to education over quality of education, creates unintended consequences and erects new boundaries between different groups of students linked to language and experience during the genocide.

The Mixed Impact of Educational Reforms and Policies in Postconflict Contexts

Education is inherently political and contested in a postconflict context. Reforms surrounding access to education, the nature of the curricula, and the language of instruction privilege some groups over others and create new boundaries (Bush and

Saltarelli 2000; Davies 2004). How students learn about the past and develop a national identity can be profoundly shaped by reforms to the curriculum, such as changes to the content of history and civics education, by expanding or reducing the amount of time spent teaching these subjects, and by changing the manner in which they are taught (E. Cole 2007a). Yet, the impact of some reforms can be significantly diluted by other reforms. For instance, changes to *what* is taught about citizenship, identity, and the genocide in school will have limited impact if *the amount of time* devoted to those sensitive subjects is modest. At the time of my research, in 2011, students at the lower secondary or ordinary level spent only one hour a week studying political education (civics) and only two studying history; and only students in the humanities concentration studied history as a subject at the upper secondary level.

The language of instruction, the availability of scholarships, the membership of school clubs, and a host of other school practices can also have important ramifications for identity construction and reconciliation. For instance, clubs and scholarships for student survivors inevitably exclude other students and create competition over limited resources.

Evidence from this book highlights the fact that donors, policy makers, practitioners, and educators working in postconflict contexts need to be mindful of the limitations of education as a solution to past conflict. While education can be a powerful and constructive tool for promoting reconciliation, it also has restrictions and complications. Although curricular and other education reforms to address the past are necessary to build peace, rarely are these changes sufficient to heal past societal divisions, and they can often result in new problems. For example, implementing human rights or peace education is usually not adequate to provide students with tools for reconciliation if structural inequalities are not simultaneously acknowledged or addressed, and may in fact serve to obscure deeper problems.

Countries face the considerable challenge of constructing a unifying national identity through citizenship education (Dryden-
Peterson and Mulimbi 2017) while recounting the history of a
recent conflict.

This book also highlights the crucial but often overlooked
role of teachers, who may carry their own memories of the conflict but who are also responsible for conveying the government's interpretation of the past to a future generation of
citizens. Teachers play an important role in postconflict settings
(Novelli and Sayed 2016; Rubagiza, Umutoni, and Kaleeba
2016). However, teachers, as Zvi Bekerman and Micahlinos
Zembylas (2011) find in the cases of Israel and Cyprus, "bear
their own internal struggles, concerns and ambivalences," and
are thus not always open to dialogue with students from different groups (4). In this sense, teachers' identity, as well as students'
identity, must be taken into account when formulating curricula
and pedagogy. Moreover, professional development often omits
difficult or contested issues related to history and citizenship.
More attention on the part of national governments, donors,
and organizations working in the field should be given to these
challenging areas.

My findings problematize the notion that education, by
itself, can be used to achieve societal reconciliation and transitional justice. Reforms to the education system are also shaped
and limited by the historical, political, and economic context
(Davies 2004; Novelli and Lopes Cardozo 2008). Whether a
minority or majority group controls the state influences the
process of societal reconciliation, as does the level of democracy
and the amount of political stability that a country enjoys. For
instance, oppressive regimes tend to limit or prohibit discussion
of the past in an open, critical, and constructive manner. Issues
of power and who controls the larger narrative of the past, as
well as how local actors contest metanarratives, have important
implications for what is taught in schools.

The dilemmas faced in Rwanda are not unique to the Rwandan case; they occur in some form whenever a postconflict society seeks to advance its national goals by drawing on global constructs around human rights and peacebuilding. Often, countries draw on these global tropes to bolster their image globally and to seek international legitimacy (Hafner-Burton and Tsutsui 2005; Russell 2015). And often, the use of these global frameworks leads to mixed results.

In Rwanda, as in any postconflict country striving to overcome deep divisions while promoting a prescribed version of the past, a focus on the future and on development, in conjunction with a restricted discussion of past events (which must stay within the confines of the official government narrative), is likely to result in contested narratives about the past in schools.

While the Rwandan government seeks to achieve a version of reconciliation that has been customized to suit the national agenda, the prospect of achieving real reconciliation is hampered by the political and social context. Although the official discourse of unity and reconciliation is pervasive, genuine reconciliation, trust, and open discussion of the past are impeded at the school level. Indeed, fear surrounds the teaching and discussion of the genocide and ethnicity, which discourages the expression of alternative narratives of the genocide experience. While the intent of the national-level policy is to use education to create a unified civic identity and to promote reconciliation, there is a discrepancy between the aim of the official discourse for the promotion of social cohesion and actual practices in schools, which reproduce new boundaries and inequalities among students. This refusal to discuss ethnicity and past violence candidly undermines the national project of reconciliation and peacebuilding.

In the quarter century since the genocide, Rwanda has made impressive gains in terms of development goals. The country has almost reached the health and education targets set in the Millennium Development Goals, extending access to basic health care and education to the majority of the population (Abbott, Sapsford, and Binagwaho 2017; Abbott, Sapsford, and Rwirahira 2015). The Rwandan government has also been successful in promoting gender equality, and the country now boasts the highest proportion of women in parliament in the world (Inter-Parliamentary Union 2016).

At the same time, however, the government's single-minded focus on development and unity has made the government unresponsive to those Rwandans whose stories have not been given voice. The RPF regime has grown more authoritarian, not less, and continues to consolidate power and restrict political and civil freedoms (Longman 2017; Straus and Waldorf 2011). This has significantly affected the peacebuilding project within the education sector, given that open and critical examination and discussions of present and past human rights violations are limited. The lived realities and perceptions of teachers and students often do not correspond with the government's prescribed narrative, demonstrating the complexities of a state-mandated project for peace and reconciliation.

The case of Rwanda spotlights the need for future research into education reform in postconflict contexts. Researchers could examine how countries both in sub-Saharan Africa and in other regions use education for peacebuilding and transitional justice, drawing cross-national comparisons in order to understand what factors might predict how countries teach about their pasts. Important factors might include different levels of democracy, the type of conflict (whether genocidal or civil war), whether the majority or the minority is in power after the conflict, the time elapsed since the conflict, and the degree to which transitional justice mechanisms are integrated into the educational system. Under what conditions is education for transitional justice and peacebuilding more likely to be effective? Under what circumstances is decoupling between policies and implementation likely to occur, particularly in divided societies or fragile contexts? What are the implications of this decoupling for local actors?

This book attests to both the potential power and the limitations of education in creating a new national identity and promoting human rights, reconciliation, and sustainable peace in a postconflict context. While the country has made impressive strides in expanding access to education and reforming the curriculum, what is taught in the classrooms does not openly and honestly address the past conflict. The findings also problematize the idea of education as a solution for resolving conflict and fostering a new identity. Can education promote reconciliation and a unified civic identity in the absence of a democratic and politically open environment? To what extent is education contributing to the broader sustainable peace agenda in Rwanda? Without solidarity across ethnic groups and newly created groups based on language and country of relocation, a more equitable distribution of resources, respect for human rights, and tolerance for diversity, reconciliation and sustainable peace may be difficult to obtain.

Research Methods
and Data Analysis

National Level: Policy, Curricula, and Textbooks

OFFICIAL DISCOURSE, AS codified in national-level curricula and textbooks, provides a proxy for "legitimate knowledge" sanctioned by the state (Apple and Christian-Smith 1991). In order to analyze the national policy discourse on education policy and reconciliation, I collected the available national education policies (N = 9), national curricula (N = 5), and textbooks (N = 11) for history, political education (civics), general paper (interdisciplinary social sciences course; GP), and social studies courses spanning the years 1999 through 2011. All of the textbooks in my sample were produced or approved by the national government of Rwanda and are thus representative of textbooks used in both government and private schools. In addition to analyzing national education documents, I conducted interviews with key informants (N = 11) in government institutions and academia in order to understand the influences and rationales underlying curricular and language policy, as well as to corroborate and elaborate on content in national education policy documents.

SURVEY DATA

I administered a survey with close-ended questions and scaled responses to gather data on students' views of education policies and curricula. Data gathered from the survey were used to assess students' attitudes on civic identity / citizenship, human rights, and reconciliation. I selected a random sample of 536 secondary school students in fifteen schools. I purposively selected three districts in three different provinces (Eastern, Western, and Kigali) in order to capture geographic variation and differences across urban-rural areas, the composition of the population, the dominant language, and the level of development. Level of development was measured through the proxy of poverty levels: according to household survey data, the three provinces, Kigali has the lowest levels of population living below the poverty line (16.8 percent), followed by the Eastern Province (42.6 percent) and the Western Province (48.4 percent) (National Institute of Statistics of Rwanda 2012, 14). I selected one district in the urban capital area of Kigali, one district in the Western Province near the border with the Democratic Republic of Congo (DRC), and one district in the Eastern Province near the Ugandan border (see figure 1).

I selected five schools in each district stratified by type of school (government, government-aided, private), location (urban/semiurban, rural/semirural), and level of school (basic education school, secondary school) from a comprehensive list of schools provided by the Ministry of Education. Table A.1 provides an overview of school characteristics in the sample. The schools were divided evenly between Kigali and the Eastern and Western Provinces, and between urban, semiurban, and rural locations. Approximately half of the schools (N = 8 in the sample were government schools, and the other half were government-aided (N = 3) or private schools (N = 4); the majority of schools had a religious affiliation (N = 10). Half of

TABLE A.I
School Characteristics (N = 15)

	Frequency
Province	
Kigali	5
East	5
West	5
Location	
Urban	4
Semiurban	6
Rural	5
Type	
Government	8
Government-aided	3
Private	4
Religious affiliation	
Secular	5
Religious	10
Level	
Nine years basic education	8
Secondary	7

the schools were nine-year basic education schools, and the other half were secondary boarding schools.

Within each school, I randomly selected between thirty and forty students, with an equal number of boys and girls, across different grade levels (senior 2–senior 6) to participate in the survey.[1] Table A.2 illustrates student characteristics. The sample was divided evenly between male and female students. A significant percentage (38 percent) of the students were orphans, meaning they have lost one or both of their parents. The age of students ranged from fifteen to twenty-four, with an average age

Table a.2
Student Characteristics (N = 536)

	Percentage/ Mean
Gender	
Male	48.88%
Female	51.12%
Family status	
Orphan (one or both parents)	38.43%
Identity	
Hutu	80.60%
Tutsi (survivor/returnee)	19.40%
Religion	
Catholic	38.25%
Protestant	29.48%
Other	32.37%
Second language (at home)	
English	38.90%
French	12.50%
Swahili	10.80%
Age	
Age (15–24)	17 (mean)
Grade	
Grade (S2–S6)	S3 (mean)

of seventeen, meaning that most of the students in the sample were born after the genocide or were very young during the genocide. Thus, memories and knowledge of the genocide are generally transmitted from the parents and family rather than from personal experience. Although one cannot directly ask a student to identity his/her ethnic identity, I used proxy questions, such as whether or not the student received the FARG (Fond d'Assistance aux les Rescapés du Génocide) scholarship (for Tutsi survivors) and whether they belonged to the AERG (Association des Etudiants et Elèves Rescapés du Génocide) club for Tutsi survivors and returnees in order to approximate ethnic identity. Since most of the students who receive the FARG scholarship or who participate in AERG are likely to be identified as "Tutsi," these serve as reliable indicators of identity.[2] Approximately 19 percent of the students in the sample were identified as survivors or returnees ("Tutsi"). While the majority of students speak Kinyarwanda at home, 39 percent reported speaking English at home and 13 percent as speaking French at home. Due to the higher proportion of students from schools in the Eastern Province and in Kigali, the sample has more Anglophone than Francophone students.

Paper surveys were administered to students during school hours in Kinyarwanda (the local language) with the help of two Rwandan research assistants.[3] Surveys were confidential and took approximately forty to sixty minutes for students to complete.[4]

In analyzing the survey data, I disaggregated responses by school and student level characteristics including region, urban/rural location, type of school, age, grade level, gender, and ethnicity. I ran descriptive statistics and comparisons of means across types of schools and students using STATA. I then created composite indexes across similar questions to explore themes in the data including civic identity and reconciliation. For certain indexes, such as reconciliation, I ran a multiple regression analysis (see chapter 5).

INTERVIEWS AND OBSERVATIONS

In order to supplement the survey data, I carried out interviews and observations in seven selected schools. I purposively selected seven schools from the three districts in order to maximize variation across the type of school and the location. Six of the schools were selected from the fifteen schools that participated

TABLE A.3

School Profiles: Interviews and Observations (N = 7)

	Government-Aided	Private	Government
Western	Semiurban, religious secondary school (School 1)		Rural, government basic education school (School 2)
Eastern		Rural, private, religious secondary school (School 3)	Semiurban, government secondary school (School 4)
Kigali	Urban, religious secondary school (School 7)	Semiurban, private secondary school (School 5)	Urban, government secondary school (School 6)

in the survey. A seventh school was included as a comparison case of a school that actively engages in teaching about the genocide and previously received support from an international NGO, Facing History and Ourselves.[5] In each district, I selected an urban and a rural school, including one government school (public school) and either a government-supported religious school or a private school.[6] I also selected a combination of basic education schools and regular secondary schools and religious and secular schools.[7] Hence, each selected school represents a case study of a particular prototype of school across the types of schools (government / government-supported / private and religious / secular), levels of quality (as measured by outcomes on the national exams and material resources), degree of assimilation into the English medium of instruction, and proximity to a neighboring country (Uganda or the DRC). Table A.3 provides an overview of the selected schools.

In each of the case study schools, I first met with the school director in order to learn general information about the student body, curricula, and school. I then conducted group and individual interviews with students, individual interviews with teachers, and classroom observations in history, civics, and GP courses. During group and individual interviews, I asked students semistructured questions about education policy and the curriculum—and specifically about topics related to citizenship, human rights, gender, reconciliation, and the genocide.[8] Interviews were carried out in Kinyarwanda, English, or French, or a mixture of several languages, depending on the preferences of the students. I worked with Rwandan research assistants when conducting interviews with students, as the students were not always fluent or comfortable speaking in English or French. The research assistants also served as cultural interpreters and helped the students feel more at ease.

Group Interviews with Students
I conducted three group interviews in each of the seven schools for a total of twenty-one group interviews with 109 students. I randomly selected three to six students who had also participated in the survey to participate in the group interview. I conducted group interviews with a mix of boys and girls, all boys, and all girls, from across different grade levels and ages, in order to observe differences in the group dynamic in mixed and same-sex discussions. I utilized a group interview technique with students to create a comfortable environment for students to share their ideas. Group interviews are useful when interviewing adolescents, as they may be more inclined to talk in a group. Further, group interviews improve the reliability of responses by allowing for the verification of multiple ideas across a group or for "consensus views" to emerge (Lewis 1992). The group interviews included questions about students' demographic and personal backgrounds (such as age, grade, religion, parents' occupation and education, funding for school, and clubs) and open-ended questions related to the language of instruction, topics in the curriculum (human rights, gender, citizenship), the genocide, and reconciliation.

Individual Interviews with Students

In addition to group interviews, I also conducted fourteen individual interviews with seven girls and seven boys from the group interviews in each of the schools. I purposively selected students for the individual interviews with the aim of maximizing heterogeneity across different student characteristics, including grade, age, religion, ethnic identity, and language (Seidman 2006). The individual student interviews provided an opportunity to further explore student views on more private or sensitive topics related to identity, ethnic groups, or the genocide.

Observations

In order to complement survey and interview data, I conducted ethnographic observations in the seven schools to understand students' experiences in the classroom and the interactions among students and between students and teachers. I spent approximately three to four weeks in each school over a period of seven months, attending different schools on different days, observing classes, and informally talking to teachers and students during breaks between classes and during lunch. I also attended several club meetings and observed extracurricular activities, including sports, art activities, and traditional dance. In addition, I read through student notebooks to understand what they were learning. I also observed twenty civics, history, and GP teachers across the seven schools teach three to eight lessons, depending on the class and the school. In total, I observed more than seventy hours of direct classroom instruction in history, political education (civics), and GP in the seven case study schools.

Interviews with Teachers

After I observed multiple classes and built a rapport and gained the trust of teachers, I then conducted individual interviews with twenty civics, history, and GP teachers across the seven

TABLE A.4
Teacher Characteristics (N = 20)

	Percentage/ Mean
Gender	
Male	85%
Female	15%
Identity	
Hutu	55%
Tutsi (survivor/returnee)	15%
Ugandan	30%
Language	
English	40%
French	60%
Religion	
Catholic	50%
Protestant	35%
Other	15%
Age	
Age (23–62)	35 (mean)
Level of education	
BA	80%
Diploma	20%

schools.[9] While the survey and interviews with students provide insight into the perspectives and knowledge of students, observations and interviews with teachers complement the student perspective. Teachers provide a link between the official national-level curriculum and what students perceive and understand; they serve as the conduits of information and knowledge, and thus play an important role in disseminating national ideas for building a national identity and in shaping understandings of the past. Table A.4 provides an overview of teacher characteristics.

The majority of the teachers were male (85 percent); only three teachers (15 percent) were female. While 15 percent of teachers self-identified as "survivors" or returnees, the majority (55 percent) was determined to be "Hutu." Additionally, 30 percent of the teachers were Ugandans who had come to Rwanda to work.[10] The majority of teachers were Francophone (60 percent), while 40 percent were Anglophone. Although the sample of teachers is small and not nationally representative, the characteristics are generally aligned with national trends.

ANALYSIS

For the analysis of qualitative interview and observation data, I conducted iterative content analysis of interview transcripts and field notes and coded for themes using NVivo qualitative software. I drew on both a deductive and an inductive approach for analysis, coding for predetermined and emergent codes. Predetermined codes derived from my theoretical construct and were linked to global norms such as human rights, global citizenship, gender, and reconciliation; emergent codes were common topics that appeared in the data.

I coded the interview transcriptions and field notes through an initial "open coding," in order to identify important themes and core unifying concepts; thereafter, I conducted a "focused" coding from a list of specifically defined codes that I identified (Emerson, Fretz, and Shaw 1995, 143). Throughout the coding process, I wrote coding memos on emerging ideas, themes, and connections across codes.

LIMITATIONS AND ISSUES
OF VALIDITY

Several issues and limitations arise in the process of collecting field data in a postconflict and politically restrictive context. One limitation of my research is linked to the sensitive nature of perceptions of human and citizenship rights, civic culture, ethnicity, reconciliation, and genocide. Due to the difficulties of openly discussing these topics, respondents do not always answer truthfully, particularly around sensitive issues. However, King (2009) argues that the methodological challenges in carrying out research in post-genocide Rwanda, including the contested historical memories and divergent group narratives, actually provide insight into societal structures. While it was not always possible to pose direct questions about identity or the genocide, the use of various data sources, including observations, allowed for the validation and expansion of findings from the survey data though interview and observation data. Furthermore, divergent narratives across groups provided insight into circumstances under which individuals present the official narrative as their own perspective or present narratives that depart from the official narrative.

I utilized multiple data sources across the national and school levels in order to provide a more reliable measure of attitudes and perceptions among students and teachers. The survey data provide an overview of general trends in the selected schools; however, the sample of students is not nationally representative and cannot necessarily be generalized beyond the selected schools. The survey instrument was pretested in order to ensure internal validity. However, due to the response bias inherent in surveys, especially in restrictive political environments, it is likely that not all students answered all of the questions truthfully. I attempted to address these concerns by reassuring all respondents that surveys were anonymous. The interviews and observations allowed me to explore in detail specific issues that arose from the survey data. Data from interviews and classroom observations were selected to maximize variation; thus, the information gleaned from the selected case study schools is not necessarily generalizable to other schools in Rwanda or to other postconflict countries.

TABLE A.5
Mean Reconciliation Index across Groups

	Mean	Test Statistic	Significance
Gender		0.297	0.767
Girl	0.013		
Boy	−0.013		
Identity		1.989	0.047
Tutsi	0.178		
Hutu	−0.042		
Father's SES		3.39	0.035
High	−0.113		
Middle	−0.158		
Low	0.085		
School type		9.05	0.0001
Government	0.145		
Government-aided	−0.017		
Private	−0.290		
Province		5.07	0.006
Eastern	0.184		
Western	−0.039		
Kigali	−0.147		

NOTE: Two-sided T-test conducted for groups with two categories; F-test conducted for groups with three categories. SES = socioeconomic status.

DESCRIPTIVE AND MULTIVARIATE
ANALYSIS OF SURVEY DATA

Table A.5 illustrates the variation in the mean reconciliation across different groups and schools. Although girls have a slightly higher mean value compared to boys, the difference is not statistically significant. Tutsi students have a higher and statically significant reconciliation index compared to Hutu students; students from poorer backgrounds have a higher (and

Table a.6
Descriptive Statistics (N = 536)

Variable	Mean	SD	Min	Max
Reconciliation index	0.00	1.00	−3.06	1.51
Gender	0.51	0.50	0	1
Age	17.23	1.68	15	24
Tutsi	0.19	0.40	0	1
English at home	0.39	0.49	0	1
Trust neighbors	2.88	0.88	1	4
Citizenship	2.58	0.66	1	3
Father SES	1.45	0.64	1	3
Catholic	0.38	0.49	0	1
Government-aided school	0.20	0.40	0	1
Government school	0.54	0.50	0	1
Western Province	0.34	0.47	0	1
Eastern Province	0.33	0.47	0	1
Urban	0.27	0.44	0	1
Semiurban/rural	0.40	0.49	0	1

NOTE: SES = socioeconomic status.

statistically significant) value on the index compared to those from middle and low socioeconomic backgrounds. Students in government schools have a higher, statistically significant mean level of reconciliation compared to students in government-aided and private schools. Students in schools in the Eastern Province have a higher and statistically significant mean on the reconciliation index compared to students in the Western Province and Kigali.

Table A.6 shows the descriptive statistics from the survey data.

Table A.7 shows the results from the multivariate analysis of the reconciliation index. Model 1 includes student demographic

TABLE A.7

Predictors of Reconciliation Index with Multivariate Regression (OLS)

	Model 1	Model 2	Model 3
Girl	0.016	0.098	0.125+
	(0.070)	(0.070)	(0.070)
Age	−0.035	−0.031	−0.011
	(0.020)	(0.020)	(0.020)
Tutsi	0.221+	0.163	0.231+
	(0.120)	(0.100)	(0.110)
Home language English	0.069	0.058	0.092
	(0.060)	(0.060)	(0.060)
Father's SES	−0.161+	−0.152*	−0.08
	−0.08	−0.06	−0.06
Catholic	0.017	0.018	0.026
	(0.100)	(0.090)	(0.080)
I can trust my neighbors		0.179*	0.178**
		(0.060)	(0.060)
Identify as a citizen of Rwanda		0.378***	0.343***
		(0.090)	(0.080)
Government-aided school			0.184
			−0.17
Government school			0.276+
			(0.150)
Western Province			0.085
			(0.130)
Eastern Province			0.264+
			(0.130)
Constant	0.747+	−0.840*	−1.553**
	(0.380)	(0.360)	(0.450)
N	531	530	530
R2	0.0214	0.1215	0.1482

NOTE: ***p < .001; **p < .01; *p < .05; +p < .10. SES = socioeconomic status. *Reference categories*: Tutsi–Hutu; Catholic–non-Catholic; Western Province–Eastern Province–Kigali.

TABLE A.8

Multinomial Logistic Regression Results Used to Calculate Marginal Analysis (Low Level of Reconciliation as Baseline) (N = 531)

	Medium vs. Low Level of Reconciliation	High vs. Low Level of Reconciliation
Girl	0.265 (0.246)	0.403★ (0.172)
Age	−0.122 (0.081)	−0.016 (0.073)
Tutsi	0.119 (0.218)	0.436+ (0.262)
Home language English	−0.143 (0.262)	0.220 (0.176)
Father's SES	0.186 (0.214)	−0.335 (0.246)
Catholic	−0.224 (0.387)	0.039 (0.253)
Government-aided school	−0.013 (0.183)	−0.004 (0.348)
Private school	−0.402+ (0.205)	−0.521 (0.385)
Eastern Province	0.446 (0.273)	0.480 (0.353)
Western Province	0.649★★ (0.226)	0.031 (0.422)
Trust my neighbors		
Somewhat disagree	0.701 (0.558)	−0.228 (0.408)
Somewhat agree	1.297★ (0.558)	0.015 (0.398)
Strongly agree	1.733★★ (0.652)	1.111★ (0.461)
Identify as citizen of Rwanda		
Somewhat	0.317 (0.524)	0.791★ (0.315)
A lot	0.630 (0.489)	1.322★★★ (0.284)

NOTE: ★★★p < .001; ★★ p <.01; ★p < .05; +p < .10. SES = socioeconomic status.

variables, including gender, age, ethnic identity, whether the subject spoke English at home, father's socioeconomic status, and religion (Catholic). Results show that Tutsi students, meaning that they are genocide survivors or returnees (as measured by participation in FARG and AERG), have higher levels of reconciliation compared to non-Tutsi students. Students from higher socioeconomic backgrounds are less likely to support the reconciliation narrative compared to those from lower levels, although this difference becomes nonsignificant in model 3. Model 2 includes students' perception of trust—the degree to which they trust their neighbors—and the degree to which they identify as citizens of Rwanda as proxies for national identity. Both measures are positive and highly significant, meaning that students who have higher degrees of trust and strongly identify as citizens of Rwanda are more likely to have higher levels of reconciliation. Model 3, which explains the most variation (R-squared of 14 percent), includes school-level variables, such as whether or not the school was a government or government-aided school (compared to a private school) and the location of the school in the Western and Eastern Provinces (compared to Kigali).

Results from model 3, which includes both student and school-level variables, indicate that, controlling for other background variables, girls have higher levels on the reconciliation index compared to boys. Students with a Tutsi ethnic identity exhibit higher values on the reconciliation index (significant at the p < .10 level). Students who report higher levels of trust and who strongly identify as citizens of Rwanda have significantly higher reported levels on the reconciliation index (significant at the p < .001 level). In terms of school variables, students in government schools report marginally significant higher levels on the reconciliation index compared to students in private schools; students in schools in the Eastern Province have higher levels of ·reconciliation as compared to students in Kigali.

Table A.8 shows the results from the multinomial logistic regression of the reconciliation index divided into low, medium, and high levels of reconciliation and the results used to calculate the predicted probabilities of statistically significant variables controlling for background variables.

APPENDIX B

National Policy Documents, Curricula, and Textbooks

BELOW IS A purposeful selection of the main national policy documents related to education, curricula, and textbooks used in the post-genocide period, which I used in my analysis.

NATIONAL POLICY DOCUMENTS

Ministry of Education (MINEDUC). 2003a. *Education for All (EFA) Plan of Action.* Kigali: MINEDUC.

————. 2003b. *Education Sector Policy.* Kigali: MINEDUC.

————. 2006. *Education Sector Strategic Plan, 2006–2010.* Kigali: MINEDUC.

————. 2008a. *Education Sector Strategic Plan, 2008–2012.* Kigali: MINEDUC.

————. 2008b. *Girls' Education Policy.* Kigali: MINEDUC.

————. 2008c. *Nine Years Basic Education Implementation.* Kigali: MINEDUC.

————. 2010. *Education Sector Strategic Plan, 2010–2015.* Kigali: MINEDUC.

Ministry of Finance and Economic Planning (MINECOFIN). 2000. *Rwanda Vision 2020.* Kigali: MINECOFIN.

————. 2007. *Economic Development and Poverty Reduction Strategy (PRSP), 2008–2012.* Kigali: MINECOFIN.

Textbooks

Bamusananire, Emmanuel. 2011. *History of Africa for Rwanda Secondary Schools: Advanced Level*. Kampala, Uganda: Fountain Publishers.

Bamusananire, Emmanuel, Joseph Byiringiro, Augustine Munyakazi, and Johnson Ntagaramba. 2006a. *Primary Social Studies: Pupil's Book 4*. Kigali: Macmillan Rwanda.

———. 2006b. *Primary Social Studies: Pupil's Book 5*. Kigali: Macmillan Rwanda.

———. 2006c. *Primary Social Studies: Pupil's Book 6*. Kigali: Macmillan Rwanda.

Bamusananire, Emmanuel, and Dorothy Ntege. 2010a. *New Junior Secondary History Book 1*. Kampala, Uganda: Netmedia Publishers.

———. 2010b. *New Junior Secondary History Book 2*. Kampala, Uganda: Netmedia Publishers.

———. 2010c. *New Junior Secondary History Book 3*. Kampala, Uganda: Netmedia Publishers.

Direction des Programmes de l'Enseignement Secondaire. 1989. *Histoire du Rwanda*: 2nd Partie. Kigali: Direction des Programmes de l'Enseignement Secondaire.

Munezero, Catherine, Pharouk Isaac, Thomas Gichana, and Martin Habimana. 2017. *Social Studies for Rwandan Primary Schools*. Nairobi, Kenya: Spotlight Publishers.

National Curriculum Development Center (NCDC). 2004. *A Guide to Civic Education: Life Skills for Rwanda Primary Schools, Upper Primary Level*. Kigali: NCDC.

———. 2008a. *A Guide to Political Education: Volume 1*. Kigali: NCDC.

———. 2008b. *A Guide to Political Education: Volume 2*. Kigali: NCDC.

———. 2010a. *The History of Rwanda Secondary Schools—Teacher's Guide*. Kigali: NCDC.

Sebazungu, Theophile, Assa Okoth, and Ndaloh Agumba. 2016. *History and Citizenship for Rwandan Schools.* Kigali: East African Education Publishers.

CURRICULA

National Curriculum Development Center (NCDC). 1999. *Political Education Programme for Advanced Level.* Kigali: NCDC.
————. 2008c. *History Program for Ordinary Level.* Kigali: NCDC.
————. 2008d. *Political Education Curriculum for Secondary Schools.* Kigali: NCDC.
————. 2010b. *History Program for Advanced Level Secondary School.* Kigali: NCDC.
————. 2010c. *Social Studies Curriculum: Grade 1–6.* Kigali: NCDC.
————. 2011. *General Paper Curriculum for Secondary Schools: Advanced Level.* Kigali: NCDC.
Rwanda Education Board (REB). 2015. *Competence-Based Curriculum Framework Pre-Primary to Upper Secondary.* Kigali: REB/MINEDUC.

Acknowledgments

I am immensely grateful to everyone who has made this book possible. I would first like to thank my mentors at Stanford, who provided feedback and inspiration for the foundation of this endeavor: Francisco Ramirez, John Meyer, Prudence Carter, Christine Min Wotipka, and Richard Roberts. I am especially grateful to Francisco Ramirez and John Meyer for the continued feedback on various iterations of my book, and to Prudence Carter for her advice on the book proposal.

I would also like to thank my friends and colleagues who provided insightful feedback on different parts of the book and support throughout the process: Elizabeth Buckner, Naomi Moland, and Julia Lerch for their great input and inspiring conversations over the past few years; Tim Williams for his careful reading and particular attention to the case of Rwanda; and Oren Pizmony-Levy for his constant encouragement and feedback on my analysis sections. I would also like to thank Margaret Irving, Brenda Jarillo Rabling, Magda Gross, Dijana Tiplic, and Max Retig for comments and input on earlier versions. I am also grateful to those friends and colleagues who provided advice at different stages of the project, including Lesley Bartlett, Elizabeth Anderson Worden, Dana Burde, Rachel Wahl, Bill Gaudelli, Elisabeth King, Monisha Bajaj, Patricia Bromley, and Michelle Bellino.

My amazing students at Teachers College, Columbia University also read various sections and provided great comments, as well as research support. I owe my gratitude to Sandra Sirota,

215

Marlana Salmon-Letelier, Kayum Ahmed, Diana Rodríguez-Gómez, Anya Azayerva Valente, Kevin Nascimento, Sarah Lewinger, and Paula Mantilla-Blanco. And special thanks to Danielle Falk, who provided not only incredible feedback on the entire manuscript but also amazing research assistance and support throughout the writing of this book. Thank you for your endless enthusiasm and your detail-oriented approach and knowledge of Rwanda.

I am thankful to my colleagues at Teachers College for their support and collegiality throughout this process: Herve Varenne, Gita Steiner-Khamsi, Mary Mendenhall, Regina Cortina, Carol Bensen, Felisa Tibbitts, Hope Leichter, Nicholas Limerick, Fenot Aklog, Camilla Addy, and Tom James.

I would also like to especially thank Nigel Quiney for his amazing developmental editorial support and for helping me to reframe my research for a broader audience, as well as for his careful editing. And thank you to Lisa Banning and her team at Rutgers University Press for all of their great work. I would also like to thank the three anonymous reviewers who provided detailed feedback on the manuscript, which strengthened the book.

Additionally, I am especially grateful for the amazing community in Rwanda who inspired and supported me during my field research—in particular, my fabulous research assistants, as well as my wonderful friends. In addition, I would like to thank Dr. Shirley Randall at the Center for Gender, Development, and Culture at the Kigali Institute of Education for all of her support throughout the research process and for welcoming me into her home and helping me to establish my initial contacts. I would also like to acknowledge all of the amazing teachers and students I met during my research—thank you for all that you have taught me about Rwanda. Also, I would like to acknowledge the translation assistance provided by my research assistants at Stanford, Annie Kramer and Aimee Uwilingiyimana.

My research and fieldwork in Rwanda and subsequent writing would not have been possible without the support of numerous grants and fellowships, including the National Science Foundation (NSF) Sociology Dissertation Grant, the Boren Language Fellowship, the Stanford Center for International Conflict Negotiation (SCICN) Goldsmith Grant, the Stanford Center on Philanthropy and Civil Society (PACS) Grant, the Stanford Vice-Provost for Graduate Education (VPGE) Diversity Dissertation Research Opportunity (DDRO) Grant, the Stanford Graduate School of Education Dissertation Support Grant (DSG), and the Clayman Graduate Dissertation Fellowship (GDF).

On a more personal note, I would like to thank my family for all of their love and emotional support throughout this process—my parents, David and Susan; my late grandmother, Jean; my cousins Barbara, Kate, and Chidi and the girls; and especially my sister Alexandra. I am so grateful for all of your support and input on every stage of this project, and especially for your amazing editing skills. I also would like to thank my closest friends, who have sustained me from near and far: Mia, Sarah M., Caitrin, Hannah, Ilanit, Kate, Janie, Ewa, Maria, Momo, Sierra, and Sarah P. And last, I would like to thank my husband, Khalid, for his constant encouragement and love throughout the process and for inspiring me to pursue my passion. And of course our son, Rafa, for all his love and patience while I wrote the book.

Notes

Chapter 1 Introduction

1. I use "Hutu" and "Tutsi" to refer to the singular and plural of these groups; however, others refer to Hutus and Tutsis in the plural.
2. For general social science literature on peacebuilding, see, for example, Autesserre (2014); Barnett (2006); Berdal and Suhrke (2012); Doyle and Sambanis (2000); Lederach (1997).
3. The Government of National Unity, composed of both Hutu and Tutsi politicians, was based on power-sharing arrangements across political parties as outlined in the 1993 Arusha Peace Agreement.
4. Information on the National Unity and Reconciliation Commission is available at http://www.nurc.gov.rw/.
5. The survey was written in English and then translated by my Rwandan research assistants into Kinyarwanda. Students completed the survey in Kinyarwanda.
6. I use pseudonyms to protect students' and teacher's identities.
7. General paper is a mandatory interdisciplinary social sciences course, at the advanced level of secondary schools. The course covers a range of topics, including health, society, politics, and culture.
8. All of the interviews were transcribed in the original language and then translated into English by my Rwandan research assistants. I double-checked the interviews translated from French to English to ensure that the translations were accurate.

Chapter 2 The Role of Education in Transitional Justice, Peacebuilding, and Reconciliation

1. For more information on the ICTR, see http://unictr.unmict.org/en/tribunal.
2. The *gacaca* courts were created through the Organic Law No. 40/2000 of January 26, 2001.
3. The net enrollment rate is defined by the UNESCO Institute of Statistics as the "total number of pupils or students in the theoretical age group for a given level of education enrolled in that level, expressed as a percentage of the total population in that age group." http://glossary.uis.unesco.org/glossary/en/term/2048/en.

219

4. The gross enrollment ratio is defined by the UNESCO Institute of Statistics as the "number of pupils or students enrolled in a given level of education, regardless of age, expressed as a percentage of the official school-age population corresponding to the same level of education." http://glossary.uis.unesco.org/glossary/en/term/2048/en.

5. The transition rate is defined by the UNESCO Institute of Statistics as "the number of pupils admitted to the first grade of a higher level of education in a given year, expressed as a percentage of the number of pupils enrolled in the final grade of the lower level of education in the previous year." http://glossary.uis.unesco.org/glossary/en/term/2048/en.

6. The linguistic shift was also viewed as a political move to distance Rwanda from the Francophone community. Several political issues precipitated the announcement of the policy, including strained relations between Rwanda and France stemming from France's support of the genocidal government through Opération Turquoise, which created a safe zone that benefited the Hutu Interahamwe, or government-supported militia groups. In 2006, France issued a controversial report addressing responsibility for the assassination of former Rwandan president Habyarimana, accusing President Kagame and the RPF of shooting down the president's plane. In response, Rwanda closed the French embassy for three years. In 2008, the Rwandan government formed a committee to document France's role in the genocide. Thus, political tensions between Rwanda and France were a factor in the switch from French to English.

7. The NCDC is now under the auspices of the Rwandan Education Board, which was established in 2011.

8. "Ordinary level" refers to lower secondary level (grades 7, 8, 9); "advanced level" refers to the upper secondary level (grades 10, 11, 12).

9. These history books were published through a Ugandan publishing house, but were approved by the national government and follow the official government narrative regarding the genocide.

Chapter 3 Constructing Citizenship and a Post-Genocide Identity

1. Although there are three ethnic groups in Rwanda (Hutu, Tutsi, and Twa), Twa constitute only 1 to 3 percent of the population and are generally not included in debates about ethnicity. However, in post-genocide Rwanda, Twa are referred to as the "historically marginalized group" (*abasigajwe ihyuma n'amateka*) and are thus singled out as a separate group.

2. Translated from original document in Kinyarwanda on Ndi

Umunyarwanda available on the NURC website, http://www.nurc
.gov.rw/fileadmin/templates/nurc/documents/NDI_UMUNYA
RWANDA.pdf.

3. I also tested for differences by socioeconomic status, gender, religion, ethnicity, and school level but did not find statistically significant differences.

4. The World Values Survey is a cross-national survey on political and social attitudes.

5. In Kinyarwanda, *ubwoko*, or *amoko* in the plural, means both ethnic group and clan. Clan is defined as the origin of one's ancestors, whereas ethnic group refers to Tutsi, Hutu, or Twa. The distinction is dependent on the context in which the word is used.

6. The terms "social groups" and "social classes" were first used in Rwanda in the precolonial period to refer to differences among so-called ethnic groups.

7. Those who were in Rwanda during the genocide and are not "survivors" are assumed to be *génocidaires*, complicit in the killings, or children of *génocidaires* by virtue of their Hutu identity (see Burnet [2009]; Eltringham [2004]; Vidal [2004]).

8. For more information on FARG, see http://www.farg.gov.rw.

9. Discussing war crimes committed by the RPF after the genocide is also a taboo topic.

10. FARG determines one's status as a survivor in consultation with local authorities, who form a committee at the *utugari* (cell) level comprising survivors, local authorities, and representatives of the *imidugudu* (villages). The committee creates a list of student survivors in their area that is sent to the sector (*imirenge*) and the district (*uturere*) levels.

11. NAR clubs are supported by the NGO of the same name, which was founded with the intention of bringing together students from different backgrounds—survivors, returnees, and children of *génocidaires*—to foster dialogue and peacebuilding (Interview, September 2012).

12. For more information about AERG, see http://www.aerg.org.rw.

13. These informal terms are used to refer to different groups of returnees based on where they were living before the genocide; these returnees are assumed to be Tutsi. Hutu who fled to the DRC in 1994 following the genocide and who returned in 1996 and 1997 are known as *abahutse* or *abatingitingi*; these refugees are distinguished from Tutsi refugees who fled to the Congo, Burundi, Uganda, and Tanzania between 1959 and 1964 and who returned after the genocide and are known collectively as *abarutashye* (Burnet 2009, 89).

14. An estimated 40 percent of the post-genocide Rwandan population returned from other countries after the genocide (Purdeková 2015, 5). This number includes an estimated 700,000

"old caseload refugees," or Tutsi returnees who fled to other countries before the genocide, primarily in 1959, and returned after the genocide (Prunier 1995). Approximately 2 million "new caseload refugees," or Hutu, fled in 1994 to Tanzania and to the DCR and returned in 1996 and 1997 (Bruce 2007).

15. A 2009 study funded by the British Council found that less than 10 percent of secondary teachers were proficient in English at the upper intermediate level (Lynd 2010).

Chapter 4 Using and Abusing Human Rights Norms

1. Women hold 63.8 percent of the seats in parliament according to 2016 data from the Inter-Parliamentary Union.

2. For more details on alleged human rights violations in the DRC, see the UN Security Council Resolution 1533 (2012) (http://www.nytimes.com/interactive/2012/12/01/world/africa/01congo-document.html) and Human Rights Watch (http://www.hrw.org/news/2012/11/20/dr-congo-us-should-urge-rwanda-end-m23-support).

3. The Genocide Ideology Law (2008) was revised in 2013 to eliminate ambiguous language.

4. "Interahamwe" refers to the perpetrators of the genocide who fled to the DRC.

Chapter 5 Addressing the Genocide and Promoting Reconciliation

1. This contradiction was evident at the closing ceremony of *gacaca* in June 2012, where President Kagame contrasted the value and effectiveness of *gacaca* as a local Rwandan solution with the record of the ICTR. In the same speech, however, he also thanked Rwanda's development partners for supporting *gacaca*. For the full transcript of the speech, see http://gacaca.rw/opinion/speech-by-president-paul-kagame-at-the-closing-of-the-gacaca/.

2. For more details on official memorial sites, see http://cnlg.gov.rw/genocide/memorial-sites/; for more on unofficial sites, see http://maps.cga.harvard.edu/rwanda/home.html.

3. For more information on the CNLG, see http://cnlg.gov.rw.

4. For more information on Kwibuka, see https://kwibuka.rw/.

5. Children between the ages of twelve and eighteen convicted of the crime of genocide ideology serve their sentences in a rehabilitation center, according to Article 9 of Law No. 18/2008 of July 7, 2008, "Relating to the Punishment of the Crime of Genocide Ideology"; see http://www.cnlg.gov.rw/genocide-laws.

6. Translated from the original in French: "La population Rwandaise

proprement dite se divise en trois groupes socialement différenciés et hiérarchisés. Il y a les Batwa, les Bahutu et les Batutsi."

7. For more information on the World Values Survey, see http://www.worldvaluessurvey.org/.

8. Survey questions were combined into a scale using confirmatory principal-component factor analysis. The scale has a high degree of reliability, as measured by the Cronbach's alpha value of .78. The reconciliation index range has a maximum value of 1.5 and a minimum value of −3, with a mean of 0.

9. I used cluster robust standard errors to account for the fact that students are clustered across different schools so that regression model errors could be correlated within schools.

APPENDIX A: RESEARCH METHODS AND DATA ANALYSIS

1. I randomly selected an equal number of boys and girls across different grade levels from a list of all students enrolled in the school.

2. In an effort to avoid the reification of an identity that is generally considered taboo and illegal, I do not always identify respondents through their "ethnic identity." Rather, I sought to identify them in terms of pertinent experiences. However, in some cases and in particular contexts, the respondents signaled their "ethnic identity" directly or indirectly; in these instances, I include a proxy of "ethnic identity" where it is important for interpretation.

3. The survey instrument was translated from English to Kinyarwanda and pretested with a class of students in order to check for consistency and internal reliability of the questions.

4. Students were briefed about the project, and the Institutional Review Board protocol was explained. Informed consent was received orally from all participants.

5. More information about Facing History and Ourselves is available at http://www.facing.org/.

6. Government schools receive funding from the government; government-supported schools receive funding from the government to pay for teachers' salaries and are usually religious schools; private schools do not receive government funds but must follow the national curricula.

7. Basic education schools are primary schools that were recently converted into nine-year and twelve-year basic education schools, whereas regular secondary schools are generally boarding schools of higher quality.

8. I use pseudonyms for the names of students and teachers.

9. I conducted interviews with two to four teachers in each school, depending on the configuration in each school. In some schools,

the same teacher taught both the history and political education classes or GP classes.

10. With the change from French to English, the government has made an effort to bring in Anglophone teachers from Uganda and Kenya. Ugandans constituted a noticeable portion of the teachers in my sample, particularly in the higher-quality schools.

References

Abbott, Pamela, Roger Sapsford, and Agnes Binagwaho. 2017. "Learning from Success: How Rwanda Achieved the Millennium Development Goals for Health." *World Development* 92(Supplement C): 103–116.

Abbott, Pamela, Roger Sapsford, and John Rwirahira. 2015. "Rwanda's Potential to Achieve the Millennium Development Goals for Education." *International Journal of Educational Development* 40: 117–125.

Abowitz, Kathleen Knight, and Jason Harnish. 2006. "Contemporary Discourses of Citizenship." *Review of Educational Research* 76(4): 653–690.

Abramowitz, Sharon, and Mary H. Moran. 2012. "International Human Rights, Gender-Based Violence, and Local Discourses of Abuse in Postconflict Liberia: A Problem of 'Culture'?" *African Studies Review* 55(2): 119–146.

Aegis Trust. 2017. *Education for Sustainable Peace in Rwanda*. Kigali: Aegis Trust.

Akhavan, Payam. 2001. "Beyond Impunity: Can International Criminal Justice Prevent Future Atrocities?" *American Journal of International Law* 95(1): 7–31.

Almond, Gabriel A., and Sidney Verba. 1963. *The Civic Culture: Political Attitudes and Democracy in Five Nations*. Princeton, NJ: Princeton University Press.

Amnesty International. 2010. *Safer to Stay Silent: The Chilling Effect of Rwanda's Laws on "Genocide Ideology" and "Sectarianism."* London: Amnesty International.

———. 2012. *Rwanda: Annual Report*. London: Amnesty International. http://www.amnesty.org/en/region/rwanda/report-2012.

———. 2017. *Setting the Scene for Elections: Two Decades of Silencing Dissent in Rwanda*. London: Amnesty International.

Anderson, Benedict. 2006. *Imagined Communities: Reflections on the Origin and Spread of Nationalism*. Rev. ed. London: Verso.

Anderson-Levitt, Kathryn M. 2012. "Complicating the Concept of Culture." *Comparative Education* 48(4): 441–454.

225

Ansoms, An, and Giuseppe D. Cioffo. 2016. "The Exemplary Citizen on the Exemplary Hill: The Production of Political Subjects in Contemporary Rural Rwanda." *Development and Change* 47(6): 1247–68.

Apple, Michael W., and Linda K. Christian-Smith. 1991. *The Politics of the Textbook*. New York: Routledge.

Arendt, Hannah. 1985. *The Human Condition*. Chicago: University of Chicago Press.

Assman, Aleida. 2012. "Limits of Understanding: Generational Identities in Recent German Memory Literature." In *Victims and Perpetrators: 1933–1945*, edited by L. Cohen-Pfister and D. Wienroeder-Skinner, 29–48. Berlin: De Gruyter.

Autesserre, Séverine. 2014. *Peaceland: Conflict Resolution and the Everyday Politics of International Intervention*. New York: Cambridge University Press.

Avery, Patricia G., and Annette M. Simmons. 2001. "Civic Life as Conveyed in United States Civics and History Textbooks." *International Journal of Social Education* 15(2): 105–130.

Badat, Saleem, and Yusuf Sayed. 2014. "Post-1994 South African Education: The Challenge of Social Justice." *Annals of the American Academy of Political and Social Science* 652(1): 127–148.

Bajaj, Monisha. 2011a. "Human Rights Education: Ideology, Location, and Approaches." *Human Rights Quarterly* 33(2): 481–508.

———. 2011b. *Schooling for Social Change: The Rise and Impact of Human Rights Education in India*. New York: Continuum.

Banks, James A. 2004. "Teaching for Social Justice, Diversity, and Citizenship in a Global World." *Educational Forum* 68(4): 296–305.

Barahona De Brito, Alexandra, Carmen Gonzalez Enriquez, and Paloma Aguilar, eds. 2001. *The Politics of Memory and Democratization: Transitional Justice in Democratizing Societies*. Oxford: Oxford University Press.

Barnett, Michael. 2006. "Building a Republican Peace: Stabilizing States after War." *International Security* 30(4): 87–112.

Bar-Tal, Daniel, and Yigal Rosen. 2009. "Peace Education in Societies Involved in Intractable Conflicts: Direct and Indirect Models." *Review of Educational Research* 79(2): 557–575.

Bartlett, Lesley, and Frances Vavrus. 2016. *Rethinking Case Study Research: A Comparative Approach*. New York: Routledge.

Barton, Keith C. 2015. "Young Adolescents' Positioning of Human Rights: Findings from Colombia, Northern Ireland, Republic of Ireland and the United States." *Research in Comparative and International Education* 10(1): 48–70.

Bass, Gary Jonathan. 2014. *Stay the Hand of Vengeance: The Politics of War Crimes Tribunals*. Princeton, NJ: Princeton University Press.

Beck, Colin J., Gili S. Drori, and John W. Meyer. 2012. "World Influences on Human Rights Language in Constitutions: A Cross-National Study." *International Sociology* 27(4): 483–501.

Bekerman, Zvi, and Michalinos Zembylas. 2011. *Teaching Contested Narratives: Identity, Memory and Reconciliation in Peace Education and Beyond.* Cambridge: Cambridge University Press.

Bellino, Michelle J. 2015. "So That We Do Not Fall Again: History Education and Citizenship in 'Postwar' Guatemala." *Comparative Education Review* 60(1): 58–79.

———. 2017. "Whose Past, Whose Present? Historical Memory among the 'Postwar' Generation in Guatemala." In *(Re)Constructing Memory: School Textbooks and the Imagination of the Nation*, edited by J. Williams, 131–152. Rotterdam: Sense.

Bellino, Michelle J., Julia Paulson, and Elizabeth Anderson Worden. 2017. "Working through Difficult Pasts: Toward Thick Democracy and Transitional Justice in Education." *Comparative Education* 53(3): 313–332.

Bendix, Reinhard. 1964. *Nation-Building and Citizenship: Studies of Our Changing Social Order.* New York: Wiley.

Bentrovato, Denise. 2015. *Narrating and Teaching the Nation: The Politics of Education in Pre- and Post-Genocide Rwanda.* Gottingen: Vandenhoeck & Ruprecht.

Berdal, Mats R., and Astri Suhrke, eds. 2012. *The Peace in Between: Post-War Violence and Peacebuilding.* London: Routledge.

Berry, Marie E. 2015. "When 'Bright Futures' Fade: Paradoxes of Women's Empowerment in Rwanda." *Signs* 41(1): 1–27.

Bourdieu, Pierre. 1991. *Language and Symbolic Power.* Cambridge, MA: Harvard University Press.

Boutros-Ghali, Boutros. 1992. *An Agenda for Peace: Preventive Diplomacy, Peacemaking, and Peace-Keeping.* New York: United Nations.

Bromley, Patricia, and Walter W. Powell. 2012. "From Smoke and Mirrors to Walking the Talk: Decoupling in the Contemporary World." *Academy of Management Annals* 6(1): 483–530.

Brubaker, Rogers. 2004. *Ethnicity without Groups.* Cambridge, MA: Harvard University Press.

Bruce, John W. 2007. "Returnee Land Access: Lessons from Rwanda." Humanitarian Policy Group, https://www.odi.org/sites/odi.org.uk/files/odi-assets/publications-opinion-files/4176.pdf.

Buckland, Peter. 2005. *Reshaping the Future: Education and Postconflict Reconstruction.* Washington, DC: World Bank Publications.

Buckley-Zistel, Susanne. 2006. "Dividing and Uniting: The Use of Citizenship Discourses in Conflict and Reconciliation in Rwanda." *Global Society* 20(1): 101–113.

Buckner, Elizabeth, and Susan Garnett Russell. 2013. "Portraying the Global: Cross-National Trends in Textbooks' Portrayal of Globalization and Global Citizenship." *International Studies Quarterly* 57(4): 738–750.

Bull, Anna Cento, and Hans Lauge Hansen. 2016. "On Agonistic Memory." *Memory Studies* 9(4): 390–404.

Burde, Dana. 2014. *Schools for Conflict or for Peace in Afghanistan.* New York: Columbia University Press.

Burnet, Jennie E. 2008. "Gender Balance and the Meanings of Women in Governance in Post-Genocide Rwanda." *African Affairs* 107(428): 361–386.

————. 2009. "Whose Genocide? Whose Truth? Representations of Victim and Perpetrator in Rwanda." In *Genocide: Truth, Memory, and Representation*, edited by A. L. Hinton and K. L. O'Neill, 80–109. Durham, NC: Duke University Press.

————. 2011. "Women Have Found Respect: Gender Quotas, Symbolic Representation, and Female Empowerment in Rwanda." *Politics and Gender* 7(3): 303–334.

Bush, Kenneth D., and Diana Saltarelli, eds. 2000. *The Two Faces of Education in Ethnic Conflict.* Florence, Italy: UNICEF and the Innocenti Research Centre. http://www.unicef-irc.org/publications /pdf/insight4.pdf.

Carter, Prudence L. 2012. *Stubborn Roots: Race, Culture, and Inequality in U.S. and South African Schools.* Oxford: Oxford University Press.

Cha, Yun-Kyung. 2007. "The Spread of English Language Instruction in the Primary School." In *School Knowledge in Comparative and Historical Perspective: Changing Curricula in Primary and Secondary Education*, edited by Aaron Benavot and Cecilia Braslavsky, 55–71. Dordrecht, The Netherlands: Springer Netherlands.

Chakravarty, Anuradha. 2015. *Investing in Authoritarian Rule: Punishment and Patronage in Rwanda's Gacaca Courts for Genocide Crimes.* New York: Cambridge University Press.

Cheng, Sealing. 2011. "The Paradox of Vernacularization: Women's Human Rights and the Gendering of Nationhood." *Anthropological Quarterly* 84(2): 475–505.

Christie, Pam. 2016. "Educational Change in Post-Conflict Contexts: Reflections on the South African Experience 20 Years Later." *Globalisation, Societies and Education* 14(3): 434–446.

Clark, Rob. 2010. "Technical and Institutional States: Loose Coupling in the Human Rights Sector of the World Polity." *Sociological Quarterly* 51(1): 65–95.

Cole, Elizabeth A. 2007a. *Teaching the Violent Past: History Education and Reconciliation.* Lanham, MD: Rowman and Littlefield.

————. 2007b. "Transitional Justice and the Reform of History Education." *International Journal of Transitional Justice* 1(1): 115–137.

Cole, Elizabeth A., and Judy Barsalou. 2006. *Unite or Divide? The Challenges of Teaching History in Societies Emerging from Violent Conflict.* Washington, DC: United States Institute of Peace.

Cole, Wade M. 2005. "Sovereignty Relinquished? Explaining Commitment to the International Human Rights Covenants, 1966–1999." *American Sociological Review* 70(3): 472–495.

———. 2012. "Human Rights as Myth and Ceremony? Reevaluating the Effectiveness of Human Rights Treaties, 1981–2007." *American Journal of Sociology* 117(4): 1131–1171.

Cole, Wade M., and Francisco O. Ramirez. 2013. "Conditional Decoupling: Assessing the Impact of National Human Rights Institutions, 1981 to 2004." *American Sociological Review* 78(4): 702–725.

Collins, Farren. 2017. "R1.5-Billion for Apartheid Victims but Thousands Still Waiting for Money." *Times Live*, August 28. https://www.timeslive.co.za/politics/2017-08-28-r15-billion-for-apartheid-victims-but-thousands-still-waiting-for-money/.

Colvin, Christopher. 2006. "Overview of the Reparations Program in South Africa." In *The Handbook of Reparations*, edited by P. D. De Greiff, 176–214. Oxford: Oxford University Press.

Cook, Philip, and Cheryl Heykook. 2010. "Child Participation in the Sierra Leonean Truth and Reconciliation Commission." In *Children and Transitional Justice: Truth-Telling, Accountability, and Reconciliation*, edited by S. Parmar, M. J. Roseman, S. Siegrist, and T. Sowa, 159–192. Cambridge, MA: UNICEF and the Harvard Rights Program.

Davies, Lynn. 2004. *Education and Conflict: Complexity and Chaos*. London: RoutledgeFalmer.

———. 2017. "Justice-Sensitive Education: The Implications of Transitional Justice Mechanisms for Teaching and Learning." *Comparative Education* 53(3): 333–350.

Debusscher, Petra, and An Ansoms. 2013. "Gender Equality Policies in Rwanda: Public Relations or Real Transformations?" *Development and Change* 44(5): 1111–1134.

De Greiff, Pablo. 2006. *The Handbook of Reparations*. Oxford: Oxford University Press.

———. 2012. "Theorizing Transitional Justice." In *Transitional Justice*, edited by M. S. Williams, R. Nagy, and J. Elster, 31–77. New York: New York University Press.

Des Forges, Alison. 1999. *"Leave None to Tell the Story": Genocide in Rwanda*. New York: Human Rights Watch.

Donnelly, Jack. 2013. *Universal Human Rights in Theory and Practice*. 3rd ed. Ithaca, NY: Cornell University Press.

Doyle, Michael W., and Nicholas Sambanis. 2000. "International Peacebuilding: A Theoretical and Quantitative Analysis." *American Political Science Review* 94(4): 779–801.

Dreeben, Robert. 1968. *On What Is Learned in School*. Reading, MA: Addison-Wesley.

Drumbl, Mark. 2003. "Toward a Criminology of International Crime."

Washington & Lee Public Law Research Paper No. 03-07. https://papers.ssrn.com/abstract=411780.

Dryden-Peterson, Sarah, and Bethany Mulimbi. 2017. "Pathways toward Peace: Negotiating National Unity and Ethnic Diversity through Education in Botswana." *Comparative Education Review* 61(1): 58–82.

Elliott, Michael A. 2007. "Human Rights and the Triumph of the Individual in World Culture." *Cultural Sociology* 1(3): 343–363.

Eltringham, Nigel. 2004. *Accounting for Horror: Post-Genocide Debates in Rwanda*. London: Pluto Press.

Emerson, Robert M., Rachel I. Fretz, and Linda L. Shaw. 1995. *Writing Ethnographic Fieldnotes*. Chicago: University of Chicago Press.

Erny, Pierre. 2001. *L'école coloniale au Rwanda (1900–1962)*. Paris: Editions L'Harmattan.

———. 2003. *L'enseignement au Rwanda après l'indépendance (1962–1980)*. Paris: Editions L'Harmattan.

Finnemore, Martha, and Kathryn Sikkink. 1998. "International Norm Dynamics and Political Change." *International Organization* 52(4): 887–917.

Fraser, Nancy. 1995. "From Redistribution to Recognition? Dilemmas of Justice in a 'Post-Socialist' Age." *New Left Review* 1(212): 68–93.

Freedman, Sarah Warshauer, Harvey M. Weinstein, Karen Murphy, and Timothy Longman. 2008. "Teaching History after Identity-Based Conflicts: The Rwanda Experience." *Comparative Education Review* 52(4): 663–690.

Freedom House. 2017. *Freedom in the World: Rwanda Country Report*. https://freedomhouse.org/report/freedom-world/2017/rwanda.

Fujii, Lee Ann. 2009. *Killing Neighbors: Webs of Violence in Rwanda*. Ithaca, NY: Cornell University Press.

Galtung, Johan. 1969. "Violence, Peace, and Peace Research." *Journal of Peace Research* 6(3): 167–191.

Gasanabo, Jean-Damascene. 2004. "Mémoires et histoire scolaire: Le cas du Rwanda de 1962 à 1994" [Memories and school history: The case of Rwanda from 1962 to 1994]. Doctoral thesis, University of Geneva.

———. 2006. "School History and Mechanisms for the Construction of Exclusive Identities: The Case of Rwanda from 1962 to 1994." In *Textbooks and Quality Learning for All: Some Lessons Learned from International Experiences*, edited by Cecilia Braslavsky, 365–404. Paris: UNESCO, International Bureau of Education.

Goodale, Mark. 2007. "Introduction: Locating Rights, Envisioning Law between the Global and the Local." In *The Practice of Human Rights: Tracking Law between the Global and the Local*, edited by S. E. Merry and M. Goodale, 1–38. Cambridge: Cambridge University Press.

———. 2009. *Surrendering to Utopia: An Anthropology of Human Rights*. Stanford, CA: Stanford University Press.

Goodale, Mark, and Sally Engle Merry. 2007. *The Practice of Human Rights: Tracking Law between the Global and the Local.* Cambridge: Cambridge University Press.

Hafner-Burton, Emilie M., and Kiyoteru Tsutsui. 2005. "Human Rights in a Globalizing World: The Paradox of Empty Promises." *American Journal of Sociology* 110(5): 1373–1411.

———. 2007. "Justice Lost! The Failure of International Human Rights Law to Matter Where Needed Most." *Journal of Peace Research* 44(4): 407–425.

Halbwachs, Maurice. 1992. *On Collective Memory.* Edited by L. A. Coser. Chicago: University of Chicago Press.

Hayner, Priscilla B. 2011. *Unspeakable Truths: Transitional Justice and the Challenge of Truth Commissions.* 2nd ed. New York: Routledge.

Hinton, Alexander Laban. 2010. *Transitional Justice: Global Mechanisms and Local Realities after Genocide and Mass Violence.* New Brunswick, NJ: Rutgers University Press.

Hirsch, Marianne. 2008. "The Generation of Postmemory." *Poetics Today* 29(1): 103–128.

Hoben, Susan J. 1989. *School, Work, and Equity: Educational Reform in Rwanda.* Boston: African Studies Center, Boston University.

Hobsbawm, Eric, and Terence Ranger, eds. 2012. *The Invention of Tradition.* Cambridge: Cambridge University Press.

Hogg, Carey. 2013. "Women's Political Representation in Post-conflict Rwanda: A Politics of Inclusion or Exclusion?" *Journal of International Women's Studies* 11(3): 34–55.

Honeyman, Catherine A. 2016. *The Orderly Entrepreneur: Youth, Education, and Governance in Rwanda.* Stanford, CA: Stanford University Press.

Human Rights Watch. 2008. *Law and Reality: Progress in Judicial Reform in Rwanda.* New York: Human Rights Watch.

———. 2010. "Rwanda: Silencing Dissent ahead of Elections." August 2. https://www.hrw.org/news/2010/08/02/rwanda-silencing-dissent -ahead-elections.

———. 2012. *Rwanda Country Summary.* New York: Human Rights Watch.

———. 2017a. "Rwanda: Politically Closed Elections." August 18. https://www.hrw.org/news/2017/08/18/rwanda-politically-closed -elections.

———. 2017b. *"We Will Force You to Confess": Torture and Unlawful Military Detention in Rwanda.* Amsterdam: Human Rights Watch.

———. 2018. *Rwanda Country Summary.* New York: Human Rights Watch.

Ingelaere, Bert. 2016. *Inside Rwanda's Gacaca Courts: Seeking Justice after Genocide.* Madison: University of Wisconsin Press.

Institute for Research and Dialogue for Peace. 2010. *Ethnic Identity and*

Social Cohesion in Rwanda: Critical Analysis of Political, Social and Economic Challenges. Kigali: Institute for Research and Dialogue for Peace (IRDP).

Inter-Parliamentary Union. 2016. "Women in National Parliaments." http://www.ipu.org/wmn-e/classif.htm.

Jara, Daniela. 2016. *Children and the Afterlife of State Violence: Memories of Dictatorship*. New York: Palgrave Macmillan.

Jelin, Elizabeth. 2003. *State Repression and the Struggles for Memory*. Minneapolis: University of Minnesota Press.

Johnson, David, and Frances Stewart. 2007. "Education, Ethnicity and Conflict." *International Journal of Educational Development* 27(3): 247–251.

Joppke, Christian. 2007. "Immigration and the Identity of Citizenship: The Paradox of Universalism." *Citizenship Studies* 12(6): 533–546.

Kapferer, Bruce. 1988. *Legends of People, Myths of State: Violence, Intolerance, and Political Culture in Sri Lanka and Australia*. Washington, DC: Smithsonian Institution Press.

Keck, Margaret, and Kathryn Sikkink. 1998. *Activists beyond Borders: Advocacy Networks in International Politics*. Ithaca, NY: Cornell University Press.

Kent, Lia. 2016. "Transitional Justice and Peacebuilding." in *An Introduction to Transitional Justice*, edited by O. Simic, 201–222. New York: Routledge.

King, Elisabeth. 2009. "From Data Problems to Data Points: Challenges and Opportunities of Research in Postgenocide Rwanda." *African Studies Review* 52(3): 127–148.

———. 2014. *From Classrooms to Conflict in Rwanda*. Cambridge: Cambridge University Press.

Kitson, Alison. 2007. "History Teaching and Reconciliation in Northern Ireland." In *Teaching the Violent Past: History Education and Reconciliation*, edited by E. A. Cole, 123–154. Lanham, MD: Rowman and Littlefield.

Koo, Jeong-Woo, and Francisco O. Ramirez. 2009. "National Incorporation of Global Human Rights: Worldwide Expansion of National Human Rights Institutions, 1966–2004." *Social Forces* 87(3): 1321–1353.

Kritz, Neil J. 1996. "Coming to Terms with Atrocities: A Review of Accountability Mechanisms for Mass Violations of Human Rights." *Law and Contemporary Problems* 59(4): 127–152.

Kruss, Glenda. 2001. "Towards Human Rights in South African Schools: An Agenda for Research and Practice." *Race Ethnicity and Education* 4(1): 45–62.

Kymlicka, Will. 2001. *Politics in the Vernacular: Nationalism, Multiculturalism, and Citizenship*. Oxford: Oxford University Press.

Lambourne, Wendy. 2009. "Transitional Justice and Peacebuilding after Mass Violence." *International Journal of Transitional Justice* 3(1): 28–48.

Lange, Matthew. 2012. *Educations in Ethnic Violence: Identity, Educational Bubbles, and Resource Mobilization*. Cambridge: Cambridge University Press.

Laplante, Lisa J. 2008. "Transitional Justice and Peace Building: Diagnosing and Addressing the Socioeconomic Roots of Violence through a Human Rights Framework." *International Journal of Transitional Justice* 2(3): 331–355.

Lauren, Paul Gordon. 2011. *The Evolution of International Human Rights: Visions Seen*. Philadelphia: University of Pennsylvania Press.

Lederach, John Paul. 1997. *Building Peace: Sustainable Reconciliation in Divided Societies*. Washington, DC: United States Institute of Peace.

———. 2006. "Theoretical Challenges of Peacebuilding with and for Youth." In *Troublemakers or Peacemakers? Youth and Post-Accord Peacebuilding*, edited by S. McEvoy-Levy, 259–280. Notre Dame, IN: University of Notre Dame Press.

Lemarchand, René. 2009. *The Dynamics of Violence in Central Africa*. Philadelphia: University of Pennsylvania Press.

Lewis, Ann. 1992. "Group Child Interviews as a Research Tool." *British Educational Research Journal* 18(4): 413–421.

Lira, Elizabeth. 2006. "The Reparations Policy for Human Rights Violations in Chile." In *The Handbook of Reparations*, edited by P. D. De Greiff, 55–100. Oxford: Oxford University Press.

Longman, Timothy. 2006. "Rwanda: Achieving Equality or Serving an Authoritarian State?" In *Women in African Parliaments*, edited by G. Bauer and H. E. Britton, 133–150. Boulder, CO: Lynne Rienner.

———. 2010. *Christianity and Genocide in Rwanda*. Cambridge: Cambridge University Press.

———. 2011. "Limitations to Political Reform: The Undemocratic Nature of Transition in Rwanda." In *Remaking Rwanda: State Building and Human Rights after Mass Violence*, edited by Scott Straus and Lars Waldorf, 25–47. Madison: University of Wisconsin Press.

———. 2017. *Memory and Justice in Post-Genocide Rwanda*. Cambridge: Cambridge University Press.

Longman, Timothy, and Theoneste Rutagengwa. 2004. "Memory, Identity, and Community in Rwanda." In *My Neighbor, My Enemy: Justice and Community in the Aftermath of Mass Atrocity*, edited by E. Stover and H. M. Weinstein, 162–182. Cambridge: Cambridge University Press.

Lutz, Ellen L., and Kathryn Sikkink. 2000. "International Human Rights Law and Practice in Latin America." *International Organization* 54(3): 633–659.

Lynd, Mark. 2010. *Assessment Report and Proposal for an Education Strategy*. Kigali: USAID/Rwanda.

Mahmoud, Youssef, and Anupah Makoond. 2017. "Sustaining Peace: What Does It Mean in Practice?" International Peace Institute, April 8. https://www.ipinst.org/2017/04/sustaining-peace-in-practice.

Mamdani, Mahmood. 2001. *When Victims Become Killers: Colonialism, Nativism, and the Genocide in Rwanda*. Princeton, NJ: Princeton University Press.

Mani, Rama. 2008. "Dilemmas of Expanding Transitional Justice, or Forging the Nexus between Transitional Justice and Development." *International Journal of Transitional Justice* 2(3): 253–265.

McEvoy, Kieran. 2007. "Beyond Legalism: Towards a Thicker Understanding of Transitional Justice." *Journal of Law and Society* 34(4): 411–440.

McEvoy-Levy, Siobhán. 2006. *Troublemakers or Peacemakers? Youth and Post-Accord Peace Building*. Notre Dame, IN: University of Notre Dame Press.

———. 2011. "Children, Youth, and Peacebuilding." In *Critical Issues in Peace and Conflict Studies: Theory, Practice, and Pedagogy*, edited by T. Matyók, J. Senehi, and S. Byrne, 159–176. Lanham, MD: Lexington Books.

McLean Hilker, Lyndsay. 2009. "Everyday Ethnicities: Identity and Reconciliation among Rwandan Youth." *Journal of Genocide Research* 11(1): 81–100.

———. 2011. "The Role of Education in Driving Conflict and Building Peace: The Case of Rwanda." *Prospects* 41(2): 267–282.

Meernik, J., and K. L. King. 2001. "The Effectiveness of International Law and the ICTY—Preliminary Results of an Empirical Study." *International Criminal Law Review* 1(3): 343–372.

Meierhenrich, Jens. 2011. "Topographies of Remembering and Forgetting: The Transformation of Lieux de Mémoire in Rwanda." In *Remaking Rwanda: State Building and Human Rights after Mass Violence*, edited by Scott Straus and Lars Waldorf, 283–296. Madison: University of Wisconsin Press.

Melvin, Jennifer. 2010. "Reconstructing Rwanda: Balancing Human Rights and the Promotion of National Reconciliation." *International Journal of Human Rights* 14(6): 932–951.

Mendeloff, David. 2004. "Truth-Seeking, Truth-Telling, and Postconflict Peacebuilding: Curb the Enthusiasm?" *International Studies Review* 6(3): 355–380.

Merry, Sally Engle. 2006. *Human Rights and Gender Violence: Translating International Law into Local Justice*. Chicago: University of Chicago Press.

Meyer, John W. 1977. "The Effects of Education as an Institution." *American Journal of Sociology* 83(1): 55–77.

————. 2010. "World Society, Institutional Theories, and the Actor." *Annual Review of Sociology* 36(1): 1–20.

Meyer, John W., John Boli, George M. Thomas, and Francisco O. Ramirez. 1997. "World Society and the Nation-State." *American Journal of Sociology* 103(1): 144–181.

Meyer, John W., Patricia Bromley, and Francisco O. Ramirez. 2010. "Human Rights in Social Science Textbooks: Cross-National Analyses, 1970–2008." *Sociology of Education* 83(2): 111–134.

Meyer, John W., and Brian Rowan. 1977. "Institutionalized Organizations: Formal Structure as Myth and Ceremony." *American Journal of Sociology* 83(2): 340–363.

Mgbako, Chi. 2005. "Ingando Solidarity Camps: Reconciliation and Political Indoctrination in Post-Genocide Rwanda." *Harvard Human Rights Journal* 18: 201–224.

Minow, Martha. 1998. *Between Vengeance and Forgiveness: Facing History after Genocide and Mass Violence.* Boston: Beacon Press.

————. 2002. "Education for Co-existence." *Arizona Law Review* 44(1): 1–29.

Moja, Teboho. 2016. "Education as Redress in South Africa: Opening the Doors of Learning to All." In *Transitional Justice and Education: Learning Peace,* edited by C. Ramírez-Barat and R. Duthie, 205–229. New York: Social Science Research Council.

Moreau, Joseph. 2003. *Schoolbook Nation: Conflicts over American History Textbooks from the Civil War to the Present.* Ann Arbor: University of Michigan Press.

Mushimiyimana, Diane. 2018. "Mindset Change Hampers Implementation of the New School Curriculum—REB Boss." *New Times,* May 29. https://www.newtimes.co.rw/news/mindset-change-hampers-implementation-new-school-curriculum-rebboss.

Nakagawa, Mana, and Christine Min Wotipka. 2016. "The Worldwide Incorporation of Women and Women's Rights Discourse in Social Science Textbooks, 1970–2008." *Comparative Education Review* 60(3): 501–529.

National Institute of Statistics of Rwanda (NISR). 2012. *The Evolution of Poverty in Rwanda from 2000 to 2001: Results from the Household Surveys (EICV).* Kigali: NISR.

Newbury, Catharine. 1988. *The Cohesion of Oppression: Clientship and Ethnicity in Rwanda, 1860–1960.* New York: Columbia University Press.

Njoroge, George. 2007. "The Reconstruction of the Teacher's Psyche in Rwanda: The Theory and Practice of Peace Education at Kigali Institute of Education." In *Addressing Ethnic Conflict through Peace Education: International Perspectives,* edited by Z. Bekerman and C. McGlynn, 215–230. New York: Palgrave Macmillan.

Nora, Pierre. 1989. "Between Memory and History: Les lieux de mémoire." *Representations* (26): 7–24.

Novelli, Mario, and Mieke T. A. Lopes Cardozo. 2008. "Conflict, Education and the Global South: New Critical Directions." *International Journal of Educational Development* 28(4): 473–488.

Novelli, Mario, Mieke T. A. Lopes Cardozo, and Alan Smith. 2017. "The 4RS Framework: Analyzing Education's Contribution to Sustainable Peacebuilding with Social Justice in Conflict-Affected Contexts." *Journal on Education in Emergencies* 3(1): 14–43.

Novelli, Mario, and Yusuf Sayed. 2016. "Teachers as Agents of Sustainable Peace, Social Cohesion and Development: Theory, Practice & Evidence." *Education as Change* 20(3): 15–37.

Nyseth Brehm, Hollie, Christopher Uggen, and Jean-Damascène Gasanabo. 2014. "Genocide, Justice, and Rwanda's Gacaca Courts." *Journal of Contemporary Criminal Justice* 30(3): 333–352.

Nzahabwanayo, S., K. Horsthemke, and T. P. Mathebula. 2017. "Identification and Critique of the Citizenship Notion Informing the Itorero Training Scheme for High School Leavers in Post-Genocide Rwanda." *South African Journal of Higher Education* 31(2): 226–250.

Obura, A. P. 2003. *Never Again: Educational Reconstruction in Rwanda.* Paris: International Institute for Educational Planning.

Office of the High Commissioner for Human Rights. 2017. "Status of Ratification." http://indicators.ohchr.org/.

Oglesby, Elizabeth. 2007. "Educating Citizens in Postwar Guatemala: Historical Memory, Genocide, and the Culture of Peace." *Radical History Review* 2007(97): 77–98.

Paluck, Elizabeth Levy, and Donald P. Green. 2009. "Deference, Dissent, and Dispute Resolution: An Experimental Intervention Using Mass Media to Change Norms and Behavior in Rwanda." *American Political Science Review* 103(4): 622–644.

Paulson, Julia. 2006. "The Educational Recommendations of Truth and Reconciliation Commissions: Potential and Practice in Sierra Leone." *Research in Comparative and International Education* 1(4): 335–350.

———. 2011. *Education and Reconciliation: Exploring Conflict and Post-conflict Situations.* London: A & C Black.

———. 2015. "'Whether and How?' History Education about Recent and Ongoing Conflict: A Review of Research." *Journal on Education in Emergencies* 1(1): 14–47.

———. 2017. "From Truth to Textbook: The Peruvian Truth and Reconciliation Commission, Educational Resources, and the Challenges of Teaching about Recent Conflict." In *(Re)Constructing Memory: Education, Identity, and Conflict*, edited by M. J. Bellino and J. H. Williams, 291–311. Rotterdam: Sense Publishers.

Paulson, Julia, and Michelle J. Bellino. 2017. "Truth Commissions, Education, and Positive Peace: An Analysis of Truth Commission Final Reports (1980–2015)." *Comparative Education* 53(3): 351–378.

Paxton, Will, and Lillian Mutesi. 2012. *School Funding and Equity in Rwanda*. Kigali: Institute of Policy Analysis and Research–Rwanda.

Pearson, Pamela. 2014. "Policy without a Plan: English as a Medium of Instruction in Rwanda." *Current Issues in Language Planning* 15(1): 39–56.

Penal Reform International. 2010. *Final Monitoring and Research Report on the Gacaca Process*. https://www.penalreform.org/resource/final-monitoring-research-report-gacaca-process/.

Pham, Phuong N., Harvey M. Weinstein, and Timothy Longman. 2004. "Trauma and PTSD Symptoms in Rwanda: Implications for Attitudes toward Justice and Reconciliation." *Journal of the American Medical Association* 292(5): 602–612.

Pollock, Mica. 2004. *Colormute: Race Talk Dilemmas in an American School*. Princeton, NJ: Princeton University Press.

Pottier, Johan. 2002. *Re-imagining Rwanda: Conflict, Survival and Disinformation in the Late Twentieth Century*. Cambridge: Cambridge University Press.

Pozen, Joanna, Richard Neugebauer, and Joseph Ntaganira. 2014. "Assessing the Rwanda Experiment: Popular Perceptions of Gacaca in Its Final Phase." *International Journal of Transitional Justice* 8(1): 31–52.

Prunier, Gérard. 1995. *The Rwanda Crisis: History of a Genocide*. New York: Columbia University Press.

Purdeková, Andrea. 2008. "Building a Nation in Rwanda? De-ethnicisation and Its Discontents." *Studies in Ethnicity and Nationalism* 8(3): 502–523.

———. 2011. *Rwanda's Ingando Camps: Liminality and the Reproduction of Power*. Oxford: Refugee Studies Centre, University of Oxford.

———. 2015. *Making Ubumwe: Power, State and Camps in Rwanda's Unity-Building Project*. New York: Berghahn Books.

Ramirez, Francisco, David Suárez, and John Meyer. 2007. "The Worldwide Rise of Human Rights Education." In *School Knowledge in Comparative and Historical Perspective: Changing Curricula in Primary and Secondary Education*, edited by Aaron Benavot and Cecilia Braslavsky, 35–52. Dordrecht, The Netherlands: Springer Netherlands.

Ramírez-Barat, Clara, and Roger Duthie. 2016. *Transitional Justice and Education: Learning Peace*. New York: Social Science Research Council.

Reisner, Edward Hartman. 1922. *Nationalism and Education since 1789: A Social and Political History of Modern Education*. New York: Macmillan.

Republic of Rwanda. 1999. Law No. 22/99 to Supplement Book 1 of the Civil Code and to Institute Part Five regarding Matrimonial Regimes, Liberalities and Successions. Kigali: Republic of Rwanda.

———. 2001. Law No. 47/2001 on Prevention, Suppression and Punishment of the Crime of Discrimination and Sectarianism. Kigali: Republic of Rwanda. http://www.refworld.org/type,LEG ISLATION,,,4ac5c4302,0.html.

———. 2003. *The Constitution of the Republic of Rwanda*. Kigali: Republic of Rwanda.

———. 2008a. Law No. 18/2008 relating to the Punishment of the Crime of Genocide Ideology. Kigali: Republic of Rwanda.

———. 2008b. Law No. 59/2008 on Prevention and Punishment of Gender-Based Violence. Kigali: Republic of Rwanda.

———. 2012. *Summary of the Report Presented at the Closing Ceremony of the Gacaca Court Activities*. Kigali: National Service of the Gacaca Courts.

Republic of Rwanda, Ministry of Gender and Family Promotion. 2010. *National Gender Policy*. Kigali: Ministry of Gender and Family Promotion.

Republic of Rwanda, Ministry of Justice. 2017. *The National Human Rights Action Plan of Rwanda: 2017–2020*. Kigali: Ministry of Justice.

Republic of Rwanda, National Unity and Reconciliation Commission (NURC). 2010. *Rwanda Reconciliation Barometer*. Kigali: NURC. http://www.nurc.gov.rw/fileadmin/Documents/RWANDA _RECONCILIATION_BAROMETER.pdf.

———. 2015. *Rwanda Reconciliation Barometer*. Kigali: NURC. http:// www.nurc.gov.rw/fileadmin/Documents/RWANDA_RECON CILIATION_BAROMETER.pdf.

Rettig, Max. 2008. "Gacaca: Truth, Justice, and Reconciliation in Postconflict Rwanda?" *African Studies Review* 51(3): 25–50.

Reyntjens, Filip. 2004. "Rwanda, Ten Years on: From Genocide to Dictatorship." *African Affairs* 103(411): 177–210.

Ricoeur, Paul. 2004. *Memory, History, Forgetting*. Translated by Kathleen Blamey and David Pellauer. Chicago: University of Chicago Press.

Risse-Kappen, Thomas, Stephen C. Ropp, and Kathryn Sikkink. 1999. *The Power of Human Rights: International Norms and Domestic Change*. Cambridge: Cambridge University Press.

Roht-Arriaza, Naomi. 1995. *Impunity and Human Rights in International Law and Practice*. New York: Oxford University Press.

———. 2004. "Reparations Decisions and Dilemmas." *Hastings International and Comparative Law Review* 27: 157–219.

———. 2006. "The New Landscape of Transitional Justice." In *Transitional Justice in the Twenty-First Century: Beyond Truth versus Justice*, edited by Naomi Roht-Arriaza and Javier Mariezcurrena, 1–16. Cambridge: Cambridge University Press.

Roht-Arriaza, Naomi, and Javier Mariezcurrena, eds. 2006. *Transitional Justice in the Twenty-First Century: Beyond Truth versus Justice.* Cambridge: Cambridge University Press.

Rubagiza, Jolly, Jane Umutoni, and Ali Kaleeba. 2016. "Teachers as Agents of Change: Promoting Peacebuilding and Social Cohesion in Schools in Rwanda." *Education as Change* 20(3): 202–224.

Rubagiza, Jolly, Edmond Were, and Rosamund Sutherland. 2011. "Introducing ICT into Schools in Rwanda: Educational Challenges and Opportunities." *International Journal of Educational Development* 31(1): 37–43.

Russell, S. Garnett, Sandra Sirota, and Kayum Ahmed. 2019. "Human Rights Education in South Africa: Ideological Shifts and Curricular Reforms." *Comparative Education Review* 63(1): 1–27.

Russell, Susan Garnett. 2015. "Global Civil Society and Education Policy in Post-Genocide Rwanda." *International Sociology* 30(6): 599–618.

———. 2016. "Global Gender Discourses in Education: Evidence from Post-Genocide Rwanda." *Comparative Education* 52(4): 492–515.

Russell, Susan Garnett, and Laura J. Quaynor. 2016. "Constructing Citizenship in Post-Conflict Contexts: The Cases of Liberia and Rwanda." *Globalisation, Societies and Education* 15(2): 248–270.

Russell, Susan Garnett, and David F. Suárez. 2017. "Symbol and Substance: Human Rights Education as an Emergent Global Institution." In *Human Rights Education: Theory, Research, Praxis,* edited by Monisha Bajaj, 19–46. Philadelphia: University of Pennsylvania Press.

Russell, Susan Garnett, and Dijana Tiplic. 2018. "Conflict-Resolution and Transitional Justice Mechanisms in School Textbooks, 1950–2010." Unpublished manuscript.

Rutayisire, John, John Kabano, and Jolly Rubagiza. 2004. "Redefining Rwanda's Future: The Role of Curriculum in Social Reconstruction." In *Education, Conflict and Social Cohesion,* edited by S. Tawil and A. Harley, 315–373. Paris: UNESCO, International Bureau of Education.

Salomon, Gavriel. 2006. "Does Peace Education Really Make a Difference?" *Peace and Conflict* 12(1): 37–48.

Samuelson, Beth Lewis, and Sarah Warshauer Freedman. 2010. "Language Policy, Multilingual Education, and Power in Rwanda." *Language Policy* 9(3): 191–215.

Schissler, Hanna, and Yasemin Nuhoğlu Soysal. 2005. *The Nation, Europe, and the World: Textbooks and Curricula in Transition.* New York: Berghahn Books.

Schulz, Wolfram, John Ainley, Julian Fraillon, David Kerr, and Bruno Losito. 2010. *ICCS 2009 International Report: Civic Knowledge, Attitudes, and Engagement among Lower-Secondary School Students in 38 Countries.* Amsterdam: International Association for the Evaluation of Educational Achievement.

Scott, James C. 1990. *Domination and the Arts of Resistance: Hidden Transcripts.* New Haven, CT: Yale University Press.

Seidman, Irving. 2006. *Interviewing as Qualitative Research : a Guide for Researchers in Education and the Social Sciences.* 3rd ed. New York: Teachers College Press.

Shaw, Rosalind, Lars Waldorf, and Pierre Hazan. 2010. *Localizing Transitional Justice: Interventions and Priorities after Mass Violence.* Stanford, CA: Stanford University Press.

Shepler, Susan. 2014. *Childhood Deployed: Remaking Child Soldiers in Sierra Leone.* New York: New York University Press.

Sikkink, Kathryn, and Carrie Booth Walling. 2007. "The Impact of Human Rights Trials in Latin America." *Journal of Peace Research* 44(4): 427–445.

Smith, Alan. 2005. "Education in the Twenty-First Century: Conflict, Reconstruction and Reconciliation." *Compare: A Journal of Comparative and International Education* 35(4): 373–391.

Smith, Alan, and Tony Vaux. 2003. *Education, Conflict and International Development.* London: Department for International Development (DFID). http://eprints.ulster.ac.uk/11468.

Smith, Anthony D. 1991a. *The Ethnic Origins of Nations.* Oxford: Blackwell.

———. 1991b. *National Identity.* Reno: University of Nevada Press.

Smith Ellison, Christine. 2012. "The Role of Education in Peacebuilding: An Analysis of Five Change Theories in Sierra Leone." *Compare: A Journal of Comparative and International Education* 44(2): 186–207.

Soysal, Yasemin Nuhoğlu. 1994. *Limits of Citizenship: Migrants and Postnational Membership in Europe.* Chicago: University of Chicago Press.

———. 2000. "Citizenship and Identity: Living in Diasporas in Post-War Europe?" *Ethnic and Racial Studies* 23(1): 1–15.

Sriram, Chandra Lekha. 2007. "Justice as Peace? Liberal Peacebuilding and Strategies of Transitional Justice." *Global Society* 21(4): 579–591.

Stacy, Helen. 2009. *Human Rights for the 21st Century: Sovereignty, Civil Society, Culture.* Stanford, CA: Stanford University Press.

Stearns, Jason, and Federico Borello. 2011. "Bad Karma: Accountability for Rwandan Crimes in the Congo." In *Remaking Rwanda: State Building and Human Rights after Mass Violence*, edited by Scott Straus and Lars Waldorf, 152–172. Madison: University of Wisconsin Press.

Stern, Steve J., and Scott Straus. 2014. *The Human Rights Paradox:*

Universality and Its Discontents. Madison: University of Wisconsin Press.

Stevick, E. Doyle, and Bradley A. U. Levinson, eds. 2007. *Reimagining Civic Education: How Diverse Societies Form Democratic Citizens*. Lanham, MD: Rowman and Littlefield.

Stover, Eric, and Harvey M. Weinstein, eds. 2004. *My Neighbor, My Enemy: Justice and Community in the Aftermath of Mass Atrocity*. Cambridge: Cambridge University Press.

Straus, Scott. 2006. *The Order of Genocide: Race, Power, and War in Rwanda*. Ithaca, NY: Cornell University Press.

Straus, Scott, and Lars Waldorf, eds. 2011. *Remaking Rwanda: State Building and Human Rights after Mass Violence*. Madison: University of Wisconsin Press.

Suárez, David F., and Francisco O. Ramírez. 2007. "Human Rights and Citizenship: The Emergence of Human Rights Education." In *Critique and Utopia: New Developments in the Sociology of Education in the Twenty-First Century*, edited by C. A. Torres and A. Teodoro, 43–64. Lanham, MD: Rowman and Littlefield.

Sundberg, Molly. 2016. *Training for Model Citizenship: An Ethnography of Civic Education and State-Making in Rwanda*. London: Palgrave Macmillan.

Teitel, Ruti G. 2003. "Transitional Justice Genealogy." *Harvard Human Rights Journal* 16: 69–94.

Terra, Luke. 2013. "New Histories for a New State: A Study of History Textbook Content in Northern Ireland." *Journal of Curriculum Studies* 46(2): 225–248.

Theidon, Kimberly. 2012. *Intimate Enemies: Violence and Reconciliation in Peru*. Philadelphia: University of Pennsylvania Press.

Thomson, Susan, and Rosemary Nagy. 2011. "Law, Power and Justice: What Legalism Fails to Address in the Functioning of Rwanda's Gacaca Courts." *International Journal of Transitional Justice* 5(1): 11–30.

Tibbitts, Felisa. 2002. "Understanding What We Do: Emerging Models for Human Rights Education." *International Review of Education* 48(3/4): 159–171.

———. 2008. "Human Rights Education." In *Encyclopedia of Peace Education*, edited by M. Bajaj, 99–108. Charlotte, NC: Information Age Publishing.

Tibbitts, Felisa, and William R. Fernekes. 2011. "Human Rights Education." In *Teaching and Studying Social Issues: Major Programs and Approaches*, edited by S. Totten and J. E. Pedersen, 87–117. Charlotte, NC: Information Age Publishing.

Tibbitts, Felisa L., and Gail Weldon. 2017. "History Curriculum and Teacher Training: Shaping a Democratic Future in Post-Apartheid South Africa?" *Comparative Education* 53(3): 442–461.

Torney-Purta, Judith. 2002. "The School's Role in Developing Civic Engagement: A Study of Adolescents in Twenty-Eight Countries." *Applied Developmental Science* 6(4): 203–212.

Torney-Purta, Judith, Britt Wilkenfeld, and Carolyn Barber. 2008. "How Adolescents in 27 Countries Understand, Support, and Practice Human Rights." *Journal of Social Issues* 64(4): 857–880.

Transparency International. 2012. *Rwanda Public Expenditure Tracking Survey in Education (9YBE)*. Kigali: Transparency International Rwanda.

Tsutsui, Kiyoteru, and Christine Min Wotipka. 2004. "Global Civil Society and the International Human Rights Movement: Citizen Participation in Human Rights International Nongovernmental Organizations." *Social Forces* 83(2): 587–620.

Tumwebaze, Peterson. 2017. "REB Recalls Textbook with Content Trivialising Genocide." *New Times*, June 19. http://www.newtimes.co.rw/section/read/214509.

Tyack, David. 1966. "Forming the National Character: Paradox in the Educational Thought of the Revolutionary Generation." *Harvard Educational Review* 36(1): 29–41.

———. 1999. "Monuments between Covers: The Politics of Textbooks." *American Behavioral Scientist* 42(6): 922–932.

UNDP Rwanda. 2014. *Millennium Development Goals Rwanda: Final Progress Report*. Kigali: UNDP Rwanda.

UNICEF. 2015. *Evaluation of UNICEF's Peacebuilding, Education and Advocacy Programme (PBEA)*. New York: UNICEF.

United Nations. 2004. *The Rule of Law and Transitional Justice in Conflict and Post-conflict Societies: Report of the Secretary General*. New York: United Nations.

———. 2016. Security Council Resolution 2282. New York: United Nations.

U.S. Department of State. 2017. *Presidential Election in Rwanda*. Washington, DC: U.S. Department of State.

Uvin, Peter. 1998. *Aiding Violence: The Development Enterprise in Rwanda*. West Hartford, CT: Kumarian Press.

Uwizeyimana, Dominique E. 2014. "Aspects and Consequences of the Rwandan Law of Genocide Ideology: A Comparative Analysis." *Mediterranean Journal of Social Sciences* 5(23): 2370–2379.

Uworwabayeho, Alphonse. 2009. "Teachers' Innovative Change within Countrywide Reform: A Case Study in Rwanda." *Journal of Mathematics Teacher Education* 12(5): 315–324.

Vansina, Jan. 2004. *Antecedents to Modern Rwanda: The Nyiginya Kingdom*. Madison: University of Wisconsin Press.

Vidal, Claudine. 2004. "La commémoration du génocide au Rwanda: Violence symbolique, mémorisation forcée et histoire officielle"

[The commemoration of the genocide in Rwanda: Symbolic violence, compulsory memorization and official history]. *Cahiers d'Etudes Africaines* 44(175): 575–592.

Vinjamuri, Leslie, and Jack Snyder. 2004. "Advocacy and Scholarship in the Study of International War Crime Tribunals and Transitional Justice." *Annual Review of Political Science* 7(1): 345–362.

Wahl, Rachel. 2017. *Just Violence: Torture and Human Rights in the Eyes of the Police*. Stanford, CA: Stanford University Press.

Waldorf, Lars. 2007. "Rwanda's Failing Experiment in Restorative Justice." In *Handbook of Restorative Justice: A Global Perspective*, edited by D. Sullivan and L. Tifft, 422–434. London: Routledge.

———. 2009. "Revisiting Hotel Rwanda: Genocide Ideology, Reconciliation, and Rescuers." *Journal of Genocide Research* 11(1): 101–125.

———. 2011. "Instrumentalizing Genocide: The RPF's Campaign against 'Genocide Ideology.'" In *Remaking Rwanda: State Building and Human Rights after Mass Violence*, edited by Scott Straus and Lars Waldorf, 48–66. Madison: University of Wisconsin Press.

Weber, Eugen. 1976. *Peasants into Frenchmen: The Modernization of Rural France, 1870–1914*. Stanford, CA: Stanford University Press.

Weinstein, Harvey M., Sarah Warshauer Freedman, and Holly Hughson. 2007. "School Voices Challenges Facing Education Systems after Identity-Based Conflicts." *Education, Citizenship and Social Justice* 2(1): 41–71.

Wertsch, James V. 2002. *Voices of Collective Remembering*. Cambridge: Cambridge University Press.

Wielenga, Cori. 2012. "Narrative Research and Human Rights Law: A Case Study of Rwanda." In *Beyond the Law: Multi-disciplinary Perspectives on Human Rights*, edited by F. Viljoen, 253–273. Pretoria, South Africa: PULP.

Williams, Timothy P. 2017. "The Political Economy of Primary Education: Lessons from Rwanda." *World Development* 96: 550–561.

Williams, Timothy P., Pamela Abbott, and Alfred Mupenzi. 2015. "'Education at Our School Is Not Free': The Hidden Costs of Fee-Free Schooling in Rwanda." *Compare: A Journal of Comparative and International Education* 45(6): 931–952.

Wippman, David. 1999. "Atrocities, Deterrence, and the Limits of International Justice." *Fordham International Law Journal* 23: 473–488.

World Bank. 2011. *Rwanda—Education Country Status Report: Toward Quality Enhancement and Achievement of Universal Nine Year Basic Education—an Education System in Transition; a Nation in Transition*. http://documents.worldbank.org/curated/en/2011/01/13171101 /rwanda-education-country-status-report-toward-quality-en hancement-achievement-universal-nine-year-basic-education -education-system-transition-nation-transition.

———. 2017. "The World Bank in Rwanda." http://www.worldbank
.org/en/country/rwanda/overview.

———. 2018. "Education Statistics—Rwanda." http://datatopics
.worldbank.org/education/country/rwanda.

World Values Survey. 2007. "World Values Survey Rwanda: Field
Technical Record." http://www.worldvaluessurvey.org/WVSDoc
umentationWV5.jsp.

———. 2012. "World Values Survey Rwanda: Technical Record."
http://www.worldvaluessurvey.org/WVSDocumentationWV6.jsp.

Zorbas, Eugenia. 2009. "What Does Reconciliation after Genocide
Mean? Public Transcripts and Hidden Transcripts in Post-Genocide
Rwanda." *Journal of Genocide Research* 11(1): 127–147.

INDEX

civic identity, 17; as "being
Rwandan," 56; characteristics
of, *69*; in the curriculum,
62–72; defined, 58; discussion
of rights, *71*; global, *67*; minimal
conceptualization of, 72;
national, *67*; promoted by
government, 55; regional, *67*;
by school type, *68*. *See also*
citizenship
civics/citizenship education, 39,
102; conventional notions of,
57–59; in curricula and
textbooks, 63–65, 108–109;
revision of, 51–52, 63, 189.
See also political education
civil/political rights *vs.* eco-
nomic/social rights, as taught
in school, 114–115, 129
civil war (1990–1993), 2, 96,
140–141, 146, 152, 157
civil war, as term for 1994
genocide, 144, 192
clan (term), 61, 73–75
collective memory, 132–133,
133–137; of children survivors,
135; control over narrative of,
136, 140; defined, 135–136;
memorialization of, 137;
official, 135, 138, 140, 178
colonialism/colonization, 8–10,
55, 59–61, 73–76, 143, 146–148,
160. *See also* Belgian colonial
government
conflict, past, teaching about, 38
crimes against humanity, prosecution of, 34
criminal justice, 34–35
curriculum: authoritarianism in,
129; civics in, 6, 14, 25, 63–68,

73–76, 96; civil/political rights
de-emphasized, 129; global
awareness in, 63; human rights
in, 26, 99–101, 108–110, 117,
129; under Hutu Republics,
11–12; reconciliation in,
158–160; reforms in, 16, 39, 40,
49, 51–53; social/economic
rights emphasized, 129; standards, 129; time devoted to
sensitive subjects, 189. *See also*
specific curricular programs (e.g.,
education; social studies)

decoupling, defined, 20
Democratic Republic of Congo
(DRC): human rights violations committed in, 106;
returnees from, 83, 86–89
development: in educational
content, 63–65, 142, 182; focus
of RFP government, 16; gender
equality and, 121–124, 128;
linked to sustaining peace,
5–6, 30. *See also* national
development
divisionism, 15, 56, 74, 149, 153,
172, 178. *See also* genocide
ideology
double genocide (term), 151–152

East African Community, 51, 66
écoles libres subsidées, 10
Economic Development and Poverty
Reduction Study 2008–2012
(Ministry of Education), 104
economic rights. *See* civil/political
rights *vs.* economic/social rights
education: access to, 16, 38, 39;
civics, 6, 14, 63; limits of on

About the Author

S. GARNETT RUSSELL is assistant professor of international and comparative education at Teachers College, Columbia University, and director of the George Clement Bond Center for African Education. Her research focuses on citizenship and human rights in conflict-affected and postconflict contexts. Recent articles have appeared in *Comparative Education Review*, *Gender and Society*, *Comparative Education*, *International Sociology*, and *International Studies Quarterly*.